Clientelism and
Democratic Representation
in Comparative Perspective

Clientelism and Democratic Representation in Comparative Perspective

Edited by Saskia Ruth-Lovell
and Maria Spirova

ecpr
PRESS

Published by the European Consortium for Political Research, Harbour House, 6–8 Hythe Quay, Colchester, CO2 8JF, United Kingdom

British Library Cataloguing in Publication Data

A catalogue record for this book is available from the British Library

ISBN: HB 978-1-78552-300-7

Library of Congress Control Number: 2019949269

ISBN 978-1-78552-300-7 (cloth)
ISBN 978-1-5381-5680-3 (pbk)
ISBN 978-1-78552-301-4 (electronic)

ecpr.eu/shop

Contents

List of Abbreviations

CHAPTER 2

DALP – Democratic Accountability and Linkages Project
ENPP – Effective Number of Parliamentary Parties
GDP – Gross Domestic Product
LAB – Latinobarometer

CHAPTER 3

DPS – the Movement for Rights and Freedoms
EC – European Commission
KDH – Hungarian Party in Slovakia
MPP – Hungarian Citizens' Party
UDMR – Democratic Union of Hungarians in Romania

CHAPTER 4

BJP – Indian People's Party (Bharatiya Janata Party)
MBCs – Most Backward Castes
NCBC – National Commission for Backward Classes
OBC – Other Backward Classes
SC – Scheduled Castes
SP– Socialist Party (Samajwadi Party)
UPA – United Progressive Alliance

CHAPTER 5

CPRF – the Communist Party of the Russian Federation
PRI – Institutional Revolutionary Party
TIK – territorial electoral commission (territorialnaya izbiratel'naya komissiya)
UIK – precinct electoral commission (utchastkoavaya izbiratel'naya komissiya)

CHAPTER 6

FSN – National Salvation Front
MPs – Members of Parliament
PDL – Democratic Liberal Party
PNG – New Generation Party
PNL – National Liberal Party
PPDD – People's Party Dan Diacinescu
PR – Proportional Representation
PRM – Greater Romania Party
PSD – Social Democratic Party
SEAP – Electronic System for Public Procurement
USL – Social Liberal Union

CHAPTER 7

GDP – Gross Domestic Product
OECD – Organisation for Economic Co-Operation and Development

CHAPTER 8

CCTs – Conditional Cash Transfers
DALP –Democratic Accountability and Linkages Project
ENPP – Effective Number of Parliamentary Parties
IMR – Infant Mortality Rate
LA – Latin American Region
PCSE – Panel-Corrected Standard Errors
VDem – Varieties of Democracies Project
WDI – Worldwide Development Indicators

CHAPTER 9

GMM – Generalized Method of Moments
GP Index – Golden and Picci Normalized Index
IRAP – the Regional Tax on Economic Activities
NHS – National Health Service
PBCs – Political Budget Cycles

CHAPTER 10

CSWs – Centres for Social Work
HDZ – Croatian Democratic Union
MFVAIS – Ministry of the Family, Veterans' Affairs and Intergenerational
        Solidarity
NPG – New Public Governance
NPM – New Public Management
NWS – Neo-Weberian State

CHAPTER 11

BI – Banco Industrial
BNDE – the National Economic Development Bank
DAS – Direcao e Assessoramento Superior
DASP – Department for Administrative Services
EBAPE – the Brazilian School for Public Administration and Enterprise
ENA – the French National School of Administration
ENAP – the National School of Public Administration
ESAF – the Higher School of Financial Administration
FUNDAP – the Foundation for Administrative Development
INAP – the Institute for Public Administration
OCV – Inter-Annual Variations in the Organizational Charts
PRN – only mentioned once without the full name
SINAPA – the National System for the Administrative Profession
TORs – units change depending on turnovers
UCRI – the Intransigent Radical Union Party

List of Figures and Tables

LIST OF FIGURES

LIST OF TABLES

Chapter One

Introduction

Clientelism and Democratic Representation in Comparative Perspective

Saskia Ruth-Lovell

Research on political clientelism has experienced a revival in recent years. Though the decline of clientelistic practices – such as vote buying and patronage – in democratic contexts has often been predicted, they have proven to be a highly adaptive electoral strategy and a means for party building (Kopecký, Mair, and Spirova 2012, 209; Roniger 2004). The puzzling persistence of the phenomenon in new and old democracies inspired researchers to investigate its micro-foundations and causes (e.g., Kitschelt & Kselman 2013; Kramon 2017; Stokes, Dunning, Nazareno, & Brusco 2013; Szwarcberg 2015). Within the last two decades researchers have begun to uncover the behavioural logic driving clientelistic actors' choices as well as institutional contexts which favour such state-society relationships through different theoretical and empirical approaches (e.g., Hilgers 2009; Isaksson & Bigsten 2017; Kitschelt & Wilkinson 2007b; Nichter 2018; Tomsa & Ufen 2013). Recently scholars have also turned their attention to the effects of clientelism on the functioning and quality of different democratic institutions (e.g., Abente Brun & Diamond 2014; Hilgers 2013; Keefer 2007).

This volume seeks to contribute to this new line of research on the consequences of clientelism, in particular, for democratic representation. The contributors to this book argue that clientelistic practices impinge on democratic representation in several distinct ways. In the first part of this volume, we investigate how political clientelism may cause accountability failures and lead to adverse selection of political representatives through the electoral process. In the second part of the volume we turn our attention to the relationship between political clientelism and the responsiveness of elected representatives as well as the substantive outputs of the democratic process, that is public policies. To set the stage, this introductory chapter will first revisit the variety of overlapping and conflicting definitions of clientelism researchers are confronted with as well as give an overview of the problems that arise when researchers aim to measure the phenomenon for the purpose of empirical analyses. Afterwards, I will then turn to the two main themes the contributors in this volume address in more detail and give a short overview of the chapters in this book.

DEFINING AND MEASURING POLITICAL CLIENTELISM

This volume builds on a long history of studies on the phenomenon of clientelism. Due to this history as well as the presence of clientelism in very different contexts, researchers are confronted with a variety of overlapping and conflicting definitions. According to the origins of the concept, traditional clientelism describes a dyadic, personal relationship between unequals that builds on fear or obligation as bonds, for example between landowners (patron) and their peasants (clients) in agrarian societies (Eisenstadt & Roniger 1984; Piattoni 2001; Roniger 2004). With democratization and mass enfranchisement, clientelistic relationships adapted to changing political circumstances. Hence, contemporary definitions of political clientelism, in contrast, directly relate to the democratic process and therefore extend to political exchanges between parties (patron) and voters (clients), like vote buying and patronage (Kopecký et al. 2012; Schaffer & Schedler 2007). As the term 'clientelism' is widely used and prone to conceptual stretching, we limit its conception for the purpose of this book to those practices which directly relate to the democratic process (see Gans-Morse, Mazzuca, & Nichter 2014; Kitschelt & Wilkinson 2007b; Stokes et al. 2013).

More specifically, we define political clientelism as a political strategy based on the distribution of selective benefits to voters and supporters, like consumer goods, access to social security programs, or jobs in exchange for their support (e.g., Kitschelt & Wilkinson 2007a; Piattoni 2001). This general definition covers both patronage and vote-buying practices, two specific subtypes of the clientelistic exchange. Following Stokes, patronage is '*the proffering of public resources (most typically, public employment) by office-holders in return for electoral support*' (Stokes 2007b, 606, italics in original), and '*vote buying is a more narrow exchange of goods (benefits, protections) for one's own vote*' (Stokes 2007b, 606, italics in original).[1] Note that clientelistic practices may extend beyond elections and serve to build long-term reciprocal exchange networks or conditional partisan loyalties (see Nichter 2018, Diaz-Cayeros, Estévez, and Magaloni 2016). Vote buying and patronage can be distinguished from other more programmatic forms of distributional strategies – like pork barrelling or constituency service – through their selectivity and the conditionality of the exchange relationship between parties and voters (see, especially, Schaffer & Schedler 2007; Stokes et al.

2013). While programmatic political actors mobilize support by promising to implement specific policies that do not distinguish between co-partisans and non-partisans when they vote for them, clientelistic actors provide only selective benefits (like consumer goods, preferential access to social security programs, or employment opportunities) conditional on their clients' political support. Especially in new democracies political clientelism is prevalent and complements political parties' strategic repertoire in addition to a classical policy-based representation (e.g., Corstange 2016; Hilgers 2013; Kitschelt & Wilkinson 2007b; Kramon 2017; Mares & Young 2016; Roy 2018).

Comparative research on political clientelism also struggles with the problem of data availability. Clientelistic practices usually do not take place in the open, due to their potential illegality and the social undesirability that is attached to them in democratic contexts (Gonzalez-Ocantos, de Jonge, Meléndez, Osorio, & Nickerson 2012; Schaffer & Schedler 2007). Hence, direct and reliable comparative measures on political clientelism are difficult to find. This is why a considerable degree of research on political clientelism is based on ethnographic and qualitative case studies (e.g., Auyero 1999; Hilgers 2009; Szwarcberg 2012). Comparative studies on the phenomenon, on the other hand, often rely on proxy variables, like public employment and spending data or indices of corruption (e.g., Calvo & Murillo 2004; Keefer 2007; Remmer 2007). More recently, comparative researchers began to use different types of surveys to cover a larger number of cases and to measure clientelism directly on different analytical levels, for example on the micro-level (e.g., the Latin American Public Opinion Project [LAPOP] included several items on vote-buying practices in some of their waves; see Americas Barometer 2010), the meso-level (e.g., the Democratic Accountability and Linkages Project [DALP] asks experts to evaluate political parties' representational links with their supporters across several world regions; see Kitschelt 2013), as well as on the macro-level (e.g., the Varieties of Democracy Project [VDem] recently included a system-level indicator assessing the degree of clientelistic exchanges across a large number of countries, see Coppedge et al. 2018).

POLITICAL CLIENTELISM AND DEMOCRATIC REPRESENTATION

In theory, the quality of democratic representation is often judged according to the accountability of representatives as well as on their responsiveness towards the interests of their voters (see Bartolini 1999, 2000; Schumpeter 1950). Both *accountability* and *responsiveness* are at the core of theories on democratic representation and political competition (Powell 2004; Strøm 1992). Ideally, repeated, free, open, secret, and fair elections make political actors accountable to their electorate, and political competition between these actors induces them to be responsive to their voters' policy preferences. Policy responsiveness may, thereby, originate in two ways: First, in line with an *accountability perspective* on democratic representation, political competition enables voters to hold their representatives accountable by rewarding or punishing them retrospectively, dependent on their performance in office (Manin, Przeworski, & Stokes 1999a; Powell 2000). Thereby, institutional mechanisms ideally induce responsive behaviour of representatives to the preferences of citizens, since these are (according to theory) the voter's criteria to evaluate whether to sanction them or not. If such institutional accountability arrangements function well, incumbent public officials are induced to be directly responsive to public opinion changes due to 'rational anticipation' of the threat of turnover (Manin et al. 1999a; Stimson, Mackuen, & Erikson 1995; Wlezien & Soroka 2007). Second, according to the *mandate perspective* of democratic representation, responsiveness may also originate indirectly when voters select representatives prospectively according to their policy promises, assuming these representatives are credible to their promises, implementing the policies desired by their voters (Manin et al. 1999a; Powell 2000). Figure 1.1 gives an overview on the different links in the process of democratic representation.

Traditional theories, however, usually rest upon the assumption of policy-based behaviour of both political representatives and voters (Manin et al. 1999a; Powell 2004). But elected representatives will respond to voters' policy interests only if they are selected and judged by this logic. Thus, representative institutions structure only the scope of political actors' behavior but do not determine the substance on which they are accountable and responsive to their voters (Caramani 2017; Schweber 2016; Thomassen 1994).

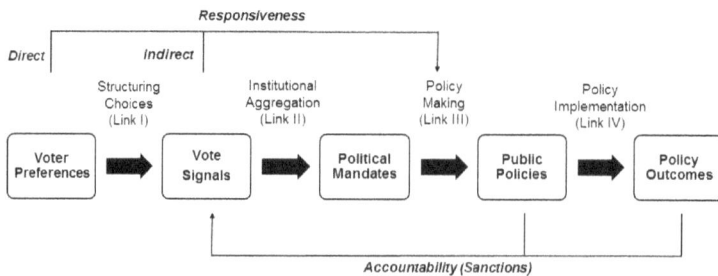

Figure 1.1   The Process of Representation
Source: Adapted from Manin, Przeworski, and Stokes (1999b, 9) as well as Powell (2005, 63).

The predominant focus on procedural and substantive conceptions of representation is conditioned by developments in the field of representation studies itself. Research on democratic representation draws heavily on Hannah Pitkin's canonical book *The Concept of Representation* (1967). However, Pitkin theorizes that representation can be conceived of in four ways: (1) formalistic representation through procedures that authorizes representatives to act on behalf of their represented; (2) substantive representation that puts an emphasis on 'acting in the interest of the represented, in a manner responsive to them' (1967, 209); (3) descriptive representation in which representatives 'stand for' their represented based on some attributive characteristic; and, finally, (4) symbolic representation which also conceives of representing as 'standing for' by means of ideas, rituals, or practices. Although Pitkin asserts that all of these views are part of the general concept of representation ('making present *in some sense* of something', 1967, 8, italics in original), she elevated substantive representation above other modes of representation, and for decades to come researchers have not contested this supremacy and shied away from critical engagement with this framework (Brito Vieira 2017; Urbinati & Warren 2008). Since the 1990s, however, the study of democratic representation experienced a wave of renewed attention. Representation scholars have taken interest in the inclusiveness and exclusiveness of representation, which led them to move beyond elitist conceptions (e.g., Manin 1997; Williams 1997; Young 2000). Moreover, contributions in the area of gender and ethnic studies sparked research on formerly neglected modes of descriptive and symbolic representation (e.g., Lombardo & Meier 2018; Zuber 2015) and contributed to the development of new ways to incorporate these different modes of representation into an integrated model of democratic representation (e.g., Hänni 2016; Meier & Verge 2017; Schwindt-Bayer & Mishler 2005).

The aim of this edited book is to add to this literature by highlighting potential distortions in the process of democratic representation through non-programmatic political behaviour, and political clientelism, more specifically. As previous research indicates, clientelism may impact on the democratic representative process in several ways. First, research on the behavioural foundations of clientelistic exchanges indicates that clientelism may pervert the representative link between parties and voters, making the latter accountable to the former (see Gans-Morse et al. 2014; Stokes 2005)[2] and makes the distribution of benefits dependent on previous political support (see links II through IV in Figure 1.1). Second, several researchers highlight that unlike programmatic parties, clientelistic parties do not offer consistent policy cues to their voters nor do they provide for mechanisms of interest aggregation (Kitschelt 2000; Piattoni 2001; Ruth 2016). Consequently, clientelistic mobilization renders the vote signal useless to determine voter's policy preferences (i.e., it severs the first link in the ideal process of representation, see Figure 1.1).

Qualitative as well as quantitative research on clientelism identified two societal groups that are more likely to be targeted by clientelistic parties: poor voter groups and ethnic voter groups (e.g., Chandra 2007; Kramon 2019; Stokes et al. 2013; Weitz-Shapiro 2014).[3] Concerning the former, the marginal utility theorem states that poor voters are more receptive to direct material incentives, because they value side payments more than future benefits from the provision of public goods (Calvo & Murillo 2013; Dixit & Londregan 1996; Szwarcberg 2015). Hence, clientelistic parties have a genuine interest in maintaining the status quo of poverty or income inequality (Shefner 2013; Stokes 2007a). Concerning ethnic voters another rationale applies. Especially in new democracies where uncertainty in the political realm is high, political parties may use ethnic attributes to identify and mobilize voters belonging to such categories (e.g., Dunning & Nilekani 2013; Isaksson & Bigsten 2017). Thus, when ethnic voters elect representatives belonging to the same ethnic category, this fosters descriptive representation based on ethnic markers (language, religion, etc.). Thereby, ethnic elites may capture state institutions by promising to grant their ethnic group privileged access to state resources instead of catering for voter groups through specific policy programs (van de Walle 2007). Furthermore, neither poverty nor ethnicity are categories that circumscribe homogeneous groups. Other criteria like regional differences, class characteristics, or multi-ethnic fragmentation – to name just a few – may lead to different representation patterns within these groups of likely clients.

However, political clientelism does not just impinge on the input side of democratic representative systems (Easton 1965; Schmidt 2013), since these practices aim at the exploitation of state resources for the benefit of few clearly delimitable groups of voters (i.e., particularistic, private goods) and not at the implementation of general welfare-enhancing policies (i.e., universalistic, public goods).[4] Recently, researchers have turned their attention to these so-called second-tier effects of clientelistic practices (Desposato 2007) on democratic throughput and output. This is highly relevant, since once clientelistic actors reach governmental positions they may have a greater 'margin of safety' (Stimson et al. 1995) to follow other policy interests than those of their voters and nevertheless become re-elected as long as they provide selective benefits. Hence, clientelistic practices induce political parties or candidates to collect votes based on one rational while representing only a segmented fraction of their voters based on their policy preferences (Gibson 1997; Luna 2014; Tzelgov and Wang 2016). Hence, the connection between clientelism and low (policy) responsiveness of political elites to the policy interests of their clients seems to be intuitively straightforward. On these grounds, it is often assumed that clientelistic parties' primary interest in the legislative arena lies in the introduction of new policies that expand their leverage on public resources (*rent-seeking*), in safeguarding public funds at their disposal from legislative interference (*rent-preserving*), which might include the blocking of meritocratic public service reforms or transparency requirements in public administration (see Geddes 1996; Lyne 2008; Pribble 2013). Studies on clientelism and policy implementation offer additional theoretical and empirical insights. Recent research, for example shows how clientelism may distort the implementation of public policies through political manipulation (e.g., Abente Brun & Diamond 2014; Cruz & Keefer 2015; Diaz-Cayeros, Estévez, & Magaloni 2016; Nichter 2018) as well as under which contexts political actors refrain from distributing public benefits in clientelistic ways (see Beck Fenwick 2015; De La O 2013; Weitz-Shapiro 2014).

OUTLINE OF THE BOOK

Studying the effects of clientelism on democratic representation is most relevant. For one, by targeting specific voter groups political clientelism capitalizes on social and economic inequalities and translates them into unequal political power (Shefner 2013), which should reflect on the quality of democratic inputs as well as democratic outputs (Stokes et al. 2013; Weitz-Shapiro 2014). To address these two theoretical consequences of clientelistic practices systematically, this volume is structured along the lines of the democratic process. The first part of the book comprises five chapters that focus on the input side of the representative process, that is electoral politics. The second part of this volume also comprises five chapters that analyse questions related to the output side of democratic governance, that is public policies.

The contributions in the first part of the volume theorize and empirically test arguments about the interplay of voter characteristics (e.g., socio-economic groups, identity groups) and context conditions (e.g., heterogeneity, electoral system) in order to examine the consequences of particularistic practices for the quality of democratic representation.

In chapter 2, Saskia P. Ruth-Lovell analyses the distortive impact clientelistic practices may have on the representation of voter's policy preferences. Hence, this chapter focuses on the first part of the representative process (link I in Figure 1.1). Ruth-Lovell hypothesizes a negative association between clientelistic practices and one of the most common indicators of substantive representation, policy congruence. By means of quantitative analyses she shows how clientelism impedes one of the desirable outcomes of the representative process, i.e. policy responsiveness. Relatedly, in their contribution to this volume (chapter 3), Petr Kopecký and Maria Spirova investigate the link between clientelism and descriptive representation. By means of a comparative case study of the role of ethnic minority parties in Bulgaria and Romania, they investigate how particularistic organizational party strategies may jeopardize the representation of the preferences of minority groups within ethnically divided societies. Hence, this chapter identifies another logic how clientelism may distort the input side of the representative process.

Frank de Zwart, in chapter 4, looks at how difficult it is to design institutional structures aimed to counter clientelistic practices. Focusing on the Indian affirmative action quota rules, he exemplifies the adaptability of the clientelistic strategy to changing conditions in the institutional context as well as how fluid ethnic identity categories may serve as clientelistic mobilization tool.

In chapter 5, Inga A.-L. Saikkonen investigates how spatial patterns of clientelistic turnout buying in Russia contribute to the stabilization of a competitive authoritarian regime. As such the chapter highlights the distortive potential of clientelism on the second link in the representative process, that is institutional aggregation (see Figure 1.1). Therefore, Saikkonen analyses presidential election data from 2000 to 2012 in one of the most stable electoral authoritarian systems in recent history.

Chapter 6 – by Sergiu Gherghina and Clara Volintiru – analyses how the funding of clientelistic networks by private donors helps clientelistic actors to survive in public office and how they contribute to a cartelization process of democratic representation. They propose a bi-dimensional mechanism as to how exogenous resources, provided by private donors, shift the locus of responsiveness towards another set of actors (horizontal linkage) beyond voters.

The second part of this volume focuses on the influence of clientelistic practices on policy programs, policy implementation and evaluation, as well as the relationship between clientelism and the potential for policy reform. Hence, this part of the book aims at analysing second-tier effects of particularistic practices (Desposato 2007). Contributions in this part of the edited volume analyse the behaviour of clientelistic actors within different institutional settings and with respect to different public policies.

Juha Ylisalo, in chapter 7, highlights the interactive relationship between the institutional context of party competition, government formation, and non-programmatic spending behaviour of governments, illuminating the impact clientelistic practices can have on the third link in the process of representation (policy-making, see Figure 1.1). By means of quantitative analyses he analyses the association between clientelism, government fragmentation, and fiscal spending patterns in both Western and Eastern European countries (from 1990/1995 to 2012).

Chapter 8 – by Sarah Berens and Saskia P. Ruth-Lovell – focuses on the relationship between clientelistic practices and the persistence of particularistic welfare states in Latin America. As such the chapter illuminates how social policy advocacy as well as social policy outcomes may be distorted in contexts with high levels of clientelism. Hence, the chapter adds to the investigation of the impact of clientelism on policy-making (link III in Figure 1.1). To test their claims they use public opinion and expert survey data to estimate cross-sectional as well as time-series regression models.

In chapter 9 on health policy in Italy, Francesco Stolfi analyses the relationship between social capital and clientelistic spending patterns. His contribution highlights how the clientelistic practice of patronage may be associated to electoral cycles in distributive spending. Using a sub-national comparative design, he analyses how the degree of clientelism distorts regional spending in the health sector in Italy for electoral purposes.

Looking at the connection between clientelism and policy implementation as well as reform in Croatia, Anka Kekez analyses the fourth link in the representative process depicted in Figure 1.1 (chapter 10). Building on an in-depth case study design she highlights how a patronage-driven strategy of the incumbent impacts the organizational structures of public service delivery and reform.

Luciana Cingolani focuses on the role of the bureaucracy as an opportunity structure for neopatrimonialism in chapter 11. She develops an original measure of the extent to which new administrations 'appropriate' bureaucratic structures and compares the trajectories of Argentina and Brazil between 1990 and 2010. The chapter analyses several political economy reasons that are argued to explain the resulting contrast between the countries, with Argentina displaying more opportunities for neopatrimonial practices.

In the last chapter, Maria Spirova and Saskia P. Ruth-Lovell draw conclusions.

NOTES

1. Related practices are, for example, turnout and abstention buying (see Gans-Morse, Mazzuca and Nichter 2014).

2. With respect to vote-buying practices, especially in democratic contexts where the secrecy of the vote is given (de jure), clientelistic actors need to invest in monitoring and enforcement procedures to secure compliance to the quid-pro-quo nature of these exchanges over time (see, e.g., Finan & Schechter 2012; Nichter 2008; Szwarcberg 2015; Wang & Kurzman 2007).

3. Beyond these two most likely target groups it is still a matter of debate if clientelistic actors rather target swing- versus core-voters or if they use selective benefits to mobilize or to persuade clients to support them (Cox 2010; Hidalgo & Nichter 2016; Nichter 2008; Stokes et al. 2013).

4. For a debate on whether clientelistic exchanges may be considered as a substitute to the welfare state in contexts with low state capacity and, as such, pose a viable option from a client's perspective, see chapter 8 in this volume, as well as, among others, Auyero (1999), Hilgers (2009), and Kitschelt (2015).

REFERENCES

Abente Brun, D., & Diamond, L. (2014). *Clientelism, Social Policy, and the Quality of Democracy*. Baltimore: Johns Hopkins University Press.

AmericasBarometer. (2010). Latin American Public Opinion Project (LAPOP).

Auyero, J. (1999). 'From the Client's Point(s) of View': How Poor People Perceive and Evaluate Political Clientelism. *Theory and Society, 28*, 297–334.

Bartolini, S. (1999). Collusion, Competition and Democracy: Part I. *Journal of Theoretical Politics, 11*(4), 435–470.

Bartolini, S. (2000). Collusion, Competition and Democracy: Part II. *Journal of Theoretical Politics, 12*(1), 33–65.

Beck Fenwick, T. (2015). *Avoiding Governors: Federalism, Democracy, and Poverty Alleviation in Brazil and Argentina*. Notre Dame, IN: University of Notre Dame Press.

Brito Vieira, M. (2017). Introduction. In M. Brito Vieira (Ed.), *Reclaiming Representation: Contemporary Advances in the Theory of Political Representation* (pp. 1–21). New York: Routledge.

Calvo, E., & Murillo, M. V. (2004). Who Delivers? Partisan Clients in the Argentine Electoral Market. *American Journal of Political Science, 48*(4), 742–757.

Calvo, E., & Murillo, M. V. (2013). When Parties Meet Voters: Assessing Political Linkages Through Partisan Networks and Distributive Expectations in Argentina and Chile. *Comparative Political Studies, 46*(7), 851–882.

Caramani, D. (2017). Will vs. Reason: The Populist and Technocratic Forms of Political Representation and Their Critique to Party Government. *American Political Science Review, 111*(1), 54–67.

Chandra, K. (2007). Counting Heads: A Theory of Voter and Elite Behavior in Patronage Democracies. In H. Kitschelt & S. I. Wilkinson (Eds.), *Patrons, Clients, and Policies. Patterns of Democratic Accountability and Political Competition* (pp. 84–109). Cambridge: Cambridge University Press.

Coppedge, M., Gerring, J., Knutsen, C. H., Lindberg, S. I., Skaaning, S-E., Teorell, J., Altman, D., Bernhard, M., Cornell, A., Fish, M. S., Gjerlow, H., Glynn, A., Hicken, A., Krusell, J., Lührmann, A., Marquardt, K. L., McMann, K., Mechkova, V., Olin, M., Paxton, P., Pemstein, D., Seim, B., Sigman, R., Staton, J., Sundtröm, A., Tzelgov, E., Uberti, L., Wang, Y-T., Wig, T., and Ziblatt, D. (2018). V-Dem Codebook v8. In V. o. D. V.-D. Project (Ed.).

Corstange, D. (2016). *The Price of a Vote in the Middle East: Clientelism and Communal Politics in Lebanon and Yemen*. Cambridge: Cambridge University Press.

Cox, G. W. (2010). Swing Voters, Core Voters, and Distributive Politics. In I. Shapiro, S. C. Stokes, E. J. Wood, & A. S. Kirshner (Eds.), *Political Representation* (pp. 342–357). Cambridge: Cambridge University Press.

Cruz, C., & Keefer, P. (2015). Political Parties, Clientelism, and Bureaucratic Reform. *Comparative Political Studies, 48*(14), 1942–1973.

De La O, A. (2013). Do Conditional Cash Transfers Affect Electoral Behavior? Evidence from a Randomized Experiment in Mexico. *American Journal of Political Science, 57*(1), 1–14.

Desposato, S. W. (2007). How Does Vote Buying Shape the Legislative Arena? In F. C. Schaffer (Ed.), *Elections for Sale: The Causes and Consequences of Vote Buying* (pp. 101–122). Boulder, CO: Lynne Rienner.

Diaz-Cayeros, A., Estévez, F., & Magaloni, B. (2016). *The Political Logic of Poverty Relief: Electoral Strategies and Social Policy in Mexico*. Cambridge: Cambridge University Press.

Dixit, A., & Londregan, J. (1996). The Determinants of Success of Special Interests in Redistributive Politics. *Journal of Politics, 58*(4), 1132–1155.

Dunning, T., & Nilekani, J. (2013). Ethnic Quotas and Political Mobilization: Caste, Parties, and Distribution in Indian Village Councils. *American Political Science Review, 107*(1), 35–56.

Easton, D. (1965). *A System Analysis of Political Life*. New York: McGraw-Hill.

Eisenstadt, S. N., & Roniger, L. (1984). *Patrons, Clients and Friends: Interpersonal Relations and the Structure of Trust in Society*. Cambridge: Cambridge University Press.

Finan, F., & Schechter, L. (2012). Vote-Buying and Reciprocity. *Econometrica, 80*(2), 863–881.

Gans-Morse, J., Mazzuca, S. L., & Nichter, S. (2014). Varieties of Clientelism: Machine Politics During Elections. *American Journal of Political Science, 58*(2), 415–432.

Geddes, B. (1996). *Politician's Dilemma: Building State Capacity in Latin America*. Berkeley: University of California Press.

Gibson, E. L. (1997). The Populist Road to Market Reform: Policy and Electoral Coalitions in Mexico and Argentina. *World Politics, 49*(3), 339–370.

Gonzalez-Ocantos, E., de Jonge, C. K., Meléndez, C., Osorio, J., & Nickerson, D. W. (2012). Vote Buying and Social Desirability Bias: Experimental Evidence from Nicaragua. *American Journal of Political Science, 56*(1), 202–217.

Hänni, M. (2016). Presence, Representation, and Impact: How Minority MPs Affect Policy Outcomes. *Legislative Studies Quarterly, 42*(1), 97–130.

Hidalgo, F. D., & Nichter, S. (2016). Voter Buying: Shaping the Electorate Through Clientelism. *American Journal of Political Science, 60*(2), 436–455.

Hilgers, T. (2009). 'Who Is Using Whom?' Clientelism from the Client's Perspective. *Journal of Iberian and Latin American Research, 15*(1), 51–75.

Hilgers, T. (Ed.). (2013). *Clientelism in Everyday Latin American Politics*. Basingstoke: Palgrave Macmillan.

Isaksson, A-S., & Bigsten, A. (2017). Clientelism and Ethnic Divisions in African Countries. *African Affairs, 116*(465), 621–647.

Keefer, P. (2007). Clientelism, Credibility, and the Policy Choices of Young Democracies. *American Journal of Political Science, 51*(4), 804–821.

Kitschelt, H. (2000). Linkages Between Citizens and Politicians in Democratic Polities. *Comparative Political Studies, 33*(6–7), 845–879.

Kitschelt, H. (2013). *Democratic Accountability and Linkages Project*. Durham: Duke University Press.

Kitschelt, H. (2015). *Social Policy, Democratic Linkages, and Political Governance*. Paper presented at the Quality of Government and the Performance of Democracies, Gothenburg.

Kitschelt, H., & Kselman, D. M. (2013). Economic Development, Democratic Experience, and Political Parties' Linkage Strategies. *Comparative Political Studies*.

Kitschelt, H., & Wilkinson, S. I. (2007a). Citizen-Politician Linkages: An Introduction. In H. Kitschelt & S. I. Wilkinson (Eds.), *Patrons, Clients, and Policies: Patterns of Democratic Accountability and Political Competition* (pp. 1–49). Cambridge: Cambridge University Press.

Kitschelt, H., & Wilkinson, S. I. (Eds.). (2007b). *Patrons, Clients, and Policies: Patterns of Democratic Accountability and Political Competition*. Cambridge: Cambridge University Press.

Kopecký, P., Mair, P., & Spirova, M. (2012). *Party Patronage and Party Government in European Democracies*. Oxford: Oxford University Press.

Kramon, E. (2019). Ethnic Group Institutions and Electoral Clientelism. *Party Politics*, *25*(3), 435–447.

Kramon, E. (2017). *Money for Votes: The Causes and Consequences of Electoral Clientelism in Africa*. Cambridge: Cambridge University Press.

Lombardo, E., & Meier, P. (2018). Good Symbolic Representation: The Relevance of Inclusion. *PS: Political Science & Politics*, *51*(2), 327–330.

Luna, J. P. (2014). *Segmented Representation: Political Party Strategies in Unequal Democracies*. Oxford: Oxford University Press.

Lyne, M. M. (2008). *The Voter's Dilemma and Democratic Accountability: Latin America and Beyond*. University Park: The Pennsylvania State University Press.

Manin, B. (1997). *The Principles of Representative Government*. Cambridge: Cambridge University Press.

Manin, B., Przeworski, A., & Stokes, S. C. (1999a). Elections and Representation. In A. Przeworski, S. C. Stokes, & B. Manin (Eds.), *Democracy, Accountability, and Representation* (pp. 29–54). Cambridge: Cambridge University Press.

Manin, B., Przeworski, A., & Stokes, S. C. (1999b). Introduction. In A. Przeworski, S. C. Stokes, & B. Manin (Eds.), *Democracy, Accountability, and Representation* (pp. 1–26). Cambridge: Cambridge University Press.

Mares, I., & Young, L. (2016). Buying, Expropriating, and Stealing Votes. *Annual Review of Political Science*, *19*(1), 267–288.

Meier, P., & Verge, T. (2017). Conceptual and Methodological Challenges in the Study of Symbolic Representation – an Introduction. *Politics, Groups, and Identities*, *5*(3), 478–481.

Nichter, S. (2008). Vote Buying or Turnout Buying? Machine Politics and the Secret Ballot. *American Political Science Review*, *102*(1), 19–31.

Nichter, S. (2018): *Votes for Survival. Relational Clientelism in Latin America*. Cambridge: Cambridge University Press.

Piattoni, S. (2001). Clientelism in Historical and Comparative Perspective. In S. Piattoni (Ed.), *Clientelism, Interests, and Democratic Representation* (pp. 1–30). Cambridge: Cambridge University Press.

Pitkin, H. F. (1967). *The Concept of Representation*. Berkeley: University of California Press.

Powell, G. B. (2000). *Elections as Instruments of Democracy: Majoritarian and Proportional Visions*. New Haven, CT: Yale University Press.

Powell, G. B. (2004). Political Representation in Comparative Politics. *Annual Review of Political Science*, *7*(1), 273–296.

Powell, G. B. (2005). The Chain of Responsiveness. In L. Diamond & L. Morlino (Eds.), *Assessing the Quality of Democracy* (pp. 62–76). Baltimore: Johns Hopkins University Press.

Pribble, J. (2013). *Welfare and Party Politics in Latin America*. Cambridge: Cambridge University Press.

Remmer, K. L. (2007). The Political Economy of Patronage: Expenditure Patterns in the Argentine Provinces, 1983–2003. *The Journal of Politics*, *69*(2), 363–377.

Roniger, L. (2004). Political Clientelism, Democracy, and Market Economy. *Comparative Politics*, *36*(3), 353–375.

Roy, I. (2018). *Politics of the Poor: Negotiating Democracy in Contemporary India*. Cambridge: Cambridge University Press.

Ruth, S. P. (2016). Clientelism and the Utility of the Left-Right Dimension in Latin America. *Latin American Politics and Society*, *58*(1), 72–97.

Schaffer, F. C., & Schedler, A. (2007). What Is Vote Buying? In F. C. Schaffer (Ed.), *Elections for Sale: The Causes and Consequences of Vote Buying* (pp. 17–30). Boulder, CO: Lynne Rienner.

Schmidt, V. A. (2013). Democracy and Legitimacy in the European Union Revisited: Input, Output and 'Throughput'. *Political Studies*, *61*(1), 2–22.

Schumpeter, J. A. (1950). *Capitalism, Socialism & Democracy*. New York: Harper & Brothers.

Schweber, H. (2016). The Limits of Political Representation. *American Political Science Review*, *110*(2), 382–396.

Schwindt-Bayer, L. A., & Mishler, W. (2005). An Integrated Model of Women's Representation. *The Journal of Politics*, *67*(2), 407–428.

Shefner, J. (2013). What Is Politics For? Inequality, Representation, and Needs Satisfaction Under Clientelism and Democracy. In T. Hilgers (Ed.), *Clientelism in Everyday Latin American Politics* (pp. 41–59). Basingstoke: Palgrave Macmillan.

Stimson, J. A., Mackuen, M. B., & Erikson, R. S. (1995). Dynamic Representation. *American Political Science Review*, *89*(3), 534–565.

Stokes, S. C. (2005). Perverse Accountability: A Formal Model of Machine Politics with Evidence from Argentina. *American Political Science Review*, *99*(3), 315–325.

Stokes, S. C. (2007a). Is Vote Buying Undemocratic? In F. C. Schaffer (Ed.), *Elections for Sale: The Causes and Consequences of Vote Buying* (pp. 81–99). Boulder, CO: Lynne Rienner.

Stokes, S. C. (2007b). Political Clientelism. In C. Boix & S. C. Stokes (Eds.), *The Oxford Handbook of Comparative Politics* (pp. 604–627). Oxford: Oxford University Press.

Stokes, S. C., Dunning, T., Nazareno, M., & Brusco, V. (Eds.). (2013). *Brokers, Voters, and Clientelism. The Puzzle of Distributive Politics*. Cambridge: Cambridge University Press.

Strøm, K. (1992). Democracy as Political Competition. *American Behavioral Scientist*, *35*(4–5), 375–396.

Szwarcberg, M. (2012). Revisiting Clientelism: A Network Analysis of Problem-Solving Networks in Argentina. *Social Network*, *34*, 230–240.

Szwarcberg, M. (2015). *Mobilizing Poor Voters: Machine Politics, Clientelism, and Social Networks in Argentina*. Cambridge: Cambridge University Press.

Thomassen, J. (1994). Empirical Research into Political Representation: Failing Democracy or Failing Models? In M. K. Jennings & T. E. Mann (Eds.), *Elections at Home and Abroad* (pp. 237–264). Ann Arbor: University of Michigan Press.

Tomsa, D., & Ufen, A. (Eds.). (2013). *Party Politics in Southeast Asia: Clientelism and Electoral Competition in Indonesia, Thailand and the Philippines*. London: Routledge.

Tzelgov, E., & Wang, Y-T. (2016). Party Ideology and Clientelistic Linkage. *Electoral Studies, 44*, 374–387.

Urbinati, N., & Warren, M. E. (2008). The Concept of Representation in Contemporary Democratic Theory. *Annual Review of Political Science, 11*(1), 387–412.

van de Walle, N. (2007). Meet the New Boss, Same as the Old Boss? The Evolution of Political Clientelism in Africa. In H. Kitschelt & S. I. Wilkinson (Eds.), *Patrons, Clients, and Policies: Patterns of Democratic Accountability and Political Competition* (pp. 50–67). Cambridge: Cambridge University Press.

Wang, C-S., & Kurzman, C. (2007). The Logistics: How to Buy Votes. In F. C. Schaffer (Ed.), *Elections for Sale: The Causes and Consequences of Vote Buying* (pp. 61–78). Boulder, CO: Lynne Rienner.

Weitz-Shapiro, R. (2014). *Curbing Clientelism in Argentina: Politics, Poverty, and Social Policy*. Cambridge: Cambridge University Press.

Williams, M. (1997). *Voice, Trust, and Memory: Marginalized Groups and the Failings of Liberal Representation*. Princeton: Princeton University Press.

Wlezien, C., & Soroka, S. N. (2007). The Relationship Between Public Opinion and Policy. In R. Dalton & H-D. Klingemann (Eds.), *Oxford Handbook of Political Behavior* (pp. 799–817). Oxford: Oxford University Press.

Young, I. M. (2000). *Inclusion and Democracy*. Oxford: Oxford University Press.

Zuber, C. I. (2015). Reserved Seats, Political Parties, and Minority Representation. *Ethnopolitics, 14*(4), 390–403.

Chapter Two

Linkage Strategies and Policy Congruence in Latin American Democracies

Saskia Ruth-Lovell[1]

INTRODUCTION

In line with a substantive conception, democratic representation is understood as the connection between citizens' political preferences and the political preferences or behaviour of elected representatives (see Manin, Przeworski, & Stokes 1999; Pitkin 1967; Powell 2004). Empirical research on this topic has a long history in advanced democracies (e.g., Blais & Bodet 2006; Huber & Powell 1994; Miller & Stokes 1963) and has recently been applied to new democracies like those in Latin America (e.g., Belchior, Sanches, & José 2018; Luna & Zechmeister 2005; Otero-Felipe & Rodríguez-Zepeda 2010).

However, assumptions frequently made in studies on advanced democracies may not be easily transferred to contexts of new democracies. As research on party politics shows, the role of political parties in new democracies seems less central and political parties and politicians maintain other forms of relationships with society than the classic programmatic linkage form predominant in (most) advanced democracies (e.g., Coppedge 2001; Kitschelt 2000). Especially outside Western European democracies political parties do not just compete in programmatic ways; they may pursue additional or completely different electoral mobilization strategies like personalism and clientelism (Kitschelt & Wilkinson 2007; Stokes 2007b; Webb, Poguntke, & Kolodny 2012). The idealization of policy representation through programmatic competition, therefore, hampers awareness of other modes of political representation.

The aim of this chapter is to investigate the impact of different party-society linkages on the congruence or incongruence between political parties' advocated policies and the policy interests of their supporters. More

15

specifically, the research question is twofold: On the one hand, I address how different linkage strategies affect the degree of policy congruence between political parties and their supporters. On the other hand, I examine the direction of misrepresentation in the case of incongruence between political parties and their supporters. Do political parties position themselves systematically to the right or to the left of their supporters preferred policy interests?[2] These arguments are then tested empirically through multinomial logistic regression analyses, using public opinion and expert survey data covering eighty political parties from eighteen Latin American democracies.

By answering these questions, this study contributes to research on democratic accountability and democratic representation in new democracies.

DEMOCRATIC REPRESENTATION, POLICY CONGRUENCE, AND PARTY-SOCIETY LINKAGES

Political representation is usually described as a principal-agent relationship, in which a principal selects an agent who is then supposed to act in the best interest of the principal. In representative democratic terms this means that the citizens (principal) select – by some voting rule determined by the electoral system – their representatives (agents) for public offices. These elected representatives are expected to act in accordance with the interests of their voters. By means of this substantive representative link citizens may, therefore, insert their interests or policy preferences into the democratic process. Thus, the connection between citizens' policy preferences and preferences or behaviour of policymakers is at the heart of representative democracy (see Manin et al. 1999; Powell 2005; Stimson 1999).

A common way to conceptualize and measure this substantive representational link between a principal and her agent(s) is to assess the degree of congruence between voters' policy preferences and their preferred parties' policy pledges. There are several ways to calculate *policy congruence* emphasizing alternative aspects of the representational link. Concept-measurement approaches usually differ with respect to four themes: the comparative approach, the scope of content, the timing, and the actors involved.

Concerning the comparative approach the representativeness of political actors with respect to voters' policy interests may be measured at one point in time – *cross-sectional* perspective – or over time – *dynamic* perspective (see Ezrow 2010; Spies & Kaiser 2014; Stimson, Mackuen, & Erikson 1995). Concerning the scope of the content a distinction can be made between *issue* and *ideological congruence*. Empirical research on substantive representation started in the 1960s with Miller and Stokes (1963) seminal study on policy congruence in specific issue domains (see Achen 1978; Iversen

1994; Schmitt & Thomassen 1999). Later studies turned their attention to the policy bundles political parties offer to their voters, thereby evaluating ideological congruence (e.g., Huber & Powell 1994). Concerning the timing within the democratic process, citizens' policy preferences may be compared to the *policy preferences* of political agents or their behaviour in the policy-making process, that is *policy decisions*. In the former case the focus lies on the matching of signals. This measure of political representation centres on an early stage of the democratic process, that is the agents' quality of being policy advocates (see Cox 1997; Powell 2004). Alternatively the focus may lie on the relationship between citizens' policy preferences and public policy decisions (e.g., Kedar 2005; Mansergh & Thomson 2007; Soroka & Wlezien 2005; Thomson et al. 2017).

Finally, concerning the type of actors involved one may distinguish between *dyadic* and *collective congruence*. Dyadic congruence, on the one hand, refers to the correspondence of policy preferences between voters and their individual district representative or their preferred political party (Barnes 1977; Dalton 1985; Thomassen 1994). Collective congruence, on the other hand, evaluates aggregated, institutional correspondence of citizens' preferences with the preferences of entire legislatures or governments on the system level (Powell 2006; Weissberg 1978). This may lead to different evaluations of policy congruence on different analytical levels. For one, depending on the type of electoral system and the representational link between citizens and legislators it incentivizes (i.e., candidate-centred versus party-centred electoral systems, see Shugart & Haggard 2001), the unit of analysis may refer to district-legislator dyads or party-voter dyads (Dalton 1985, 278). Furthermore, collective congruence may result from the aggregation of dyadic congruence measures, weighted by seat shares, vote shares, or cabinet portfolios. Even if party-voter dyads display considerable low degrees of policy congruence, collective congruence may still be high on the system level as long as the distortions of policy congruence are distributed equally around the country mean (Weissberg 1978, 542). Thus, by evaluating collective congruence only, representational deficits of individual parties may be overlooked because of the ecological inference problem (King 1997). Moreover, misrepresentation within party-voter dyads is most severe for the quality of representation if its distribution is systematically biased to one side of the country mean.

By now researchers came up with several explanatory factors of policy congruence on different analytical levels. On the national level especially electoral system rules, the number of political parties and their degree of polarization as well as different power sharing characteristics and recently the impact of economic crisis have been at the centre of interest (Huber & Powell 1994; Kedar 2005; Pierce 1999). However, empirical findings remain inconclusive. On the party level the effects of several party characteristics, like government participation, candidate selection processes, or the ideological position on congruence in several issue dimensions, have been tested (e.g., Dalton 1985; Spies & Kaiser 2014).

However, as this short review shows, the congruence literature explicitly focuses on a programmatic link between political parties and their supporters. Comparative research on the effects of other linkage strategies on party-voter congruence, however, is missing.[3] One explanation for this research gap is the regional segmentation of the literature on congruence – which mainly focuses on established democracies. Moreover, the sometimes-implicit application of models of programmatic party competition (like 'the responsible party model') in representational studies on advanced democracies hindered the travelling of empirical research on policy congruence to new democracies (Powell 2004; Thomassen 1994). This chapter, therefore, aims to close this gap and centres on the influence of different party-society linkages on policy congruence.

The linkage concept is a useful analytical tool to study the relationship between political parties and the electorate and, consequently, the quality of democratic representation outside established democracies and without a predetermined focus on programmatic party competition (e.g., Kitschelt 2000; Poguntke 2000). In general, the concept describes an interactive connection between the electorate and the state mediated by political elites. Linkages are driven by political parties' need for votes to win elections and to secure their survival, irrespective of whether they are motivated by office-, vote-, or policy-seeking (Poguntke 2002; Strøm 1990). The literature on representational linkages usually distinguishes between three forms of party-society relationships: programmatic, personalistic, and clientelistic linkages.

Political parties may mobilize electoral support following a programmatic linkage strategy and appeal to their voters with policy programs. These programs consist of policy bundles concerning a range of solutions to the problems in a society. Political parties' policy promises are important for the electoral process because they serve as information short cuts for voters, which have policy preferences and base their electoral decision on them (Downs 1957). In this regard, parties that pursue a programmatic linkage strategy induce voters to signal their policy preferences at election time and thus directly foster an important informational prerequisite of policy congruence.

Political parties may also maintain personalistic bonds with their voters and base their strategy on the personal skills of a (charismatic) leader. Hence, personalistic parties are often referred to as mere electoral vehicles for ambitious party leaders (Coppedge 2001; Kitschelt 2000; Roberts 2002). The promises personalistic parties make to their voters remain opaque. Their party leaders 'tend to promise all things to all people to maintain maximum personal discretion over the strategy of their party vehicle' (Kitschelt 2000, 849). In turn, voters of personalistic parties hardly reveal explicit information about their policy preferences.[4]

Finally, and in line with the general theme of this volume, political parties may rely on a clientelistic linkage strategy. Following the definition laid out in the introduction to this volume, clientelism is understood here as a mobilization strategy, where clientelistic parties offer access to private goods and public services in exchange for political support (see Ruth-Lovell, chapter 1; Kitschelt 2000; Kitschelt & Wilkinson 2007; Stokes 2007b).

There are two different perspectives with regard to the combinability of these linkage strategies. One strand in the literature supports the argument that political actors may pursue different forms of linkages at the same time and for several reasons. Such *strategy mixing* may be a consequence of either risk-aversion of political elites (Magaloni, Diaz-Cayeros, & Estévez 2007; Wantchekon 2003) or the parallel appeal to diverse constituencies which according to Gibson (1997) are then combined into one 'electoral coalition' (see also Luna 2014). Research grouped around the *trade-off hypothesis* argues that programmatic, personalistic, and clientelistic linkages are combinable only to a small degree (Cox & McCubbins 2001; Dixit & Londregan 1996; Kitschelt 2000). Based on the assumption that both programmatic and clientelistic linkage strategies require different organizational investments, parties are precluded to pursue both forms of linkage extensively. Furthermore, the personalistic linkage strategy is usually associated with a weakly institutionalized organizational structure, since party leaders do not want to limit their leverage on intraparty decision-making (Kitschelt 2000; Weyland 1999). The institutionalization of the party organization always comes at the expense of the party leader's autonomy. However, case study research and new comparative data rather support the strategy-mixing perspective than the trade-off hypothesis (see Figures 2.1-a to 1-c).

As suspected by the trade-off hypothesis, Figure 2.1-a shows a moderate negative relationship between the degree of a clientelistic and a programmatic linkage emphasis of one party ($r = -305$, $p < 0.01$). However, at least some political parties are capable to combine both programmatic and clientelistic strategies effectively at a high degree (Hilgers 2009; Magaloni et al. 2007; Singer & Kitschelt 2011). Furthermore, no political parties are observed in the lower-left corner of Figure 2.1-a. This indicates that there are no political parties in the studied sample which rely on a personalistic linkage alone. Thus, the personalistic linkage type does not appear outside of a mix with a programmatic, a clientelistic, or both of these linkages.

In addition to this, Figure 2.1-b shows a positive association between a clientelistic and a personalistic linkage strategy of political parties in the study

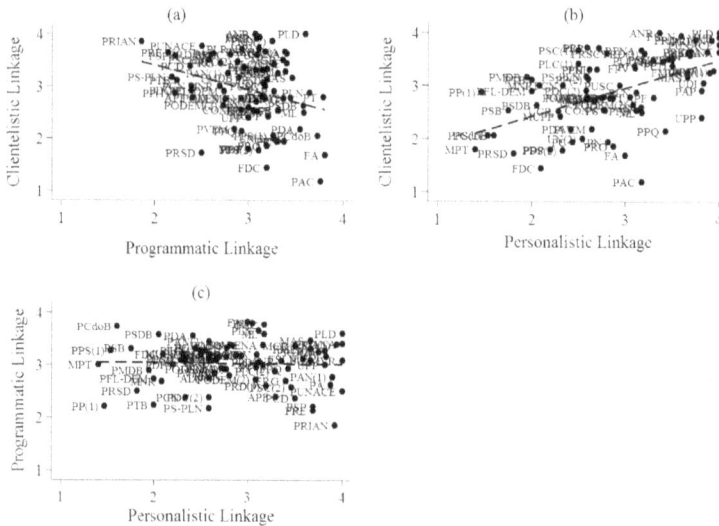

Figure 2.1 Combination of Linkage Strategies (a–c)
Source: Author's calculation based on data from the DALP survey (Kitschelt 2013). Data points are mean expert positions per party on ordinal scales ranging from 1 to 4. Party acronyms are reported in Table A2.1 in the appendix.

($r = 0.530$, $p < 0.01$). This confirms another argument made in the literature, that a personalistic appeal is most compatible with a party organization that is hierarchically structured, and is therefore likely to be combined with the clientelistic linkage strategy (Barr 2009; Pappas 2009; Roberts 2006). Finally, the relationship between a programmatic and a personalistic linkage focus appears to be unsystematic (Figure 2.1-c). A personalistic linkage strategy seems to be an asset that both parties with strong or weak programmatic profiles use if they can.

Building on analytical considerations of elites' as well as voters' behaviour in contexts marked by different party-society relationships, I develop hypotheses on how these linkages affect policy congruence in the next section. More specifically, I analyse the issue congruence of party-voter dyads as the matching between voters' signalled economic policy interests and parties' signalled economic policy programs at one point in time. A special focus is put on biased misrepresentation on the party level.

HYPOTHESES

The functioning of programmatic party competition can be interpreted as an 'iterative signalling game' (Kitschelt 1995, 452). Political parties signal to their potential voters a set of policies they promise to enact when elected into office. Programmatic voters evaluate these policy signals and base their voting decision on their evaluations (Downs 1957). Such programmatic linkage is based on trust and credibility and thus prone to path dependency effects. If victorious political parties defect from their policy pledges or engage in extreme policy switches over time, they may lose the support of voters in subsequent elections. Hence, political parties linked to their supporters by policy pledges ideally hold themselves responsive to voters' policy preferences (Manin et al. 1999; Stokes 1999). The programmatic linkage strategy, thus, constitutes the causal mechanism to bring about policy congruence between political parties and their supporters.

(Baseline) Hypothesis 1: Ceteris paribus, the stronger a political party pursues a programmatic linkage strategy, the higher is the policy congruence between this party and its supporters.

In contrast to this, both clientelistic and personalistic parties do not engage in this policy-signalling game. Instead both linkage strategies 'reduce parties to their most basic, self-referential political function: electing candidates from their ranks into public office' (Roberts 2002, 29). Votes obtained in this way do not entail any information about the policy interests of the voter and are useless for democratic deliberation and the retrospective evaluation of a representatives' policy responsiveness (Ruth 2016; Schaffer 2007; Stokes 2007a; Zechmeister 2010).

Personalistic parties, as mentioned earlier, tend to make opaque promises to their potential supporters. Voters in personalistic relationships base their voting decision on the personal skills of a party leader irrespective of the programmatic outline of the political party (Coppedge 2001; Kitschelt 2000). Furthermore, the personalistic linkage often occurs in combination with a clientelistic and/or a programmatic appeal in the present sample. Thus, if we control for other linkages the match between the policy promises of a personalistic party and the policy preferences of its supporters should reveal no systematic pattern.

Hypothesis 2: Ceteris paribus, a personalistic linkage strategy is expected to have no systematic effect on the policy congruence between a party and its supporters.

In a similar way, clientelistic parties offer no orientation in the policy space to their voters and may even cut across cleavages and cater for highly heterogeneous clients (Gay 1998; Roberts 2002). Voters in clientelistic relationships, in turn, base their voting decision on the exchange of material benefits. Furthermore, arguments in the literature hint to the fact that clientelism distorts policy congruence towards the right end of the economic dimension. The marginal utility theorem, for example states that clientelism builds on socio-economic disadvantages of some parts of the society as the costs of a vote-buying strategy rise with the income of targeted voters (Dixit & Londregan 1996, 1998; Stokes, Dunning, Nazareno, & Brusco 2013). Since the clientelistic linkage relies on direct material inducements, this strategy gets more likely the stronger voters value such side payments and the lesser they value future benefits from the provision of public goods (Kitschelt 2000). Moreover, clientelistic parties may combine vote-buying strategies to address poor constituencies with policy concessions to party brokers or private investors within the clientelistic network (Stokes 2005). Policy preferences of these patrons are assumed to be more to the right on the economic scale than the preferences of poor constituencies.[5] On the basis of these arguments two hypotheses can be stated:

> *Hypothesis 3: Ceteris paribus, the stronger a political party pursues a clientelistic linkage strategy, the lower is the policy congruence between this party and its supporters.*

> *Hypothesis 4: Ceteris paribus, the stronger a political party pursues a clientelistic linkage strategy, the more distorted its ideological congruence is to the right (pro free market) end of the economic policy dimension.[6]*

In the next sections these hypotheses will be tested by comparing cross-sectional data on political parties' linkage strategies and public opinion.

DATA AND MEASUREMENT

The following analyses draw on a cross-sectional data set of eighty political parties covering eighteen Latin American democracies. Besides the fact that different linkage strategies are prevalent in this region, I focus on Latin American party systems for two other reasons: (1) Notwithstanding the differences between new and established democracies, Kitschelt et al. (2010) showed that there are also important differences between new democracies. This is especially true for party-society linkages in Latin America, which vary between and within party systems. (2) Furthermore, Latin American countries share similar socio-economic contexts as well as institutional set-ups. For example, all countries in this study are presidential regimes and share similar structures of horizontal accountability (see Scott Mainwaring & Shugart 1997). These institutional settings are treated as scope conditions in the present study.[7] Additionally, many Latin American countries experienced phases of military rule during the 1970s and 1980s and phases of re-democratization in the 1990s.

Two further criteria were used for the selection of political parties: (1) the inclusion of a political party in the Latinobarometer surveys (hereafter LAB) from 2008 or 2009 (Latinobarómetro 1996–2015) as well as in the expert survey on democratic accountability mechanisms in Latin America (Altman, Luna, Piñeiro, & Toro 2009; Kitschelt 2013) compiled between 2007 and 2009 (hereafter DALP); (2) a minimum of five respondents per party in the public opinion survey and five expert evaluations per party in the expert survey. In total, this study covers eighty political parties from the following countries: Argentina, Bolivia, Brazil, Chile, Colombia, Costa Rica, Dominican Republic, Ecuador, El Salvador, Guatemala, Honduras, Mexico, Nicaragua, Panama, Paraguay, Peru, Uruguay, and Venezuela. For a list of political parties included in the study, see table A1 in the appendix.

Dependent Variables

In the present chapter issue congruence of party-voter dyads in the economic domain will be used as an indicator for substantive representation. The policy preferences of political parties and their respective voters are measured in a one-dimensional economic issue space. Data on positions of political parties are provided by the DALP survey, which inter alia asked experts to rank political parties on a state-market dimension using a 10-point scale:

> State role in governing the economy: [1] Party supports a major role for the state in regulating private economic activity to achieve social goals, in directing development, and/ or maintaining control over key services. [10] Party advocates a minimal role for the state in governing or directing economic activity or development. (Questionnaire DALP 2008)

To match these with the positions of party supporters, the LAB surveys from 2008 and 2009 provide a valuable database as they ask respondents about their party preference as well as to place themselves on state-market dimension using a 10-point scale:

> Some people think that the State must solve all problems because it has the resources to do it, while others think that the market will solve all problems because it distributes the resources in an efficient way. Using a scale from 1 to 10, where 1 means 'State must solve all problems' and 10 means 'Market must solve all problems'. Where would you place yourself? (Questionnaire LAB 2008, 2009, author's translation)

Another alternative would have been to use the classical left-right dimension to compare party-voter dyads in ideological terms. However, the use of the left-right policy space is debated as it may be understood differently by different units of analysis (voters, party elites, experts) and its understanding may differ depending on the context, thereby hindering cross-country comparison

(Golder & Stramski 2010; Zechmeister 2006).[8] Therefore, the economic issue dimension will be used to construct the dependent variable in this study. Figure 2.2 graphically matches the party mean position on the economic scale from the DALP survey and the mean economic position of the respective party's supporters from the LAB survey.

Different measures of policy congruence and their properties have been extensively discussed in the literature (e.g., Achen 1978; Golder & Stramski 2010). To capture the degree of congruence and the directionality of misrepresentation the median party-voter congruence (Golder & Stramski 2010) will be used:

$$\text{Median Party Voter Congruence } (\text{MPVC}) = \text{PM} - \text{MV}$$

PM is the mean party expert position on the economic scale, and MV is the median party-voter position on the economic scale. Using this operationalization we attain a measure that displays at the same time the degree of a political party's congruence and the direction of its potential 'incongruence' with their party supporters. The closer a political party's MPVC value is to 0 the more congruent the party is to its supporters. Moreover, negative values

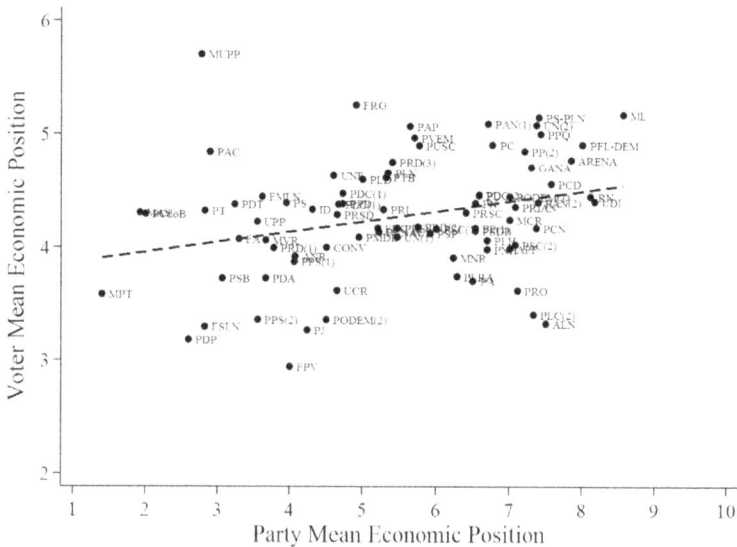

Figure 2.2 The Economic Policy Dimension
Source: Author's calculation based on data from the DALP survey and the LAB survey (Kitschelt 2013; Latinobarómetro 1996–2015). Party acronyms are reported in table A2.1 in the appendix.

indicate that a political party is positioned to the left of the median party voter on the economic dimension – promoting a stronger state interventionist stance in economic policies – while positive values indicate that a political party is positioned to the right of the median party voter on the economic dimension – promoting a free market stance in economic policies.

To use this measure as the dependent variable in a multinomial logit regression, political parties are assigned into three groups according to their value of MPVC: Congruence (C) referring to the group of political parties with a very high degree of congruence (range −0.5 to +0.5); Left distortion (LD) referring to the group of parties, which misrepresent their supporters to the state interventionist end of the economic domain (for values < −0.5); and right distortion (RD) referring to the group of political parties, which misrepresent their supporters to the free market end of the economic domain, that is less state control of the economy (for values > +0.5). The cut-off points were selected to assure comparable group sizes for the multinomial logistic regression analyses.[9]

Independent Variables

Comparative research on party-society linkages has been confronted with a problem of data availability. Due to the lack of direct and reliable comparative measures on the meso- or macro-level, research on political clientelism and personalism, on the one hand, relies on more or less adequate proxy variables, like public spending data, indices of corruption, or content analysis of political speeches (e.g., Hawkins 2010; Keefer 2007). On the other hand, a considerable degree of research on political clientelism and personalism is based on qualitative case studies (e.g., Auyero 1999; Gibson 1997).[10]

The Democratic Accountability and Linkages Project compiled a data set covering eighteen Latin American countries which provides a variety of measures of party-society linkages directly related to the concepts discussed earlier (Altman et al. 2009; Kitschelt 2013). Experts have been asked explicitly to rank political parties' emphasis on three different linkage strategies. The questions are categorical and range from 1 to 4, with higher values indicating a more frequent use of the respective linkage strategy.[11] Building the mean of the expert responses, a quasi-continuous measure of a parties' degree of each linkage strategy is derived.

Control Variables

In line with the research literature on policy congruence, two sets of control variables are included in the regression models: a set of party-level factors and a set of system-level factors. Concerning the first set of factors, several party characteristics may influence on the degree of policy correspondence between a political party and its supporters other than their linkage strategies (e.g., Dalton 1985; Ezrow, De Vries, Steenbergen, & Edwards 2011; Spies & Kaiser 2014). First, large parties may be assumed to cater for more heterogeneous voter groups than niche parties. The latter, in contrast, are assumed to send clearer signals to their potential voters (Meguid 2005). Thus, the size of a political party is expected to have a negative effect on party-voter congruence. To account for differences between large and small parties, their share of legislative seats will enter the analysis as a control variable.[12] Second, the age of a political party may also influence the substantive relationship with its voters. Parties build reputation over time and link themselves more strongly to their supporters (Scott Mainwaring & Scully 1995). Furthermore, voters are better able to evaluate political parties' policy appeals that have been around for more than one electoral cycle. Thus, party age is expected to have a positive effect on policy congruence.[13] Third, and related to the former argument, a party's political stances are more visible – and hence, easier to evaluate and be held accountable for by voters – if it holds the presidency (Pande 2011; Snyder Jr. & Strömberg 2010). Moreover, presidential office usually comes with access to additional (often discretionary) funds, amenable to clientelistic distribution (see Grzymala-Busse 2008; Hicken 2011). Hence, a dummy variable indicating which party held the presidency at the end of 2008 was added to the analysis. Data on presidents and their parties was taken from Ruth (2016). Finally, ideological orientation is another party-level factor that has been related to the degree of policy congruence of a political party. Two opposing arguments about this relationship can be found in the literature. On the one hand, a bell-shaped relationship between a party's ideological position on the policy scale and issue congruence is expected (see Dalton 1985; Klingemann 1998). This assumed relationship is based on the argument that parties with more pronounced positions to either end on the policy scale send clearer messages to their supporters than parties at the centre of the continuum (Downs 1957). On the other hand, a U-shaped relationship between the position of a political party on the policy dimension and policy congruence is assumed (Iversen 1994; Rabinowitz, Macdonald, & Listhaug 1991). This argument refers to the phenomenon that political elites take more extreme positions in the policy space than their supporters (Converse 1964, 1975). Centrist parties should therefore be more congruent with their supporters than parties at either extreme of the policy continuum. Therefore, a dummy variable accounting for centrism on the economic scale will enter the analysis as a control variable. A political party is assigned a 1 if it falls into the range of ±1 standard deviation from the party system mean on the economic dimension.

The second set of control variables accounts for three important party system-level factors.[14] First, it may be argued that the probability of voters to find a political party close to their own policy position increases with the number of political parties in a system (e.g., Pierce 1999; Schmitt & Thomassen 1999). Thus, the effective number of parliamentary parties (ENPP) is assumed to have a positive effect on party-voter congruence (Laakso & Taagepera 1979). Second, it is argued similarly that political parties differentiate themselves more clearly from each other in polarized party systems. This may influence both voter perceptions of policy differences between political parties and voter proximity to political parties (Huber & Powell 1994). Thus, party system polarization on the economic dimension is assumed to have a positive effect on party-voter congruence.[15] Finally, as differences between political parties and voters are measured on an economic scale, country-specific economic contexts may influence on the importance and visibility of policy appeals. To account for socio-economic country differences, the GDP per capita will enter the analysis as a control variable.[16]

STATISTICAL ANALYSIS

The relationship between linkage strategies and policy congruence as well as specific types of incongruence is analysed employing multinomial logistic regression models.[17] To evaluate H1 to H4, I run three models with a categorical-dependent variable (Hosmer & Lemesho, 2005; Long & Freese 2006). To account for country-specific differences, the cluster option has been used. The first model includes only the three linkage strategies of political parties, and subsequent models control for other party and system level characteristics.

Table 2.1 is structured as follows: to ease interpretation, I present three group comparisons within each model. The first group comparison contrast the group of right-distortive parties with the group of congruent parties, the second group comparison takes place between the group of left-distortive parties and the group of congruent parties, the final group comparison contrasts the group of right-distortive parties with the group of left-distortive parties. The reference category is always named second. For example, the first column in each model refers to a political parties' probability of belonging to the group of right-distortive (pro free market) parties compared to the reference category, which in this case is the group of congruent political parties.

In line with the baseline argument, the programmatic linkage should yield a positive effect on a party's policy congruence (H1); thus its beta coefficients are expected to be *negative* for the two group comparison with congruent

Table 2.1 Explaining Left or Right Distortion in Policy Congruence – Multinomial Logit Model

Variables	Model 1			Model 2			Model 3		
	RD vs. C^α	LD vs. C^α	RD vs. LD^α	RD vs. C^α	LD vs. C^α	RD vs. LD^α	RD vs. C^α	LD vs. C^α	RD vs. LD^α
Programmatic Linkage (H1)	-2.480***	1.716	-4.196***	-2.248*	1.016	-3.264***	-2.500***	0.977	-3.478***
	(0.679)	(1.081)	(0.949)	(1.161)	(1.450)	(0.873)	(0.716)	(1.383)	(1.232)
Personalistic Linkage (H2)	-0.008	-0.328	0.320	-0.115	-0.956	0.841	0.016	1.304	-1.288
	(0.353)	(0.858)	(0.755)	(0.507)	(0.681)	(0.640)	(0.354)	(1.428)	(1.531)
Clientelistic Linkage (H3&H4)	-0.919	-1.769***	0.850***	-0.696	-2.066***	1.371***	-0.872	-3.506***	2.634**
	(0.579)	(0.554)	(0.318)	(0.775)	(0.751)	(0.473)	(0.696)	(1.488)	(1.027)
Party Seat Share				-0.002	0.035	-0.037			
				(0.023)	(0.035)	(0.039)			
Party Age				-0.001	-0.016**	0.016*			
				(0.005)	(0.007)	(0.009)			
Incumbency				-0.391	0.533	-0.924			
				(1.053)	(1.205)	(1.023)			
Centrism				-0.170	-1.811**	1.641**			
				(0.569)	(0.794)	(0.763)			
Fragmentation							0.006	0.680**	-0.674**
							(0.123)	(0.318)	(0.311)
Polarization							0.128	0.755**	-0.627**
							(0.223)	(0.306)	(0.301)
GDP p.c. 2008							-0.000	-0.000**	0.000**
							(0.000)	(0.000)	(0.000)
Constant	11.673***	0.130	11.543	10.948**	4.849	6.098	11.499***	-1.397	12.896***
	(3.020)	(3.513)	(3.181)	(4.626)	(4.662)	(3.715)	(3.937)	(3.827)	(4.597)
N	80			80			80		
Log-Pseudo Likelih.	-55.546			-52.613			-49.844		
Wald-χ^2	117.08***			313,35.41***			159.54***		
Pseudo R^2	0.22			0.26			0.30		

Note: * $p < 0.10$, ** $p < 0.05$, *** $p < 0.01$. Country clustered standard errors in parentheses. The second category in each column is the reference category. α: LD = Left Distortion (state intervention), RD = Right Distortion (free market); C = Congruence.

parties as the reference category, that is the more programmatic a political party the less likely the party misrepresents its voters to the left or to the right on the economic dimension. According to H2 no effect is expected concerning the relationship between the personalistic linkage and the dependent variable, that is the coefficients of all group comparisons should be *insignificant*. According to H3 I expect an inverse relationship between a political party's emphasis on the clientelistic linkage strategy and party-voter congruence. Thus, the beta coefficient of clientelism should be *positive* for both the left- and right-distortion groups compared to the group of congruent parties. According to H4, comparing right-distortive parties to left-distortive parties, a positive significant effect of clientelism is expected.

The findings in Table 2.1 show that in accordance with the expectations outlined in H2, the coefficient of the personalistic linkage strategy remains insignificant over all models. Confidence in these results is fairly strong as the standard errors of the coefficients are very high. Concerning this first group comparison (column 1), results indicate that political parties that pursue a programmatic linkage strategy are more likely congruent than right distortive. The effect remains robust when other party and system characteristics are included as control variables in subsequent models. This confirms one part of the baseline argument that a programmatic linkage is related to a higher level of party-voter congruence (H1). However, with respect to the clientelistic linkage strategy, the results of this group comparison reveal no significant effect (H3).

As regards the second group comparison (column 2), an interesting – although counterintuitive – finding arises. The negative effect of clientelism in all models indicates that the more clientelistic a political party is the less likely it misrepresents its supporters to the left compared to being congruent (which is not in line with H3). This finding, however, relates to another argument in the literature concerning the combinability of a leftist programmatic appeal with a clientelistic linkage strategy. Party programs are usually grounded on universalistic principles which are more or less combinable with particularistic exchanges. It is, therefore, plausible that the kind of ideologically grounded universalistic principle impacts the feasibility of clientelism. Especially left-libertarian parties that focus on social inequality issues and redistribution may compromise their credibility when engaging in clientelistic practices (see Kitschelt 2000).[18]

Moreover, in line with H4 the third group comparison (column 3) shows that political parties pursuing a clientelistic linkage strategy more likely misrepresent their supporters to the free market end (right) of the economic dimension than to the state protectionist end (left). Furthermore, the opposite effect arises for programmatic parties. The unexpected strong negative effect indicates that programmatic parties misrepresent their supporters more likely to the left end of the economic scale than to the right end. Both effects are significant on a high confidence level as well as robust over all three models.

Inspecting political parties' predicted probabilities in combination with their linkage mix further confirms this picture as can be seen in Table 2.2. On the one hand, the three parties with the highest probability of misrepresenting their supporters to the right end of the economic scale score rather high with respect to their emphasis on the clientelistic linkage strategy and low with respect to their emphasis on the programmatic linkage strategy. On the other hand, the three parties with the highest probability of misrepresenting their supporters to the left end of the economic scale score extremely high with respect to their emphasis on the programmatic linkage strategy and extremely low with respect to their emphasis on the clientelistic linkage strategy. In line with H2 we find no clear pattern concerning these parties' emphasis on the personalistic linkage strategy.

These findings hint to an aggregative compensation between programmatically left-distortive parties and clientelistic right-distortive parties, corroborating the decision to analyse policy congruence on the party level as to avoid the ecological inference problem (King 1997). Further research in this respect may uncover a possible cancelling-out effect of programmatic and clientelistic linkage strategies with respect to collective policy congruence in Latin American party systems (Weissberg 1978). Moreover, this finding urges us to theorize on programmatic parties' possible intentions to misrepresent their supporters to the left as to counterbalance a systematic right distortion of clientelistic parties on the economic policy dimension.

Finally, concerning the first set of control variables, party age and centrism seem to have an effect with respect to the second group comparison

Table 2.2   Predicted Probabilities of Extreme Cases

Right-Distortive Parties			
Party Name	Predicted Probability	Programmatic Linkage	Personalistic Linkage	Clientelistic Linkage
Left-Distortive Parties			
Party Name	Predicted Probability	Programmatic Linkage	Personalistic Linkage	Clientelistic Linkage
PRIAN	97.02	1.9	3.9	3.9
PP (1)	96.63	2.2	1.5	2.9
PS-PLN	96.29	2.1	2.6	3.2
PAC	87.77	3.7	1.6	2.1
FA	83.73	3.8	3.0	1.7
PCdoB	80.06	3.8	3.2	1.2

Note: Party acronyms are reported in table A2.1 in the appendix.

(left distortion vs. congruence) as well as the third group comparison (right distortion vs. left distortion). Older parties and parties with a centrist position on the economic scale are less likely left distortive than congruent or right distortive. The finding partly confirms the argument made about the effect of party age. Parties that are around for a longer period are expected to be more congruent than younger parties. The effect of the centrism dummy confirms that centrist parties are expected to be more congruent – at least when compared to left-distortive parties. Finally, all three system-level controls are highly significant for the second and third group comparison. A higher number of political parties in a political system and a higher polarization seem to increase the probability of left distortion as compared to congruence and decrease the probability of right distortion compared to left distortion.

CONCLUSION

This chapter has argued that it is important to investigate the influence of different party-society linkages on the degree of party-voter congruence as well as the direction of potential incongruence, especially in new democracies. Several arguments about the different effects of personalistic and clientelistic linkage strategies on party-voter congruence in the economic domain have been made.

From the results of the statistical analysis, some interesting conclusions can be drawn. As expected no systematic relationship between a personalistic linkage strategy and party-voter congruence was detected. With respect to the other linkage strategies, the analysis confirms that clientelistic parties more likely misrepresent their supporters to the right (free market) end of the economic scale than to the left (state interventionist) end of the economic dimension, while a strong emphasis on a programmatic linkage induces the opposite effect. Programmatic parties misrepresent their supporters more likely to the left than to the right on the economic dimension. This might hint to the conclusion that the two forms of misrepresentation cancel each other out on the macro-level (Weissberg 1978), an effect that deserve further theoretical and empirical research. In contrast, the analysis confirms that programmatic parties are more likely congruent than right distortive (in line with H1).

Finally, with respect to the clientelistic linkage strategy the analyses indicate a positive association between clientelism and party-voter congruence when compared to left distortion. This counterintuitive effect may partly be explained by an adverse relationship between a leftist position on the economic dimension and a clientelistic linkage strategy (Kitschelt 2000) as well as data limitations, more specifically, the exclusion of non-programmatic voters in the present study. As voters of clientelistic parties base their decision on material benefits and clientelistic parties do not provide orientation for their voters in the policy space, it is highly probable that non-programmatic voters are more likely to be clientelistic party voters (Colomer & Escatel 2005; Ruth 2016).

These findings offer several avenues for future research: First, a potential counterbalancing representation effect of highly programmatic and ideologically left political parties with respect to the misrepresentation of clientelistic parties on the system level has to be analysed in more detail. Second, the discrepancy between the spread of political parties and party supporters on the economic scale as well as its consequences for the quality of representation and the application of different models of political competition may be further investigated. Finally, future research should also incorporate non-programmatic voting into models of party competition in contexts where clientelistic linkages prevail.

APPENDIX

Table 2.3   Party Acronyms, Number of Observations by Political Party, and Data Source

Country	Political Party (Acronym, N DALP/ N LAB)
Argentina	Peronist Party (PJ, 21/321), Radical Civic Union (UCR, 20/118), Front for Victory (FPV, 20/88) Republican Proposal (PRO, 9/68)
Bolivia	Movement for Socialism (MAS, 13/843), Social and Democratic Power (PODEM(1), 13/121), Revolutionary Nationalist Movement (MNR, 13/22), National Unity Front (UN(1), 13/145)
Brazil	Liberal Front Party (PFL-DEM, 17/30), Brazilian Democratic Movement Party (PMDB, 17/155), Progressive Party (PP(1), 15/24), Brazilian Socialist Party (PSB, 16/11), Brazilian Social Democracy Party (PSDB, 17/124), Workers' Party (PT, 17/614), Democratic Labor Party (PDT, 17/32), Communist Party of Brazil (PCdoB, 15/31), Popular Socialist Party (PPS(1), 16/8)
Chile	Radical Social Democratic Party (PRSD, 17/7), Independent Democratic Union (UDI, 18/113), Socialist Party of Chile (PS, 18/155), National Renewal (RN, 18/228), Christian Democratic Party (PDC(1), 18/186), Party for Democracy (PPD, 18/105)
Colombia	Colombian Liberal Party (PLC(1), 12/431), Colombian Social Conservative Party (PSC(1), 12/157), Social Party of National Unity (PU, 12/408), Radical Change (MCR, 11/21), Alternative Democratic Pole (PDA, 12/114)
Costa Rica	Citizen's Action Party (PAC, 18/166), National Liberation Parties (PLN, 18/166), Libertarian Movement Party (ML, 18/48), Social Christian Unity Party (PUSC, 17/109)
Dominican Republic	Dominican Revolutionary Party (PRD(3), 5/589), Social Christian Reformist Party (PRSC, 5/83), Dominican Liberation Party (PLD, 5/735)

Country	Political Party (Acronym, N DALP/ N LAB)
Ecuador	Social Christian Party (PSC(2), 13/93), Democratic Left (ID, 13/18), Ecuadorian Roldosist Party (PRE, 13/24), Pachakutik Plurinational Unity Movement (MUPP, 13/10), Renewal Party of National Action (PRIAN, 13/31), Patriotic Society Party (PSP, 12/74)
El Salvador	Nationalist Republican Alliance (ARENA, 13/307), Farabundo Martí National Liberation Front (FMLN, 13/615), Party of National Conciliation (PCN 11/18), Christian Democratic Party (PDC(2), 12/13)
Guatemala	Guatemalan Republican Front (FRG, 10/32), Grand National Alliance (GANA, 10/37), National Advancement Party (PAN(1), 10/11), Patriotic Party (PP(2), 10/192)
Honduras	Liberal Party of Honduras (PLH, 13/564), National Party of Honduras (PNH, 13/622)
Mexico	Institutional Revolutionary Party (PRI, 18/563), National Action Party (PAN(2), 18/412), Party of the Democratic Revolution (PRD(1), 18/158), Ecological Green Party of Mexico (PVEM, 13/26), Convergence (CONV, 12/8)
Nicaragua	Nicaraguan Liberal Alliance (ALN, 14/31), Sandinista National Liberation Front (FSLN, 17/401) Constitutionalist Liberal Party (PLC(2), 18/285)
Panama	Democratic Revolutionary Party (PRD(2), 8/437), Panameñista Party (PA, 8/213), Solidarity Party-Liberal Party (PS-PLN, 10/7), Democratic Change (PCD, 7/478)
Paraguay	National Republican Association (ANR, 14/278), Authentic Radical Liberal Party (PLRA, 14/353), Beloved Fatherland (PPQ, 14/6), National Union of Ethical Citizens (PUNACE, 14/38), Democratic Popular Party (PDP, 5/11), Tekojoja Movement (MPT, 5/24)
Peru	Union for Peru (UPP, 11/9), American Popular Revolutionary Alliance (PAP, 11/104), National Unity (UN(2), 11/157), Alliance for the Future (APF, 10/70), Center Front (FDC, 10/12)
Uruguay	National Party (PN, 17/387), Colorado Party (PC, 17/124), Broad Front (FA, 17/873)
Venezuela	Fifth Republic Movement (MVR, 12/710), Social Democracy Party (PODEM(2), 12/14)

Source: Author's calculation based on data from LAB and DALP.

NOTES

1. I gratefully acknowledge the useful comments of my former colleagues at the University of Cologne as well as the participants of the workshop on "Political Representation: Congruence of Interests in New Democracies" at the ECPR Joint Sessions in Antwerp 2012. Many thanks go to David Altman and Juan Pablo Luna from the Catholic University of Chile for sharing their data.

2. The labels 'left' and 'right' in this context are used in a mere positional sense relating to the two poles of a one-dimensional issue space and not in a substantive sense referring to the classical ideological left-to-right dimension. Furthermore, the

empirical analysis in this article centres on party-voter congruence on an economic policy dimension, where the left end of the scale refers to a state interventionist position and the right end of the scale to a free market position. For more details see the following data and measurement section.

3. Note that some interesting arguments on different programmatic party strategies of mainstream and niche parties in relation to their policy responsiveness have been discussed (see Ezrow et al. 2011).

4. The personalistic linkage strategy is often related to populism. Populist parties usually exhibit a direct, unmediated electoral appeal through personalistic leaders (e.g., Brug & Mughan 2007; Mudde 2004). Thus, populism has an affinity to the personalistic linkage strategy. But neither is populism the only form of personalistic authority nor is the personalistic linkage the only form of linkage populist parties may pursue (Barr 2009). Furthermore, a charismatic leadership is no necessary condition for a populist party, as the example of Alberto Fujimori in Peru shows.

5. However, it is also argued that clientelism constitutes a functional equivalent in developing countries to social welfare regimes like those in advanced democracies. In this sense clientelism may be seen as an appropriate party strategy in places where political institutions are dysfunctional (see Hilgers 2009, 2013). Furthermore, from a clients' perspective the exchange of particularistic goods may be perceived as a viable solution to social problems (e.g., Auyero 1999).

6. One could also argue in favour of conditional hypotheses with respect to strategic mixing of linkage strategies. However, pairwise comparisons of interaction effects (both two-way and three-way) were tested insignificant in all models.

7. For an analysis of the representativeness of presidents as opposed to political parties, see Wiesehomeier and Benoit (2009).

8. Furthermore, while the DALP survey uses a 10-point scale for the left-right dimension the LAB surveys use an 11-point scale. Transforming one scale to match the other would only partly solve the problem, as the latter scale disposes of a midpoint (5) while the former does not. This could lead to substantive differences between the two questions. Additionally, comparing item responses in the LAB between the economic and the left-right self-placement questions, the amount of non-response is nearly twice as high in the latter (7 vs. 13 per cent). This might also hint to the conclusion that respondents of the public opinion survey are less familiar with abstract concepts like left and right compared to a more specific issue-related question on the state role in the economy (see Ruth 2016).

9. Wald test statistics show that each of the three categories are clearly distinguishable, confirming that we should not merge them ($\chi^2 = 56.20$, $p < 0.000$).

10. Notable exceptions are comparative studies based on subnational data sets (e.g., Brusco, Nazareno, & Stokes 2004; Stokes 2005).

11. For question wordings see the DALP online questionnaire, available at https://sites.duke.edu/democracylinkage/, accessed August 2017.

12. Data on the distribution of seats was taken from Ruth (2016).

13. The party age indicator is operationalized by subtracting the formation year of a political party from 2008.

14. Estimating the effect of both party characteristics and party system factors on a dependent variable located on the lower level is usually addressed via multi-level

analysis. However, statistical tests revealed a very low explanatory power of party system level factors (intra-class correlation coefficients < 0.06). Therefore, the analysis presented in the next section is based on non-hierarchical regression models with standard errors clustered by country.

15. The indicator is constructed using the Taylor-Herman index of party system polarization (Taylor and Herman 1971).

16. Data for 2008 was taken from the World Development Indicator database (The World Bank Group 2017).

17. The analysis was implemented using STATA 14.

18. Furthermore, with respect to the counterintuitive effect of clientelism, the exclusion of non-programmatic voters in this study should be considered. Both policy congruence measures are based on truncated data. Respondents of the public opinion survey were included in the calculation only if they answered both questions on party preference and self-positioning on the economic scale. This procedure excludes, first, party voters that were either unable or unwilling to position themselves on the economic scale and, second, respondents who did not have or communicate a party preference independent from their ability to position themselves on the economic dimension. Especially the first reason of exclusion poses a substantive problem in relation to clientelism.

REFERENCES

Achen, C. H. (1978). Measuring Representation. *American Journal of Political Science, 22*(3), 475–510.

Altman, D., Luna, J. P., Piñeiro, R., & Toro, S. (2009). Partidos y sistemas de partidos en América Latina: Aproximaciones desde la encuesta a expertos 2009. *Revista de Ciencia Política, 29*(3), 775–798.

Auyero, J. (1999). 'From the Client's Point(s) of View': How Poor People Perceive and Evaluate Political Clientelism. *Theory and Society, 28*, 297–334.

Barnes, S. H. (1977). *Representation in Italy: Institutionalized Tradition and Electoral Choice*. Chicago: University of Chicago Press.

Barr, R. R. (2009). Populists, Outsiders and Anti-Establishment Politics. *Party Politics, 15*(1), 29–48.

Belchior, A. M., Sanches, E. R., & José, E. M. V. (2018). Policy Congruence in a Competitive Authoritarian Regime: Learning from the Angolan Case. *Journal of Asian and African Studies, 53*(2), 201–216.

Blais, A., & Bodet, M. A. (2006). Does Proportional Representation Foster Closer Congruence Between Citizens and Policy Makers? *Comparative Political Studies, 39*(10), 1243–1262.

Brug, W. van der, & Mughan, A. (2007). Charisma, Leader Effects and Support for Right-Wing Populist Parties. *Party Politics, 13*(1), 29–51.

Brusco, V., Nazareno, M., & Stokes, S. C. (2004). Vote Buying in Argentina. *Latin American Research Review, 39*(2), 66–88.

Colomer, J. M., & Escatel, L. E. (2005). La dimensión izquierda-derecha en América Latina. *Desarrollo Económico, 45*(177), 123–136.

Converse, P. E. (1964). The Nature of Belief Systems in Mass Publics. In D. E. Apter (Ed.), *Ideology and Discontent* (pp. 206–261). New York: The Free Press.

Converse, P. E. (1975). Some Mass-Elite Contrasts in the Perception of Political Spaces. *Social Science Information, 14*(3), 49–83.

Coppedge, M. (2001). Political Darwinism in Latin America's Lost Decade. In L. Diamond & R. Gunther (Eds.), *Political Parties and Democracy* (pp. 173–205). Baltimore: Johns Hopkins University Press.

Cox, G. W. (1997). *Making Votes Count: Strategic Coordination in the World's Electoral Systems*. Cambridge: Cambridge University Press.

Cox, G. W., & McCubbins, M. D. (2001). The Institutional Determinants of Economic Policy Outcomes. In S. Haggard & M. D. McCubbins (Eds.), *Presidents, Parliaments, and Policy* (pp. 21–63). Cambridge: Cambridge University Press.

Dalton, R. J. (1985). Political Parties and Political Representation: Party Supporters and Party Elites in Nine Nations. *Comparative Political Studies, 18*(3), 267–299.

Dixit, A., & Londregan, J. (1996). The Determinants of Success of Special Interests in Redistributive Politics. *Journal of Politics, 58*(4), 1132–1155.

Dixit, A., & Londregan, J. (1998). Ideology, Tactics, and Efficiency in Redistributive Politics. *The Quarterly Journal of Economics*, 497–529.

Downs, A. (1957). *An Economic Theory of Democracy*. New York: Harper & Row Publishers.

Ezrow, L. (2010). *Linking Citizens and Parties: How Electoral Systems Matter for Political Representation*. Oxford: Oxford University Press.

Ezrow, L., De Vries, C., Steenbergen, M., & Edwards, E. (2011). Mean Voter Representation and Partisan Constituency Representation: Do Parties Respond to the Mean Voter Position or to Their Supporters? *Party Politics, 17*(3), 275–301.

Gay, R. (1998). Rethinking Clientelism: Demands, Discourses and Practices in Contemporary Brazil. *European Journal of Latin American and Caribbean Studies, 65*, 7–24.

Gibson, E. L. (1997). The Populist Road to Market Reform: Policy and Electoral Coalitions in Mexico and Argentina. *World Politics, 49*(3), 339–370.

Golder, M., & Stramski, J. (2010). Ideological Congruence and Electoral Institutions. *American Journal of Political Science, 54*(1), 90–106.

Grzymala-Busse, A. (2008). Beyond Clientelism: Incumbent State Capture and State Formation. *Comparative Political Studies, 41*(4–5), 638–673. doi:10.1177/0010414007313118

Hawkins, K. (2010). *Venezuela's Chavismo and Populism in Comparative Perspective*. Cambridge: Cambridge University Press.

Hicken, A. (2011). Clientelism. *Annual Review of Political Science, 14*(1), 289–310. doi:10.1146/annurev.polisci.031908.220508

Hilgers, T. (2009). 'Who Is Using Whom?' Clientelism from the Client's Perspective. *Journal of Iberian and Latin American Research, 15*(1), 51–75.

Hilgers, T. (2013). Democratic Processes, Clientelistic Relationships, and the Material Goods Problem. In T. Hilgers (Ed.), *Clientelism in Everyday Latin American Politics* (pp. 3–22). New York: Palgrave Macmillan.

Hosmer, D. W., & Lemeshow, S. (2005). *Applied Logistic Regression*. Second Edition. Hoboken, NJ: John Wiley & Sons, Inc.

Huber, J., & Powell, G. B. (1994). Congruence Between Citizens and Policymakers in Two Visions of Liberal Democracy. *World Politics*, *46*(3), 291–326.

Iversen, T. (1994). Political Leadership and Representation in West European Democracies: A Test of Three Models of Voting. *American Journal of Political Science*, *38*(1), 45–74.

Kedar, O. (2005). When Moderate Voters Prefer Extreme Parties: Policy Balancing in Parliamentary Elections. *The American Political Science Review*, *99*(2), 185–199.

Keefer, P. (2007). Clientelism, Credibility, and the Policy Choices of Young Democracies. *American Journal of Political Science*, *51*(4), 804–821.

King, G. (1997). *A Solution to the Ecological Inference Problem: Reconstructing Individual Behavior from Aggregate Data*. Princeton, NJ: Princeton University Press.

Kitschelt, H. (1995). Formation of Party Cleavages in Post-Communist Democracies. *Party Politics*, *1*(4), 447–472.

Kitschelt, H. (2000). Linkages Between Citizens and Politicians in Democratic Polities. *Comparative Political Studies*, *33*(6–7), 845–879.

Kitschelt, H. (2013). *Democratic Accountability and Linkages Project*. Durham: Duke University Press.

Kitschelt, H., Hawkins, K. A., Luna, J. P., Rosas, G., & Zechmeister, E. J. (2010). *Latin American Party Systems*. Cambridge: Cambridge University Press.

Kitschelt, H., & Wilkinson, S. I. (2007). Citizen-Politician Linkages: An Introduction. In H. Kitschelt & S. I. Wilkinson (Eds.), *Patrons, Clients, and Policies: Patterns of Democratic Accountability and Political Competition* (pp. 1–49). Cambridge: Cambridge University Press.

Klingemann, H-D. (1998). Party Positions and Voter Orientations. In H-D. Klingemann & D. Fuchs (Eds.), *Citizens and the State* (pp. 183–205). Oxford: Oxford University Press.

Laakso, M., & Taagepera, R. (1979). 'Effective' Number of Parties. A Measure with Application to West Europe. *Comparative Political Studies*, *12*(1), 3–27.

Latinobarómetro, C. (1996–2015). *Latinobarometer Database*. Santiago de Chile, Chile.

Long, S., & Freese, J. (2006). *Regression Models for Categorical Dependent Variables Using Stata*. Second Edition. College Station: Stata Press.

Luna, J. P. (2014). *Segmented Representation: Political Party Strategies in Unequal Democracies*. Oxford: Oxford University Press.

Luna, J. P., & Zechmeister, E. (2005). Political Representation in Latin America: A Study of Elite-Mass Congruence in Nine Countries. *Comparative Political Studies*, *38*(4), 388–416.

Magaloni, B., Diaz-Cayeros, A., & Estévez, F. (2007). Clientelism and Portfolio Diversification: A Model of Electoral Investment with Applications to Mexico. In H. Kitschelt & S. I. Wilkinson (Eds.), *Patrons, Clients, and Policies: Patterns of Democratic Accountability and Political Competition* (pp. 182–205). Cambridge: Cambridge University Press.

Mainwaring, S., & Scully, T. R. (1995). *Building Democratic Institutions: Party Systems in Latin America*. Stanford, CA: Stanford University Press.

Mainwaring, S., & Shugart, M. S. (1997). *Presidentialism and Democracy in Latin America*. Cambridge: Cambridge University Press.

Manin, B., Przeworski, A., & Stokes, S. C. (1999). Introduction. In A. Przeworski, S. C. Stokes, & B. Manin (Eds.), *Democracy, Accountability, and Representation* (pp. 1–26). Cambridge: Cambridge University Press.

Mansergh, L., & Thomson, R. (2007). Election Pledges, Party Competition, and Policymaking. *Comparative Politics, 39*(3), 311–329.

Meguid, B. M. (2005). Competition Between Unequals: The Role of Mainstream Party Strategy in Niche Party Success. *American Political Science Review, 99*(3), 347–359.

Miller, W. E., & Stokes, D. E. (1963). Constituency Influence in Congress. *The American Political Science Review, 57*(1), 45–56.

Mudde, C. (2004). The Populist Zeitgeist. *Government and Opposition, 39*(4), 541–563.

Otero-Felipe, P., & Rodríguez-Zepeda, J. A. (2010). *Measuring Representation in Latin America: A Study of Ideological Congruence Between Parties and Voters.* Paper Presented at the Annual Meeting of the American Political Science Association, Washington, DC, September.

Pande, R. (2011). Can Informed Voters Enforce Better Governance? Experiments in Low-Income Democracies. *Annual Review of Economics, 3*(1), 215–237. doi:10.1146/annurev-economics-061109-080154

Pappas, T. S. (2009). Patrons Against Partisans: The Politics of Patronage in Mass Ideological Parties. *Party Politics, 15*(3), 315–334.

Pierce, R. (1999). Mass-Elite Issue Linkages and the Responsible Party Model of Representation. In W. E. Miller, R. Pierce, J. Thomassen, R. Herrera, S. Holmberg, P. Esaiasson, & B. Wessels (Eds.), *Policy Representation in Western Democracies* (pp. 9–32). Oxford: Oxford University Press.

Pitkin, H. F. (1967). *The Concept of Representation.* Berkeley: University of California Press.

Poguntke, T. (2000). *Parteiorganisation im Wandel – Gesellschaftliche Verankerung und organisatorische Anpassung im europäischen Vergleich.* Wiesbaden: Westdeutscher Verlag.

Poguntke, T. (2002). Party Organizational Linkage: Parties Without Firm Social Roots? In K. R. Luther & F. Müller-Rommel (Eds.), *Political Parties in the New Europe: Political and Analytical Challenges* (pp. 43–62). Oxford: Oxford University Press.

Powell, G. B. (2004). Political Representation in Comparative Politics. *Annual Review of Political Science, 7*(1), 273–296.

Powell, G. B. (2005). The Chain of Responsiveness. In L. Diamond & L. Morlino (Eds.), *Assessing the Quality of Democracy* (pp. 62–76). Baltimore: Johns Hopkins University Press.

Powell, G. B. (2006). Election Laws and Representative Governments: Beyond Votes and Seats. *British Journal of Political Science, 36*(2), 291–315.

Rabinowitz, G., Macdonald, S. E., & Listhaug, O. (1991). New Players in an Old Game: Party Strategy in Multiparty Systems. *Comparative Political Studies, 24*(2), 147–185.

Roberts, K. M. (2002). Party-Society Linkages and Democratic Representation in Latin America. *Canadian Journal of Latin American and Caribbean Studies, 27*(53), 9–34.

Roberts, K. M. (2006). Populism, Political Conflict, and Grass-Roots Organization in Latin America. *Comparative Politics*, *38*(2), 127–148.

Ruth, S. P. (2016). Clientelism and the Utility of the Left-Right Dimension in Latin America. *Latin American Politics and Society*, *58*(1), 72–97.

Schaffer, F. C. (2007). Why Study Vote Buying? In F. C. Schaffer (Ed.), *Elections for Sale: The Causes and Consequences of Vote Buying* (pp. 1–16). Boulder, CO: Lynne Rienner.

Schmitt, H., & Thomassen, J. (1999). Issue Congruence. In J. Thomassen & H. Schmitt (Eds.), *Political Representation and Legitimacy in the European Union* (pp. 186–208). Oxford: Oxford University Press.

Shugart, M. S., & Haggard, S. (2001). Institutions and Public Policy in Presidential Systems. In S. Haggard & M. D. McCubbins (Eds.), *Presidents, Parliaments, and Policy* (pp. 64–102). Cambridge: Cambridge University Press.

Singer, M., & Kitschelt, H. (2011). *'Do Everything' (DoE) Parties: When Can Politicians Combine Clientelistic and Programmatic Appeals*. Paper Presented at the Workshop on Democratic Accountability Strategies, Durham, May.

Snyder Jr., James M., & Strömberg, D. (2010). Press Coverage and Political Accountability. *Journal of Political Economy*, *118*(2), 355–408. doi:10.1086/652903

Soroka, S. N., & Wlezien, C. (2005). Opinion-Policy Dynamics: Public Preferences and Publich Expenditure in the United Kingdom. *British Journal of Political Science*, *35*(4), 665–689.

Spies, D. C., & Kaiser, A. (2014). Does the Mode of Candidate Selection Affect the Representativeness of Parties? *Party Politics*, *20*(4), 576–590.

Stimson, J. A. (1999). Party Government and Responsiveness. In A. Przeworski, S. C. Stokes, & B. Manin (Eds.), *Democracy, Accountability, and Representation* (pp. 197–221). Cambridge: Cambridge University Press.

Stimson, J. A., Mackuen, M. B., & Erikson, R. S. (1995). Dynamic Representation. *American Political Science Review*, *89*(3), 534–565.

Stokes, S. C. (1999). What Do Policy Switches Tell Us About Democracy? In A. Przeworski, S. C. Stokes, & B. Manin (Eds.), *Democracy, Accountability, and Representation* (pp. 98–130). Cambridge: Cambridge University Press.

Stokes, S. C. (2005). Perverse Accountability: A Formal Model of Machine Politics with Evidence from Argentina. *American Political Science Review*, *99*(3), 315–325.

Stokes, S. C. (2007a). Is Vote Buying Undemocratic? In F. C. Schaffer (Ed.), *Elections for Sale: The Causes and Consequences of Vote Buying* (pp. 81–99). Boulder, CO: Lynne Rienner.

Stokes, S. C. (2007b). Political Clientelism. In C. Boix & S. C. Stokes (Eds.), *The Oxford Handbook of Comparative Politics* (pp. 604–627). Oxford: Oxford University Press.

Stokes, S. C., Dunning, T., Nazareno, M., & Brusco, V. (Eds.). (2013). *Brokers, Voters, and Clientelism: The Puzzle of Distributive Politics*. Cambridge: Cambridge University Press.

Strøm, K. (1990). A Behavioral Theory of Competitive Political Parties. *American Journal of Political Science*, *34*(2), 565–598.

Taylor, M., & Herman, V. M. (1971). Party Systems and Governmental Stability. *American Political Science Review*, *65*, 28–37.

Thomassen, J. (1994). Empirical Research into Political Representation: Failing Democracy or Failing Models? In M. K. Jennings & T. E. Mann (Eds.), *Elections at Home and Abroad* (pp. 237–264). Ann Arbor: University of Michigan Press.

Thomson, R., Royed, T., Naurin, E., Artés, J., Costello, R., Ennser-Jedenastik, L., . . . Praprotnik, K. (2017). The Fulfillment of Parties' Election Pledges: A Comparative Study on the Impact of Power Sharing. *American Journal of Political Science*, *61*(3), 527–542.

Wantchekon, L. (2003). Clientelism and Voting Behavior: Evidence from a Field Experiment in Benin. *World Politics*, *55*, 399–422.

Webb, P., Poguntke, T., & Kolodny, R. (2012). The Presidentialization of Party Leadership? Evaluating Party Leadership and Party Government in the Democratic World. In L. Helms (Ed.), *Comparative Political Leadership* (pp. 77–98). London: Palgrave Macmillan.

Weissberg, R. (1978). Collective vs. Dyadic Representation in Congress. *The American Political Science Review*, *72*(2), 535–547.

Weyland, K. (1999). Neoliberal Populism in Latin America and Eastern Europe. *Comparative Politics*, *31*(4), 379–401.

Wiesehomeier, N., & Benoit, K. (2009). Presidents, Parties, and Policy Competition. *The Journal of Politics*, *71*(4), 1435–1447.

The World Bank Group. (2017). *World Development Indicators*.

Zechmeister, E. (2006). What's Left and Who's Right? A Q-Method Study of Individual and Contextual Influences on the Meaning of Ideological Labels. *Political Behavior*, *28*(2), 151–173.

Zechmeister, E. J. (2010). Left-Right Semantics as a Facilitator of Programmatic Structuration. In H. Kitschelt, K. A. Hawkins, J. P. Luna, G. Rosas, & E. J. Zechmeister (Eds.), *Latin American Party Systems* (pp. 96–118). Cambridge: Cambridge University Press.

Chapter Three

Clients, Patrons, and Members

Ethnic Parties and Patronage in Bulgaria and Romania

Petr Kopecký and Maria Spirova

INTRODUCTION

The representation of members of ethnic minority groups in the national political process has been a challenge for political systems of all types, and the formation of ethnic political parties has been particularly contentious. These are parties that, formally or in practice, speak for the interests of a particular ethnic group (Chandra 2011) and aim to fulfil a descriptive representative function for that group in the national political arena. The ethnic party is an interesting nexus of group-driven efforts to achieve representation and state policies regarding representation. No party can form without individuals willing to be part of it and ethnic group members willing to vote for it, making ethnic parties a reflection of the minority group's cohesiveness, socio-economic situation, and political ambition. However, the ethnic party's existence is often subject to differential treatment by the constitution and other laws of any given state because of its different nature.

There is an underlying uneasiness about both the nature of ethnic parties and their behaviour and the phenomenon of group-based, or ethnic, voting. However, we remain relatively ignorant about how ethnic parties behave in practice in terms of basic features of the political process such as organization-building efforts, electoral strategies, and coalition behaviour. Yet there are reasons to expect the ethnic party to behave differently than other parties in democratic societies because of the limited and ethnically delineated number of members, supporters, and potential voters. Ethnic parties can be expected to be constrained in terms of electoral strategies and policy positioning, just as their organizational efforts can be expected to be particularly focused on the distribution of selective benefits to the members of the ethnic group that they represent.

41

As such, ethnic parties are often seen as prime candidates for a concentration of clientelistic exchanges and this chapter investigates to what extent this proposition is correct. If they can be seen, in fact, as 'clientelistic parties', then, as the introductory chapter in this volume argues, their role as agents of representation and interest aggregation takes on an even more problematic perspective (Ruth-Lovell, this volume, page 6). This chapter sees clientelistic exchanges as an overarching framework that is supported by two organizational strategies: the recruitment of the party members and the distribution of patronage appointments. The chapter is organized as follows: after describing briefly the larger research effort of which this chapter is part, the theoretical argument establishes the links between the party's ethnic base and its organizational strategies. For doing so, we borrow from the mainstream party literature and the ethnic party literature. The chapter then goes into its empirical part to validate these propositions by investigating the experience of the ethnic parties in Bulgaria and Romania. The chapter concludes with some preliminary observations about the impact the organizational strategies of ethnic parties have on the representative functions of the parties and their functions in contemporary democracy.

ETHNIC PARTIES AND THEIR ORGANIZATIONAL STRATEGIES

Ethnic parties are defined as political parties, which, formally or in practice, speak for the interests of the particular group, which are delineated in ethnic terms (Chandra 2011) and aim to fulfil a descriptive representative function for that group in the national political arena. The ethnic nature of the group is defined by the presence of a category of attributes that are descent-based and which include only a subset of country's population (Chandra 2011).[1] A focus on the organizational nature of ethnic parties is largely absent from the traditional literature on ethnic parties. Much more frequently addressed issues involve questions of party ideology, radicalization, linkage with their electorate, and so on (Horowitz 2000; Birnir 2007). Chandra (2005) does incorporate the organizational features of the ethnic parties as one of the factors influencing their success, but for her (99–110), the type of organization is a given, just as other potential party features.

On its behalf, the literature on party organization treats the ethnic party only as an empirical category and similarly discusses the organizational feature of such parties as an empirical feature, without necessarily linking theoretically the ethnic base of the party to its organizational strategies. In fact, Gunther and Diamond (2003) note that organizational strategies of ethnic parties can vary from loose organization of traditional groups to well-established mass personal organization with ancillary groups (Gunther & Diamond 2003, 10–12).

In contrast to much of this literature, we believe that there is a reason to have certain expectations about what organizations ethnic parties will build. We start with the recruitment of party members. For any party, members provide various benefits, which often translate into electoral benefits (Tavits 2013, 85). Having members ensures that the party has a certain number of loyal and certain voters, who not only are going to turn out and vote but will also provide free advertisement (Scarrow 1994, 47). Members and local offices serve as means of communication and, even if not the only such means, still play a substantial role in election campaigns (Scarrow 1996, 86–112; Kreuzer & Pettai 2002). Members can provide valuable input for the formulation of party policies; the party members and party activists are a breeding ground for party elite. It follows that unless there is a principled reason not to have members, a party should never consider it better to have fewer members if it can have more.

In the context of the ethnic party, the usefulness of a membership organization is sometimes challenged. Given that the ties between the party and the ethnic group are tight and the group of supporters is known, there might be no reason for the party to create and cultivate an active membership organization that would provide the support, which is already there (Horowitz 2000, 332–334). In other words, voting for the party becomes a head count of the people belonging to the group. That this will necessarily happen, however, is doubtful. First of all, it assumes that the ethnic group members are highly mobilized to vote. Given a high saliency of the ethnic dimension of politics, and a context of a new democracy, this might be true (Birnir 2007). However, in circumstances where ethnicity is not a driving issue of politics, and/or democracy functions along established routes, members of the ethnic group might suffer from voter's apathy, just as any other group in society. Voting *en blok* and for the ethnic party might then not become an immediate reaction, as Horowitz expected, but might in fact require similar organizational efforts that other non-ethnic parties have to show in order to mobilize their followers. Indeed, the existing research has shown a substantial variation in the level of voter turnout among racial and ethnic minorities in various political settings (Saggar 2000, 103; Leighley; Bratton, Bhavnani, & Hse-Hsin Chen 2012; Zingher & Thomas 2012).

In addition, there could be multiple parties competing for the ethnic group's vote; in such situation, which of the ethnic parties will be the preferred choice of the ethnic group is not clear at all. This is certainly the case in sizeable ethnic groups such as the Catalans, where there is objective room for more than one party. But even smaller groups can also be faced with more than one party trying to represent them as Stroschein has shown in the case of the Hungarian minorities in Romania (Stroschein 2011).

Organizing members of the group into a structured entity thus might become a useful and even crucial strategy especially when the size of the group is not that large and no special treatment of ethnic parties is in place, and even more so when clientelistic exchanges are expected to dominate.[2] The logic of membership might then apply even to a greater extent to ethnic parties than to non-ethnic parties which are not faced with the constraints of a limited and delineated electorate. Thus the commonsense choice for ethnic parties, according to our argument, is not a relatively dormant organization, as some literature suggests, but rather a concerted organizational effort to create a strong membership organization with extensive structures across the political entity.

We now turn to the second dimension of ethnic party's organization: the distribution of party patronage. Empirical studies of party patronage revolve around various selective benefits that the party can distribute to its members, voters, and supporters. Most studies of patronage or, as it is often termed, clientelism focus on the exchange of various material goods, such as money, gifts, medicines, food packages, and specially targeted policies, such as housing subsidies, for electoral support. Other studies of patronage are, in empirical terms, somewhat more narrowly conceived and focus on the distribution of jobs within the state (see, e.g., Sorauf 1959; Wilson 1973; Goldston 1977; Müller 1989, 2006; Bearfield 2009; Kopecký et al. 2012). These studies see party patronage as a form of institutional control or of institutional exploitation that operates to the benefit of the party organization. In contrast, classic clientelistic studies see patronage as a form of vote gathering.

In this chapter we adopt the perspective that emphasizes the institutional and party organizational aspects of patronage and, consequently, focus on the (ethnic) parties' strategies to exercise control over appointments of people within state institutions. Ethnic parties should be no exception from the general proclivity observed in Europe and beyond for parties to, at least occasionally, use patronage in order to build and solidify parties as institutions. Indeed, if anything, we argue, ethnic parties should be particularly likely to engage in patronage activities, for both organizational and electoral purposes. In fact, empirical evidence from Africa (Arriola & Johnson 2013; Guha 2013) and India (Chandra 2004) points to the presence of a strong link between ethnic parties and patronage politics, but the mechanisms they describe are typical of either ethnic party systems or 'patronage democracy'. In both of these situations, there is a pre-disposition to patronage because of the need to distinguish among different potential groups of voters. But even in the situation that we consider – that is ethnic parties that exist in political party systems where ethnicity is not the main dimension of competition and in political systems which are not necessarily dominated by patronage exchanges – engaging in patronage might be particularly attracting to the ethnic party, aiming at recruiting and maintaining a stable group of members.

The main reason for this is the general feature of the ethnic parties of representing specific, particularistic, group interests (Horowitz 2000, 296; Kitschelt 2000; Gunther & Diamond 2003, 25). The inclination to use 'selective benefits' becomes in many ways a natural organizational inclination for a political party, which cannot rely exclusively on representation on ideological grounds. Ethnic groups are often diverse in socio-economic terms, making such appeals difficult to get votes from them; at the same time, appeals on socio-economic grounds are not exclusive to particular ethnic groups, reinforcing their inefficiency in securing the ethnic vote. Moreover, as Gunther and Diamond (2003, 26) also observe, the group interests themselves are likely to encourage further particularistic behaviour such as clientelism, to which patronage (i.e., appointing 'own people' within the state) is often a vehicle. Ethnic parties tend to represent minorities, which suffer from inequitable policies from the state, which encourages them, once access to the state is achieved, to consider redistribution of state resources fair and just. In addition, ethnic parties are more likely to have short-term perspective on being in government, since they are small parties, and not always considered coalitionable by the mainstream political process. Because of these tendencies, a party that represents an ethnic group is likely to be particularly prone to engage in patronage practices. That is, once in power, such party is likely to appoint people close to the party to positions of power in the state institutions, to decision-making positions in semi-state structures, or even simply to provide group members with low-level jobs in the state administration.

Ethnic parties might also look to expand their electoral base beyond their respective ethnic group. They might seek to attract members and voters from other groups, whether from the majority or other minorities in order to increase their electoral share, parliamentary representation, and potential coalition participation. This can happen because of several reasons: a party might be formally required to include members from more than one ethnic group, as is the case in Bulgaria, Albania, and other countries with official bans on ethnic parties. Alternatively, or in addition, the party might be interested in transforming itself into a larger political entity, which might necessitate the incorporation of other groups' members, a point in case here being the Russian parties in Latvia, and the BSP in India (Guha 2013). Since their group-relevant programmatic appeal is not likely to attract supporters outside the group and since changing the programmatic appeal might lose some of the within-group support, patronage might prove a useful strategy in expanding the basis of the party beyond the group.

APPLYING THE ARGUMENT: TWO ETHNIC PARTIES

The chapter investigates the propositions made in regard to ethnic parties' membership efforts and patronage inclination by looking at the parties of two ethnic minorities in two Eastern European states: the Turks of Bulgaria and the Hungarians of Romania. These two parties make for an interesting comparison because of the similarities and differences between the two states. The ethnic situation in Bulgaria and Romania is roughly similar. Ethnic Turks constitute the largest minority in Bulgaria and account for about 9.6 per cent of the total population. Bulgarians represent the majority group of around 84 per cent. Romanians constitute about 89 per cent of the population in Romania, and the Hungarian minority, 6.6 per cent of total population, is the largest one and is concentrated in several regions, similar to the Turks in Bulgaria. The two countries thus have clear dominant majorities, a single, substantial, and concentrated minority, a substantial but scattered second minority (Roma) and a multitude of smaller ethnic groups with which this chapter is only marginally concerned.[3]

The two political systems, however, provide different institutional contexts for ethnic minority representation through ethnic parties: Bulgaria opposes ethnic representation while Romania formally guarantees it. Bulgaria has formally banned the existence of parties based on ethnic, racial, and religious allegiance, making any other electoral arrangements for minorities.[4] In contrast, Romania not only allows ethnic parties but has introduced special provisions to guarantee that they have a seat in parliament and does not limit the number of minorities that can get representation.[5] Legally constituted organizations of citizens belonging to a national minority, which have not obtained at least one Deputy Seat through the general rules of the elections, have the right to a seat in parliament. The only stipulation is that they must have obtained, at national level, at least 5 per cent of the average number of the validly expressed votes needed for the elections of one deputy according to the general rules of elections (Law for the Election of the Chamber of Deputies and the Senate 1992). Through that system about fifteen minorities have, on average, gained representation in parliament in the 1990s (Juberias 2000, 44–49). Since 2004 it has become more difficult for such organizations to obtain a seat, since the 'symbolic threshold' was doubled; still, the Romanian regulatory framework remains the most permissive ones in comparative perspective, as it relates to ethnic political parties.[6]

Despite these different institutional incentives, the two minorities under study here – the Turks in Bulgaria and the Hungarians in Romania – have established their own political parties. While formally the Movement for Rights and Freedoms (DPS) in Bulgaria is not *ethnic*, and the Democratic

Union of Hungarians in Romania (UDMR) is not a *party*, both entities fit a more realistic broader definition of ethnic parties. Both are groups of people who compete in elections under a common label and are, thus, parties (Epstein 1967, 9); and both satisfy at least three of Chandra's criteria for ethnic party classification (2011, 155–626). The parties' appeals, issues, positions, and support dynamics certainly put them in the ethnic party category.

Both parties have been successful in securing a stable position in the political processes in the two countries since 1990, including continuous representation in parliament, intermittent participation in government, and representation in the European Parliament since 2007. In Bulgaria, the Movement for Rights and Freedoms (DPS) was founded officially in 1990. Since its creation, it has gained a consistent share of the vote and has been present in all legislatures. From 2001 to 2009, and again between May 2013 and August 2014, it was official coalition partner in the Bulgarian government. Because of Bulgaria's regulatory framework, the party has been making a conscious effort to present itself into a 'liberal' party concerned generally with minority rights. Especially since 2001, it has included more ethnic Bulgarians in its leadership, and joined the Liberal International. However, as Horowitz has suggested for ethnic parties in general (Horowitz 2000, 282), achieving broader electoral support has proven extremely challenging because most Bulgarians do not associate DPS with liberal values but, rather, with strong commitment to defending the interests of the Turkish minority.

Similar to the DPS in Bulgaria, the UDMR has had a substantial role in Romanian political life. It has been represented in all post-1989 parliaments at a level that roughly corresponds to the proportion of ethnic Hungarians in the Romanian population. UDMR has remained in many ways one of the more stable parties in Romanian politics, next to the communist successor party. In addition, it was part of, or has lent critical support to, the governing coalitions from 1996 until 2008.

In contrast to DPS, UDMR has not made an effort to escape its ethnic nature. Autonomy features prominently in its political demands, which have at times reached more extreme levels. UDMR threatened to leave the government coalitions in 1997 and 1998 'if demands for state funded Hungarian university were not met' (Stroschein 2001, 61). This trend has been exacerbated with an internal split in 2003 whereby UDMR radical wing advanced the issue of territorial autonomy for Transylvania. The more radical, the Hungarian Citizens' Party (MPP) supported territorial autonomy for Transylvania and presented itself as a 'purer Hungarian alternative' (Stroschein 2011, 192). Fractionalization was somewhat stymied since 2009 with the joint actions of MPP and UDMR, but the debate on what the real issue and demand of the Hungarian minority are continues (Spirova & Stefanova 2012).

Organizational Trends in the DPS and UDMR

The two parties have thus experienced quite different paths of development in terms of their ideological positioning and relationship with society overall. We now turn to a more detailed examination of the parties' organizational features, hoping that isolating any common trends will allow us to make the first step to the validation of our propositions.

Membership Recruitment

Our expectation is that ethnic parties will benefit from a membership network and will actively recruit members; this is in contrast to others' expectations of ethnic parties' loose structures relying on existing within-group channels of communication and mobilization. This expectation implies both that building a membership organization is a set party goal, but also that ethnic parties exhibit higher rates of membership preservation, especially at times when the membership rates of mainstream parties decline. This trend should be particularly strong if we look at membership in a standardized way, as the rate of members per voters for each party.[7]

In that regard, both the DPS and the UDMR conform to those expectations. Membership data for the two political parties is presented in Tables 3.1 and 3.2. Data on party membership in Bulgaria for the 2000s (Spirova 2007; van Biezen, Mair, & Poguntke 2012) points to a general rate of membership for the country higher than among European democracies – van Biezen et al. report that 5.6 per cent of the Bulgarian electorate were members of a political party, compared to an average of 4.5 per cent for the continent. At the same time, just as in most other contemporary democracies, the rate of party membership has declined since then to about 5 per cent of the electorate (*24 Chassa* 2016).

This general trend is quite in contrast to the trend in the membership figure for the Turkish party in Bulgaria, especially in the 2000s. At both 2002 and 2006, the DPS membership was second highest in absolute numbers, exceeded only by the successor party, the Bulgarian Socialist Party (Spirova 2007, 128; van Biezen et al. 2012). Furthermore, from 2002 to 2006, the party reported a substantial increase in the absolute number of its members. In the

Table 3.1   DPS Membership, 2002 and 2006

DPS	2002	2006	2016	Ranking Among All Parties
Membership	58,000	95,621	66,000	Two-third
M/V ratio	16.93%	20.45%	20.88%	Second

2010s this trend reversed slightly, because of the emergence of the popular populist GERB, which has taken on first place in terms of membership, but DPS preserves its position of a stable membership organization even in 2016.[8]

These numbers also lead to a relatively high rate of voter encapsulation, presented by the members to voters ratio (M/V), which is once again the second highest among the Bulgarian parties in both 2002 and 2006 and third highest in 2016. As a lot of the DPS electorate lives abroad – most significantly represented by the large number of Bulgarian Turks in Turkey – while it does not have party organizations outside the country, this rate is even more significant than it appears at first.

These trends of high membership recruitment and maintenance are also supported by the long-standing position of the party. In a 2003 interview, for example, the DPS leadership expressed the strongest concern with local structures and members among the Bulgarian parties then interviewed (Spirova 2007, 125–126). For them, one of their priorities over the last few years had been the development of organizational structures in all regions of the country. In addition, Kasim Dal, then DPS vice-chairman of DPS, maintained that the party had a very close connection with all their party members and supporters and valued their opinions and attitudes (Dal 2003).

The trend in UDMR membership is quite similar to that of the DPS. The party of the ethnic Hungarians is the second-largest party in the country. Data for the Romanian parties is available from a greater variety of sources, producing also quite different estimates of the UDMR membership. Table 3.2 presents numbers for 2003 and 2008, as presented in Ionascu and Soare (2012). The absolute numbers here are substantially higher than the numbers for the DPS, reflecting the higher absolute size of the ethnic Hungarian group in Romania. From within country perspective, the UDMR preserves the second place, just like the DPS in Bulgaria, after the successor to the Romanian communist party. While estimates over the years vary substantially, even the most conservative one, at 160,000 (Horvath 2005), still preserve the relative position of the UDMR as the second-most populous party in the country.

Even more telling is the rate of encapsulation of the Hungarian electorate by the party. The member-to-vote ratio is strikingly way above 50 per cent at both times, and even allowing for the lowest estimation of membership

Table 3.2   UDMR Membership, 2003 and 2008

UDMR	2003	2008	
Membership	400,000	350,000	Second
M/V Ratio	54%	82%	Second

Source: Data Sources: DPS: Spirova 2007; van Biezen et al. 2012; UDMR: Ionascu and Soare 2012; Popescu 2003.

produces a rate of 21 per cent for the 2000 election. Paralleled by the split in the UDMR brewing from 2003 and culminating in 2008 (Stroschein 2011, 190), this trend is even more impressive. What is of further note here is that the absolute number of votes for the UDMR has declined substantially over the 2000s, largely due to a massive demographic drop in the population since 2000 (Ionascu & Soare 2012). This development is in stark contrast with the increasing votes for the DPS in Bulgaria – in both absolute and relative terms – over the 2000s (Spirova & Stefanova 2012).

While we do not have first-hand impressions of the UDMR membership strategy as we have for the DPS, secondary accounts confirm the numerical trends and point to a great capacity of membership recruitment and preservation, in some ways also probably aided by the non-party status of the party in the Romanian political system and the more ambiguous party definition of membership (Ionascu & Soare 2012).

Despite the fact that this is only a first attempt at analysing the membership strategies of ethnic parties, the trends that emerge from this discussion make us believe that we are right in our hunch that ethnic parties have no reason to avoid recruiting members, and even more so, might have to do so at a higher rate than non-mainstream parties. This is clearly supported by the ranks of both DPS and UDMR as second-most populous parties in Bulgaria and Romania. In fact, using data reported in van Biezen et al. (2012), a similar trend is also observable for the Hungarians party in Slovakia (KDH), and to a lesser degree to what can be considered ethnic parties in the West – the SNP and Plaid Cymru in the UK, and the Catalan Convergence and Union in Spain (van Biezen et al. 2012).

Ethnic Parties and Patronage

With respect to the use of party patronage by ethnic political parties, we did argue that such parties are particularly prone to engage in the practice of staffing state institutions with party appointments, when given that chance. In this regard, the experience of the Turkish party in Bulgaria is quite illustrative.

Patronage is commonly practiced by Bulgarian parties in general. It is tradition inherited in many ways from the early stages of modernization, when Bulgarian parties were described as 'little more than hunting packs in pursuit of patronage'. (Crampton 1987, 40). The trend remained largely unchanged until World War II and found its perfection in the *nomenklatura* system of the Bulgarian Communist Party, which was the ultimate example of a complete marriage of party and the state. As a result, while democracy brought multiple parties and real contestation of power, it did little to curb the tradition of packing public administration with party supporters. In 2005, the European Commission observed that Bulgaria was yet to clarify the 'the division of responsibilities between the political and administrative levels of the public administration' (EC 2005, 7).

In fact, research on party patronage in Bulgaria (Georgiev 2008; Spirova 2012b) points to medium-high levels of patronage in the country, compared to other European democracies. Compared to other countries, the Bulgarian practice is characterized by higher levels of politicization at the lower levels of state administration, higher importance attributed to the political allegiance of appointees in making the patronage appointments, and a higher reward function of patronage. The latter is indicative to the more traditional use of patronage as electoral resource in which getting people jobs in the state administration is used to reward them for supporting the party. At the same time, however, we also have a clear indication that patronage in Bulgaria was used, following the trusted pattern of the Bulgarian Socialist Party, as a party-building resource: people were actively recruited to join the party with the promise of placing them in lucrative or important state positions (Spirova 2012b, 57–59).

In that context, the Movement for Rights and Freedoms (DPS) has also taken up that practice with a vengeance. At least for the period studied in detail, the ethnic party has exceeded all other Bulgarian parties in the public nature of its party appointments as well as in the institutionalization of its mechanisms. The DPS practice is best illustrated by Bulgaria's agricultural sector. Since the majority of the Turkish minority is engaged in agriculture, the Ministry of Agriculture was given to the DPS in the 2001–2005 and the 2005–2009 coalition governments, in both of which the party was a junior partner. The party proceeded to staff the ministries and its agencies, including offices such as the local forestry departments with people who belong to the party and the minority in the most extreme level. Appointments there reached further down into the ranks of the state administration than in other ministries and reached the vast majority of administrative entities (68–69).

This extensive practice was also accompanied by a very institutionalized mechanism of recruitment and distribution of patronage positions. Using its strong and numerous party ranks, the party recruited young people from the minority and educated them in order to have its own pool of qualified personnel that could be appointed to the state administration. The actual distribution of positions was very much in the hands of the central party leadership and its chairman (ibid.).

In addition to using patronage to build its own party, the party used these appointments as the stepping stone to providing further patronage and clientelistic benefits to its members. This trend is supported not only by further research but by admissions of the party itself as well outside observers such as the European Commission. A study of the organizational linkages of Bulgarian parties, for example, found that the DPS scores the highest among Bulgarian parties on the measure of clientelistic effort and attributed this to its 'integration of special business interest and its ethnically homogenous and geographically concentrated ethnic minority electorate' (Kolev 2012,

45). Similarly other academic research has found that if the majority of the Bulgarian public found the DPS problematic in the early 1990s because of the extremity of its minority-relevant positions, by the 2000s, the party was popularly seen as violating the norms of clean politics. While the ethnic model of politics was acceptable, what were not were the intertwining practices of corruption, clientelism, and authoritarian leadership that the party exhibited (Krasteva & Todorov 2011, 35).

The ex-party chairmen Dogan himself has illustrated the truth of these claims. In a now-infamous interview on the eve of the 2005 elections, Dogan publicly acknowledged that his party had a 'circle of companies' which contributed money to the party in exchange of political favours (Mediapool 2005). While the party leader later claimed that this phenomenon was 'not necessarily linked to any corrupt practices' (Mediapool 2006), it was the possibilities that the patronage appointments created for the build-up of clienteles around the EU agricultural subsidies distributed by the ministry and the agencies, which created the massive problems between Sofia and Brussels during 2007 and 2008 and led to the freeze on all funds for agricultural programs for Bulgaria (see Kolarova & Spirova 2009, 2010).

For the present purposes, however, it is somewhat more interesting to examine what this meant to the ethnic political party. There is enough evidence, we believe, to argue that the DPS was encouraged to engage in patronage, and even clientelism and corruption, at least partially, because of its ethnic nature. Serving the particular interests of its group base is one of the reasons why its engagement in rent-seeking behaviour of all kinds has been so rampant. However, this proclivity has also led to a somewhat counterintuitive consequence: not only did the membership of the party almost double during its time of governmental tenure (from 58,000 in 2003 to more than 95,000 in 2006) but, by 2007, it included about 12,000 ethnic Bulgarians as members (Mediapool 2006). We take this as an indication that membership in the DPS was seen as a pathway to a professional career by both members of the minority and opportunistic members of the majority, and later developments have confirmed this inkling. What this indicates is that, given the context of ethnic party regulation in the political system which forces the ethnic party to have a multi-ethnic facade, patronage and clientelistic practices might in fact strengthen the multi-ethnic nature of the party, or, to speculate even further, might be necessary to provide a multi-ethnic facade for the party.

Development at the higher party level also provides illustration that the practices of patronage and clientelism might be related to the expansion of the party's appeal to non-Turkish individuals. Between May 2013 and August 2014, Bulgaria was rocked by continuous public protests surrounding the appointment of a DPS member of parliament to the position of director of the Bulgarian secret service. Delyan Peevski, age thirty-three in 2013, ethnic

Bulgarian, has strong personal and family links to economic, media, and political power groups. A member of another Bulgarian party, the National Movement Simeon the Second from 2001 to 2009, Peevski became, gradually, very close to the DPS leadership. He was appointed deputy (junior) minister in the Stanishev cabinet (2005–2009) from the DPS quota and is an MP on the DPS lists since 2009. He has been named one of the 'corruption dream team' of the DPS because of his alleged involvement in various nefarious activities such as corruption schemes, meddling in political power through control of the security apparatus, and illegal media control (Capital 2005). In 2013, he emerged as one of the most important DPS MPs and despite the scandals surrounding his appointment, the subsequent resignation, and public discussions of his patronage, clientelistic and corrupt engagement has remained a very influential DPS politician (Dnevnik 2014).

Media investigations have pointed to even more convoluted interactions of ethnicity, corruption, clientelism, and patronage organized allegedly by the ethnic party. Most of the votes for the DPS that led to Peevski's election in the region of Stara Zagora have come either from the *pomaks*, a different group which has a Bulgarian ethnicity but Muslim religion, and from the Roma. According to various first-hand accounts, votes were ensured by a very intensive campaign of DPS party representatives who canvassed the Roma regions before the elections and hired local men to secure the vote in exchange of favours and small monetary payments (Capital 2013). The vote for the ethnic Turkish party came from non-Turkish voters, thus making its support multi-ethnic and laying a finely woven network of patronage and clientelistic exchanges.

Turning to Romania and its ethnic party under study here, the Democratic Union of the Hungarians in Romania, we observe indications for similar trends as we did in the case of the DPS. Regretfully we do not (yet) have as detailed data as we do for the Bulgarian case but the inklings we get from the available data point to a similar case. Romanian parties display comparable levels and characteristics of patronage appointments, as do Bulgarian ones. Patronage in the country is extensive, largely driven by motivations including the reward of members and activists and tends to benefit people who have political allegiance to the parties which appointed them, rather than high professional qualifications (Roper 2006; Gherghina, Chiru, & Bertoa 2011; Volintiru 2013). While a detailed study of the UDMR practices is clearly needed, its proclivity to use political position to further the economic well-being of its electoral base, region, and leadership (Fumurescu 2011) is an indication that tendencies similar to the ones in the Turkish party in Bulgaria might be at play in the UDMR as well. However, at this stage we do not have evidence to argue that the UDMR is especially likely to use patronage and link it any way to further forms of rent-seeking behaviour.

CONCLUSIONS

This chapter has presented a theoretical argument as well as some preliminary empirical observations on the organizational strategies of ethnic political parties. We argued that the ethnic party is, contrary to arguments by others, as much, if not even more, likely to attempt to build a strong organization because of reasons specific of its ethnic nature such as the characteristics of its electorate and the limits set on its potential voters and supporters. We further argued that ethnic parties are also particularly likely to use patronage as organizational resources not only because of its facilitation of party building but also because of the particularistic nature of the interests of the group it represents.

We apply these arguments to two ethnic parties, the parties of the Turkish minority in Bulgaria and of the Hungarian minority in Romania. The data confirms our expectation on the first dimension of part organizational strategies: both parties seem to be quite populous, especially given their smaller electorates and to try to build organizational structures actively. On the second dimension out data is limited largely to the Turkish party in Bulgaria, whose experience lends quite some credence to our argument. In the case of the Hungarians in Romania, however, we have only quite limited evidence to sustain this claim.

Overall, we believe that the chapter is first good step in outlining the theoretical arguments of why we should expect ethnic parties to organize into strong entities, similarly to some extent to the mass party, and why the use of particularistic benefits is to be expected in their case. Our analysis has also pointed to a potentially troublesome consequence. It might be that it is this particularistic feature of the ethnic political parties rather than their *ethnic* nature that might make members of the majority uneasy about them but which might come out or be interpreted as anti-minority popular positions. The consequences ethnic parties have on the general political process are thus in clear need of further theorizing and research.

What does this mean for the practice of clientelism and the way it influences the system of democratic representation? If we think of minority representation in terms of its role in the overall representative link that exists in democratic systems, it is already a difficult task to ensure that the preferences of minority groups are represented in the political decision-making process. In fact, a lot of them remain underrepresented worldwide. If, as this chapter has argued, the parties that are likely to directly represent them are also likely to engage in clientelistic behaviour in both recruiting members and exchanging jobs and other benefits for support, the quality of that democratic representation is further jeopardized.

Further, the argument presented here also points to a side effect of ethnic parties as vehicles of descriptive representation. Descriptive representation sees value in having people of the same identity group as active participants in the democratic process, and the ethnic party is certainly one of the clearest channels to increase the extent of this type of representation. In our conclusions, we add to the scholarly research, which has pointed to a potential impact of ethnic parties on the nature of ethnic relations and democracy. Most of these studies reflect an underlying uneasiness about both the nature of ethnic parties and their behaviour as they arguably tend to structure political competition along ethnic lines and, therefore, can, within the political incentive structure of a state, lead to the radicalization of ethnic demands, to outbidding among parties, to exacerbation of ethnic divisions and, ultimately, to violent ethnic conflict (Horowitz 2000, 296–363). Still, such parties tend to strengthen descriptive representation, which, according to others, brings with it other benefits for the group: heightened political efficacy and improved political legitimacy (Mansbridge 1999). That ethnic parties might further distort the political process by strengthening clientelistic relationships under the guise of descriptive representation further challenges the benefits this type of representation brings to the democratic process.

NOTES

1. This study is limited to ethnic parties and will not include parties organized purely on a regional or religious basis, although religion or region might have relevance for the differentiation of the ethnic group.

2. For a discussion of the differential treatment of ethnic parties by the party regulation in the new democracies of Eastern Europe, see Rashkova and Spirova, 2014 and Bieber (2010).

3. The Roma (Gypsies) constitute the second-largest minority in both countries. According to official statistics, they represent about 4.6 per cent of the Bulgarian population and 2.5 per cent of the Romanian population. Experts estimate the Roma population to be much bigger than official data.

4. Article 11 of the Bulgarian Constitution Article reads: 'There shall be no political parties on ethnic, racial, or religious lines, nor parties which seek the violent usurpation of state power'.

5. In contrast to the Bulgarian Constitution, Article 62(2) of the Romanian Constitution reads: 'Organizations of citizens belonging to national minorities, which fail to obtain the number of votes for representation in Parliament, have the right to one Deputy seat each, under the terms of the electoral law'.

6. For more details on the regulation of ethnic parties, see Rashkova, E. and Spirova, M. 2014.

7. Member-to-vote ratio is the ratio of the number of members to the number of votes a party has received in a general election and is used to measure the encapsulation of a party electorate by the political party (van Biezen 2003).

8. Party membership in Bulgaria, unlike in some other post-communist states, remains an important feature of party life. Because of the particularly strong presence of the Bulgarian successor party, this trend carried over to the whole party system, and the major parties in Bulgaria established organization building as the model for gaining electoral support. Further, the sequence of national and local elections has necessitated the establishment of stronger and more extensive party organizations than in countries such as Hungary and the Czech Republic (Spirova 2005). As a result, party members are an important legitimizing factor in party life in addition to providing the more direct benefits discussed in the theoretical section.

REFERENCES

Arriola, L. R. and M. C. Johnson. (2013). "Ethnic Politics and Women's Empowerment in Africa: Ministerial Appointments to Executive Cabinets," *American Journal of Political Science* 58(2): 495–510.

Bearfield, D. A. (2009). "What Is Patronage? A Critical Reexamination," *Public Administration Review*, January–February, 64–76.

Bieber, F. (2010). "National Minorities in the Party System," in V. Stojarová and P. Emerson (eds.), *Party Politics in the Western Balkans*. New York: Routledge.

van Biezen, I. (2003). *Political Parties in New Democracies: Party Organization in Southern and East-Central Europe*. Basingstoke: Palgrave Macmillan.

Biezen, I. van, P. Mair and T. Poguntke (2012). "Going, Going, . . . Gone? The Decline of Party Membership in Contemporary Europe," *European Journal of Political Research*, 51(1), 24–56.

Birnir, J. K. (2007). *Ethnicity and Electoral Politics*. Cambridge: Cambridge University Press.

Bratton, M. R. Bhavnani and H. Chen. (2012). "Voting Intentions in Africa: Ethnic, Economic or Partisan?" *Commonwealth & Comparative Politics*, 50(1), 27–52.

Capital. (2005). "Корупционният дрийм тийм" [The corruption dream team], 19 November. http://www.capital.bg/printversion.php?storyid=233808

Capital. (2013). "The Technology Used by Peevski to Increase the DPS Vote in the Stara Zagora Region," http://www.capital.bg/politika_i_ikonomika/bulgaria/2013/10/11/2159094_zaradi_desetkite_hiliadi_izbirateli/?sp=1#storystart

Chandra, K. (2004). *Why Ethnic Parties Succeed? Patronage and Ethnic Head Counts in India*. Cambridge: Cambridge University Press.

Chandra, K. (2005). "Ethnic Parties and Democratic Stability," *Perspectives on Politics*, 3, 235–252.

Chandra, K. (2011). "What Is an Ethnic Party?" *Party Politics*, 17, 151–169.

Constitution of the Republic of Bulgaria, "Bulgarian Parliament," http://parliament.bg/en/const

Crampton, R. J. (1987). *A Short History of Modern Bulgaria*, Cambridge University Press.

Dal, K. (2003). Interview.

Dnevnik. (2014). ". . . and Where Are the Puppet Masters?" 14 March, http://www.capital.bg/politika_i_ikonomika/redakcionni_komentari/2014/03/14/2261640_a_kude_sa_rejisyorite/

European Commission, (2005). Bulgaria: 2005 Comprehensive Monitoring Report, Available at: http://ec.europa.eu/enlargement/archives/pdf/key_documents/2005/sec1352_cmr_master_bg_college_en.pdf, accessed December 1, 2009.

Epstein, L. D. (1967). *Political Parties in Western Democracies*, New York: Frederick A. Praeger.

Fumurescu, A. (2011). "A Vicious Circle Ethnopolitics in Eastern European Transitions; Transylvania's Case," *mimeo.*

Georgiev, P. K. (2008). *Corruptive Patterns of Patronage in South East Europe.* Wiesbaden; VS Research.

Gherghina, S., M. Chiru and F. Casal-Bértoa. (2011). "State Resources and Pocket Money: Shortcuts for Party Funding in Romania." Working Paper Series on the Legal Regulation of Political Parties, No. 8.

Goldston, R. S. (1977). "Patronage in British Government," *Parliamentary Affairs*, 30(1), 80–96.

Guha, S. (2013). "From Ethnic to Multiethnic: The Transformation of the Bahujan Samaj Party in North India," *Ethnopolitics*, 12(1).

Gunther, R. and L. Diamond. (2003). "Species of Political Parties: A New Typology," *Party Politics*, 9(2), 167–199.

Horowitz, D. (2000). *Ethnic Groups in Conflict*. Berkeley: University of California Press.

Horváth, R. (2005). "UDMR la alegerile parlamentare din 1990-2004," *Studia Politica. Romanian Political Science Review*.

Ionascu, A. and S. Soare. (2012). "Party Members in Post Communist Settings: Extensive Organization and Weak Participation in Romania." Unpublished Manuscript.

Juberias, F. C. (2000). "Post-Communist Electoral Systems and National Minorities: A Dilemma in Five Paradigms." In Jonathan P. Stein (ed.) *The Politics of National Minority Participation in Post-communist Europe*, Armonk: M E Sharpe.

Kitschelt, H. (2000). "Linkages between citizens and politicians in democratic polities," *Comparative political studies* 33 (6–7), 845–879.

Kolarova, R. and M. Spirova. (2009). "'Bulgaria 2008' Political Data Yearbook," *European Journal of Political Research*, 49(7–8).

Kolarova, R. and M. Spirova. (2010). "'Bulgaria 2009' Political Data Yearbook," *European Journal of Political Research*, 49(7–8), 913–916.

Kolev, K. (2012). "Bulgaria" in H. Kitschelt and Y. Wang (eds), *Research and Dialogue on Programmatic Parties and Part Systems Case Study Reports.* At: https://web.duke.edu/democracy/papers/3.2.case.pdf#page=40 (accessed on 19 June 2014).

Kopecky, P., Mair, P. and Spirova, M. (2012). *Party Patronage and Party Government in European Democracies*, Oxford: Oxford University Press.

Krasteva, A. and A. Todorov. (2011). "Ethnic Minorities and Political Representation: The Case of Bulgaria," *Southeastern Europe*, 35, 8–318.

Kreuzer, M. and V. Pettai. (2002). "The Calculus of Party Affiliation in Post-Communist Democracies: Party Switching, Fusions, Fissions and the Institutionalization of the Party Systems." Paper presented at the 2002 APSA annual meeting, Boston, MA, August 29–September 2.

Law for the Election of the Chamber of Deputies and the Senate, 1992, Available at: https://www.legislationline.org/legislation/section/legislation/country/8/topic/6

Mansbridge, Jane. (1999). "Should Blacks Represent Blacks and Women Represent Women? A Contingent 'Yes'", *The Journal of Politics*, 61(3), 628–657. www.jstor.org/stable/2647821

Mediapool. (2005). "Ahmed Dogan, Interview," 26 June, http://www.mediapool.bg/доган-имаме-си-обръч-от-фирми—-те-ни-финансират-ние-им-помагаме-news106410.html

Mediapool. (2006). "Ahmed Dogan, Interview," http://www.mediapool.bg/доган-обръчът-от-фирми-не-е-обезателно-корупционна-схема-news115687.html

Müller, W. C. (1989). "Party Patronage in Austria: Theoretical Considerations and Empirical Findings," in A. Pelinka and F. Plasser (eds.), *The Austrian Party System*. Boulder, CO: Westview Press, pp. 327–355.

Müller, W. C. (2006). "Party Patronage and Party Colonization of the State," in R. S. Katz and W. J. Crotty (eds.), *Handbook of Party Politics*. London: Sage, pp. 189–194.

Popescu, M. (2003). "The Parliamentary and Presidential Elections in Romania, November 2000," *Electoral Studies*, 22(2), June, 325–335.

Rashkova, E. R. and M. Spirova (2014). "Ethnic Party Regulation in Eastern Europe," in I. van Biezen and H. ten Napel (eds.), *Political Parties and Public Law*. Leiden: Leiden University Press.

Roper, S. (2006). "The Influence of Party Patronage and State Finance on Electoral Outcomes: Evidence from Romania," *Journal of Communist Studies and Transition Politics*, 22(3), 362–382.

Saggar, S. (2000). *Race and Representation: Electoral Politics and Ethnic Pluralism in Britain*, Manchester University Press.

Scarrow, S. (1994). "The 'paradox of enrollment': Assessing the costs and benefits of party memberships," *European Journal of Political Research* 25 (1), 41–60

Scarrow, S. (1996). Parties and their members: Organizing for victory in Britain and Germany. Scarrow Oxford University Press.

Sorauf, F. (1959). "Patronage and Party," *Midwest Journal of Political Science*, 3, 115–126.

Spirova, M. (2005). "Political Parties in Bulgaria: Organizational Trends in Comparative Perspective." *Party Politics*, 11(5), 601–622, https://doi.org/10.1177/1354068805054982

Spirova, M. (2007). *Political Parties in Post-Communist Systems: Formation, Persistence, and Change*. New York: Palgrave Macmillan.

Spirova, M. (2012b). "'A Tradition We Don't Mess With': Party Patronage in Bulgaria," in P. Kopecký et al. (eds.), *Party Government and Party Patronage in European Democracies*. Oxford: Oxford University Press.

Spirova, M. and B. Stefanova. (2012). "The European Dimension of Minority Political Representation: Bulgaria and Romania Compared," *East European Politics and Societies*, 26(1), February, 75–93.

Stroschein, S. (2001). "Measuring Ethnic Party Success in Romania, Slovakia and Ukraine," *Problems of Post-Communism*, 48(4), 59–69.

Stroschein, S. (2011). "Demography in Ethnic Party Fragmentation: Hungarian Local Voting in Romania," *Party Politics*, 17(2), 189–204.

Tavits, M. (2013). *Post-Communist Democracies and Party Organization*. Cambridge University Press.

Volintiru, C. (2013). "Forms and Functions of Party Patronage: Evidence from Romania." Paper presented at the 2013 Joint Sessions of Workshop, Mainz, 22–27 March.

Wilson, J. Q. (1973) *Political Organizations*. New York: Basic Books.

Zingher, J. N. and M. S. Thomas. (2012). "Patterns of Immigrant Political Behaviour in Australia: An Analysis of Immigrant Voting in Ethnic Context," *Australian Journal of Political Science*, 47(3), 377–397.

24 Chassa. (2016). "Само 344 000 членове стоят зад партиите в парламента," 15 February, https://www.24chasa.bg/novini/article/5300656

Chapter Four

Castes, Clients, and Reservations in Indian Politics

Frank de Zwart

INTRODUCTION[1]

Susan Stokes (2011) distinguishes between 'programmatic redistributive politics', 'clientelist mobilization', and 'pork barrel politics' on the basis of one key criterion: who exactly benefits. A clientelist exchange typically benefits only those people who actually support the patron. In other words, the patron's criterion for pursuing this form of redistribution is: 'did you (will you) support me' (2). Pork-barrel politics differs because it allows all voters in a district to profit from the redistribution of goods, whether or not they actually support the patron. It is still considered problematic because pork-barrel politics often targets only a few districts while the costs are borne by all. Programmatic redistribution is different again because it targets specific *categories* of people. Who actually profits from among those who belong to these categories is irrelevant for the decision to redistribute. That is, the redistributive program, by definition, cannot exclude any person who fulfils the categorical criteria.

Our focus in this article is India's affirmative action policy. At first sight, this policy qualifies as 'programmatic redistributive politics' under Stokes' definition. It redistributes jobs and educational seats by means of quota for large population categories – the 'backward classes', for instance, are entitled to a 27 per cent quota and comprise about half the population of India. The sheer size of the target categories makes it impossible to distinguish actual and potential beneficiaries, making India's affirmative action an unlikely resource in clientelist transactions. There is no way for politicians at the national or state levels to distinguish their supporters from others within the broad categories that benefit from quota, which seemingly renders the policy useless for clientelist mobilization as conceived by Stokes (2011).

Indeed, it has often been observed, especially for northern India, that the introduction of reservations for the Backward Classes in 1990 was a final blow to the system of clientelist politics that had dominated Indian politics and kept the Congress Party in power for over four decades (Chhibber 1999; Jaffrelot 2003, 2006; Weiner 2001; Wilkinson 2014).[2] After the Congress Party lost the national elections, in 1989, a coalition government under leadership of V. P. Sing's Janata Party came to power and quickly decided to implement the so-called Mandal Report which recommended to reserve a 27 per cent quota for the Backward Classes. This report, written the second national Backward Classes Commission and named after its chairman, had already been submitted to the Government of India in 1980, but successive Congress Party governments had shelved it for a decade. The decision, in 1990, to implement it turned out to be a critical juncture because it caused a fundamental change of the party system, especially in North India. Pradeep Chhibber (1999) who studied this change in Uttar Pradesh characterizes it as the transformation of a clientelist catch-all system into a cleavage-based party system (135–157).

Before the decision to implement Mandal, both the Congress Party and its main competitor, the Janata Party, were catch-all parties specialized in vertical, clientelist mobilization. Acceptance of the Mandal report led to a turbulent period of high-caste protest and mobilization, and low-caste countermobilization (Jaffrelot 2006, 184–186). These mobilizations empowered new parties to defend caste interests and led to a political cleavage between the 'backward' and the 'forward' castes (cf. Brass 1991, 344). Chhibber shows that in the 1989 elections Congress and Janata Dal maintained their catch-all character and drew similar percentages of voters from backward and forward castes (1999, 138–139). In the 1991 elections, however, after the Mandal decision, the major parties (BJP and the Janata/SP coalition)[3] drew support from either the forward castes (BJP) or the backward castes (Janata/SP). 'Catch-all' had disappeared.

Chhibber exposed a crucial change, and most scholars and observers of Indian politics have noted and emphasized it. 'Mandalization' of politics, as some call it, basically means that the political system shifted from a clientelist structure based on vertical mobilization to a caste-based cleavage system. The introduction of reservations for the Backward Classes triggered this change, and political parties have maintained it ever since (Chandra 2005; Chhibber 1999; Jaffrelot & Kumar 2009).

The question remains, however, to what extent a clientelist system and a system of caste-based cleavages are mutually exclusive. One could argue that the ascriptive character of a caste cleavage would make clientelist mobilization redundant because people will vote for parties that represent their ascribed identity anyway. For example, Horowitz (1985, 83–87) describes a majoritarian system based on ethnic cleavages in which the election, 'intended to be a vehicle of choice, was no such thing and will be no such thing in the future; it registered not choice, but birth affiliation. This was no election – it was a census' (86). But Horowitz' election-as-census, rests on the assumption that the ethnic categories in question are given, which does not apply in India. The relevant identity categories in our case are activated, frequently adjusted, and multiplied in a political process that I call the 'logic of affirmative action'. To some extent this logic is inherent in affirmative action (e.g., Sowell 1990) but it has a particularly divisive effect in India because caste identity is segmentary and quota politics is a zero-sum game (I return to these traits in the next section). The result, I shall show, is that the large category 'Backward Classes' splits into ever-finer caste-based categories that claim quota for their own.

The cleavage system that Chhibber (1999) describes is therefore untenable. Peter Mair notes that cleavages have empirical, normative, and organizational elements, none of which can be taken for granted. Social stratification is often presumed to provide the empirical units or social categories that make up political cleavages, and thus to impact on institutions and political behaviour. But Mair points out that *the reverse is equally true* (2014, 233); institutional structure and political behaviour impact social structure too.

Chhibber emphasizes agency – *in casu* political parties – rather than taking cleavages for granted on the basis of social structure as is often mistakenly done. However, he still underestimates the logic of affirmative action. The nature of caste distinctions in combination with the institutional structure of reservation policy in India produces ongoing fission. An increasing number of political parties use the promise of 'reservation' to mobilise new subsections from within the beneficiary categories, especially the Backward Classes. This divisive process, the chapter argues, narrows the gap between actual and potential beneficiaries of quota and thus diminishes the 'over-inclusion' that characterises 'programmatic redistribution'. In effect, even though distribution is still done categorically, the logic of affirmative action pushes reservation policy closer to 'clientelism'.

CASTE CATEGORIES AND QUOTA

Many people in India agree that the state needs to mitigate durable inequality inherent in the caste system by means of affirmative action. But the nature of caste distinctions complicates the implementation of this policy. A short outline of reservation policy[4] and the categories used in it, should make this clear; relatively simple schemes such as 'election-as-census' or 'cleavage' between backward and forward castes cannot account for developments in India's political system.

The target population for reservations is divided, nationally, into several eligible categories with fixed quota of government jobs and places in institutes of higher education reserved for members. Scheduled Castes have a 15 per cent quota, Scheduled Tribes 7.5 per cent, and Other Backward Classes 27 per cent.[5] Ever since independence, the Constitution of India entitles the scheduled castes and tribes to quotas that are more or less in proportion to their share of India's population (16.2 and 8.2 per cent, respectively, according to the 2011 census). The Other Backward Classes, however, are a later addition. They are entitled to a 27 per cent quota since 1990, but that percentage is not proportional to their share of the population. The exact number of Backward Classes is unknown because there are no census data on caste identities, but the estimate is that they to comprise about half the population of India. The reason why their quota is disproportional is that the Constitution of India allots of 22.5 per cent to reservation to the Scheduled Castes and Tribes, while the Supreme Court has capped the maximum number of jobs under reservation at 50 per cent. This left 'only' 27 per cent for the Backward Classes (see Government of India 1980, 19–25).

As a consequence of the 50 per cent ceiling, the numerous new groups that mobilize to claim Backward Class status in order to qualify for quota can only be accommodated at the expense of existing entitlements; quota politics is zero-sum. Moreover, Backward Classes, Scheduled Castes, and Scheduled Tribes are umbrella categories that consist of many (thousands) of separate castes and sub-castes. These separate castes, which are named and listed in constitutional schedules (for the Scheduled Castes and Tribes) and in lists maintained by the Backward Classes Commission,[6] are both ritually and economically ranked. That is, there is significant social and economic inequality between castes and sub-castes within each of the eligible umbrella categories.

'Ritual ranking' refers to the caste system. Castes are endogamous groups with a traditional occupation and hereditary membership. The basic criterion for ranking castes is ritual purity. Purity and pollution of castes follow from their traditional occupation and stick to castes as a whole. All members of a caste – regardless of whether they follow its traditional occupation – share its rank in the hierarchy. Division between castes is most clearly manifest in patterns of marriage and commensality. Caste identity follows the segmentary principle. That is, the meaning of 'caste' is relative to context. In the context of local events castes are small endogamous groups of people with the same name, spread over a few adjacent villages. On a regional level castes are clusters of local castes, perceived by others as groups with similar status and subsumed under one name. In the context of a state or the nation, castes are clusters of regional clusters. In Indian languages all these three segments are called *jatis*, and reference to 'caste' usually refers to either of these levels.[7]

The national list of Other Backward Classes currently holds 5,013 castes, about 45 per cent of India's population.[8] These 5,000 castes are regional clusters of *jatis*, which obviously the umbrella category, but still is a stark simplification of social reality. The 2011 caste census (the first since 1931) has once more made this very clear: Census takers asked 330 million households the 'caste/tribe' identity of all household members. The instruction manual ordered them 'not to enter into any argument' with the respondents about their answer, but instead to 'record faithfully whatever Caste/Tribe is returned' (Government of India 2011, 27). The result, as recently became clear, is a list of 4.6 million entries — castes, sub-castes, synonyms, clans, and *gotras*. This outcome defeats all efforts to use these data for precision in allocating reservations, which was the main reason to hold the caste census. The census data have yet to be released. An expert group, chaired by Arvind Panagariya, is set up to 'classify' the data (*The Indian Express*, 17 July 2015).

CLASS TO CASTE

That reservations strengthen caste divisions and stimulate caste politics was not self-evident to the political elite who framed the policy in the early 1950s in a series of constitutional articles. They tried hard to avoid 'caste', hence the official classification of beneficiaries as 'Backward *Classes*'. This category was purposively created and entrenched in the Constitution of India to combat severe group inequality – commonly seen then (and now) as a consequence of the caste system – with affirmative action but without having to lend official recognition to caste identities.[9] Congress leadership feared that official recognition of caste would stimulate caste consciousness and make the policy self-defeating. Their solution was to construct a new category that could address the problem while avoiding caste identities, the Backward Classes.

However, when these constitutional articles were drafted and discussed, nobody knew exactly who the Backward Classes were. The Constituent Assembly debated this question at length in 1951. Some MPs agreed with Law Minister Ambedkar's[10] remark that '[w]hat are called the backward classes are . . . nothing else but a collection of certain castes' (quoted in Galanter 1984, 166). But most avoided mentioning this expectation, and left it at vague descriptions. According to Prime Minister Nehru, for instance, the Backward Classes were 'groups, classes, individuals, communities, if you like, who are backward' (166). Pressed harder, he replied that

> We must distinguish between the communal approach and the approach of helping our weaker, backward brothers and sisters. . . . [I]t is the backward individual citizen that we should help. Why should we brand groups and classes as backward and forward? It is a fact that certain groups or classes are backward but I do not wish to brand them as such or treat them as such. (Nehru 1994, 185)

Unable to agree, the Constituent Assembly left the definition and the selection of 'backward classes' to Backward Classes Commissions.[11] The first of these, chaired by K. Kalelkar, started its work in 1953 and reported to the government in 1955. It used a mixture of social, economic, and educational criteria, and tried, but failed, to avoid listing castes. The 'Backward Classes' in Kalelkar's report were a list of 2,392 eligible *castes*. Kalelkar explained that the commission had been 'deluged' by caste leaders and caste representatives demanding that their caste would be that their cast would be listed as backward. So even though the commission had been eager to 'eradicate the evils of the caste system' by avoiding caste identities, they could not do so. 'We tried to avoid caste', they explain, 'but we found it difficult to ignore caste in the present prevailing conditions. We wish it were easy to dissociate caste from social backwardness at the present juncture' (Government of India 1956, 41).

The Congress government shelved the report, as Chairman Kalelkar had recommended in a dissenting letter attached to the report. He regretted not having been able to avoid caste-classification, and noted that the commission's research had stimulated caste consciousness to such an extent that even Christian communities approached the commission to claim that they were low caste and should be listed as 'backward class'. Kalelkar believed it best to shelf affirmative action for Backward Classes, and that is exactly what the Congress government did.[12] The report was not discussed in parliament and in his memorandum on the report, Home Minister G. B. Pant stressed that targeting castes for development purposes did not make sense because they were bound to disappear with the further establishment of a socialist development path (quoted in Jaffrelot 2006, 178). Jaffrelot speaks of the 'resolutely modernist attitude' of the Congress government under Nehru, which 'reflected the preponderance of the notions of class and class struggle among an intelligentsia influenced by Marxism as well as Gandhi's utopia of a conflict-free society' (179).

Two decades later, in 1978, the first non-Congress government to rule in New Delhi since independence installed a second National Backward Classes Commission, the Mandal Commission. It had three tasks: to determine criteria for defining the Backward Classes, to prepare a nation-wide list of those who qualify, and to recommend steps for their advancement. However, like its predecessor, after two years of thorough research around the country, the Mandal commission eventually produced a list of castes. This time 4,339 eligible castes were listed, 52 per cent of the population of India. Unlike its predecessor, the Mandal commission also recommended that 27 per cent of government jobs and places in institutions of higher education be reserved exclusively for this category and shows no reluctance in defining the Backward Classes as collection of castes.

Mandal grounds his recommendations in an analysis of caste inequality past and present, and throughout the report stresses the enduring monopoly of upper castes on bureaucratic and political positions. The political emancipation of the lower castes, Mandal argues, cannot be realized by denying or avoiding caste identities because caste inequality is not withering away. The report quotes Rajni Kothari, who wrote in 1970 that '[t]hose in India who complain of "casteism in politics" are really looking for a sort of politics which has no basis in society' (1970, 4). Kothari's was a dissenting voice against the modernist denial of caste prevalent among the Congress elite in Delhi. Today, as we shall see below, it is a widely shared view. Mandal is quite clear about his intention, as well as the probable political impact of reservations for castes:

> It is not at all our contention that by offering a few thousand jobs . . . we shall be able to make 52 per cent of the Indian population as forward. But we must recognize that an essential part of the battle against social backwardness is to be fought in the minds of the backward people. In India government service has always been looked upon as a symbol of prestige and power. By increasing the representation of [backward classes] in government services, we give them an immediate feeling of participation in governance of this country. . . . [T]the psychological spin off . . . is tremendous, the entire community of that backward class candidate feels socially elevated. Even when no tangible benefits flow to the community at large, the feeling that now it has its 'own man' in the 'corridors of power' acts as a morale booster. (Government of India 1980, 57)

It would take another decade for Mandal to be proven right. Indira Gandhi's Congress party was back in power by the time Mandal presented his report, and did not act upon Mandal's recommendations. For now the central government remained outside reservation policy.[13] Ten years later, however, after another electoral defeat of the Congress party, Mandal's recommendations were implemented.

The 1989 elections gave power to the Janata Dal, whose leader, V. P. Singh, formed a coalition government of left parties and the Hindu nationalist BJP, which shared an anti-Congress stance. A few months after this government took office, V. P. Singh issued orders to implement Mandal's recommendations. Widespread violent reactions from the higher castes followed. Dozens of high-caste students protested by self-immolation, and in the riots that followed more than 200 people were killed. The massive resistance of upper castes against 'Mandal', and the Supreme Court's effort to appease the rioters by suspending the measures V. P. Singh had announced, triggered Backward Class leaders around the country to mobilise their followers (Jaffrelot 2006, 185). This counter-mobilization succeeded so well that it led to a profound change in the division of political power, and the caste composition of political elites.

The stakes in India's reservation policy are not just a matter of redistribution to uplift the poor and create greater socio-economic equality. Mandal had also sought to provide access for the lower 'classes' to the 'corridors of power'. Most Indians believe that political power resides in the administrative system as well in political office. Administrative and political positions are highly sought after and part of an elaborate system of patronage that has developed over time into a system of 'rent-seeking' with the business community (Weiner 2001, 204). Myron Weiner characterizes the introduction of reservations for the Backward Classes not so much as a 'promise of social justice for the poor', but primarily as 'an offer to share the spoils of office' (205; cf. Jaffrelot 2006, 183–185).

POLITICAL RISE OF THE BACKWARD CLASSES

The 1989 election was a watershed because since then India's political system 'moved from a dominant party system with governments based on party majorities in parliament to a regionalized multi-party system with coalition governments at the centre' (Rudolph 2003, 1119). Between 1984 and 2014, no national party has won a majority of seats in Delhi, and coalition governments have relied heavily on regional parties. Because castes have a regional basis, many regional parties have a specific caste-profile with members and voters belonging to either the Backward Classes or the Scheduled Castes. Gowda and Sridharan (2007) depict this change as 'party system fragmentation'. Coalition governments in Delhi, under BJP or Congress leadership, accommodate a wide range of regional or local caste-based parties.[14]

By 1989 the clientelist 'Congress system' had disappeared. Today politics is characterized by horizontal mobilization along caste lines. Many regional parties that won seats in the national parliament (*Lok Sabha*) represent sections of the Backward Classes, while the old national parties, like Congress and the BJP, increasingly give tickets and office to Backward Class leaders. The number and influence of caste-based political parties has increased, both in the states and the centre, and electoral mobilization of caste-based vote banks has replaced the vertical clientele pattern of the Congress system. As a consequence the caste composition of the national parliament has changed radically. Table 4.1 shows this for the Hindi belt, where about 40 per cent of the population of India lives and which returns the same proportion of MPs.[15]

The classification in this table with 'Backward Classes' and 'Scheduled Castes' has become a standard way of representing the electorate, which demonstrates the profound influence of reservation policy on politics. The upper castes (Brahmins and Kshatriyas) are roughly 11 per cent of the population of India, the intermediate castes (Vaishya's and Jats) comprise 6 per

Table 4.1 Castes of MPs in the Hindi Belt, 1957–2004 (in per cent)

Castes	1957	1967	1977	1989	1999	2004
Upper Castes	58.60	55.50	48.20	38.20	35.40	33.00
Intermediate Castes	1.43	2.75	6.64	8.00	7.90	7.10
Backward Classes	5.24	9.64	13.30	20.87	24.00	25.30
Scheduled Castes	18.10	18.35	17.70	17.78	18.60	17.80

Source: Based on Jaffrelot and Kumar (2009, 7).

cent, the 'Backward Classes' (Sudra's, or lower castes) are about 43 per cent, and the Scheduled Castes (former Untouchables) are 16.5 per cent of the population (Varshney 2000). Except for the untouchables these percentages are estimates, ultimately based on the last census that collected data on caste identities, in 1931.

Table 4.1 shows a decline in the upper caste share of MPs in the Hindi Belt, and a sharp rise in the number of Backward Class MPs.[16] The main cause of the rise of Backward Class MPs is the increasing number of seats, in the *Lok Sabha*, held by Backward Class parties led by Backward Class politicians. The latter are mostly regional parties, with a power base in one or a few states, but together lower-caste parties have received a considerable percentage of the national vote. In three national elections between 1996 and 1999, lower-caste parties have received between 18 and 20 per cent of the national vote. The BJP received 20 to 25 per cent, and the Congress party, 23 to 29 per cent (Varshney 2000, 6). However, the rise of Backward Class MPs is also caused by the fact that the Congress the BJP increasingly gives tickets to Backward Class candidates. Table 4.2 illustrates this phenomenon, which is a general trend in the Hindi belt, for two elections in Uttar Pradesh. Varghese George (2012) refers to it as 'Mandalization of the Congress'.

Varshney (2000) calls the rise of Backward Class politicians the 'Southernization' of North India. Kanchan Chandra (2004) speaks of the ethnification of political parties, indicating the replacement of clientele politics with horizontal, caste-specific mobilization. Jaffrelot calls it a 'silent revolution' that finally brought political dominance of India's upper castes to an end (2003, 2006, 185).[17] Some scholars argue that the present coalition politics, which accommodates lower-caste parties in grand coalitions, is a form of consociationalism (Gowda & Sridharan 2007, 6–8; Lijphart 1996). Myron Weiner (2001) calls the rise of the Backward Classes a successful movement that uprooted the traditional political dominance of the upper castes. But he adds that this

> movement for change is not a struggle to end caste; it is to use caste as an instrument for social change. Caste is not disappearing, nor is 'casteism' – the political use of caste – for what is emerging in India is a social and political system, which institutionalizes and transforms but does not abolish caste. (Weiner 2001, 196)

Frank de Zwart

Table 4.2   Caste and Community Profile of Congress Candidates in Uttar Pradesh State Elections, 2007 and 2012

Category	% of Population	% Seats 2007	% Seats 2012
Muslims and Minorities	19	15	15
Scheduled Castes	21	21	24
Backward Classes	40	20	26
Thakurs	7	17	15
Brahmins	9	17	12
Other Upper Castes	4	11	7

Source: Varghese K. George, *Hindustan Times,* 13 January 2012.

Weiner is right; to understand recent political developments in India one must abandon the 'liberal expectancy' that the saliency of traditional social distinctions such as caste or ethnicity would wither away with modernization and democratization (Glazer & Moynihan 1975, 7). The national government under Congress rule has purposively tried, for many decades, to keep caste distinctions from becoming institutionalized in India's central bureaucracy and political system. Its failure to do so has often been interpreted as a matter of the political system finally coming to terms with the 'real' cleavages in society.

THE LOGIC OF AFFIRMATIVE ACTION

As Peter Mair notes, many authors assume that social stratification provides the units of political cleavages (2014, 234–235). However, a more constructivist view would not take ascriptive cleavages for granted. The present salience of caste identities in Indian politics is not a necessary outcome, or even an overdue adjustment of the political system to social reality. Indian society has many potential cleavages – a repertory of religious, regional, language, and caste identities – and 'it is the *institutionalization* of such cleavages, rather than the mere fact of their existence, that explains the variation in democratic outcomes in India and elsewhere' (Chandra 2005, 239, italics in original).[18] India's affirmative action policy with its caste-based target categories is a textbook example of institutionalization of cleavages. The policy of reservations provides an opportunity for political leaders and parties to mobilize voters along caste lines by means of promising quota, and quota within quota. In the process, ever-finer caste distinctions become relevant for the redistribution of jobs and educational seats. Over time this pushes the India's affirmative action away from 'programmatic redistribution' toward clientelism as the gap between categorical and actual beneficiaries continuously narrows.

Given the attempts by drafters of the Constitution and the modernizing Congress elite around Nehru in the first decades after independence to keep caste out of reservation policy, the present situation appears to be an unintended but not unanticipated consequence.[19] The constitutional grounding of affirmative action for the 'Backward Classes', the work of Backward Classes Commissions, and a Supreme Court ruling that declares 'caste' to be 'also a class of citizens',[20] have all furthered institutionalization of caste identities in the political system.

However, the emergence of a cleavage between the 'backward' and 'forward' castes (Chhibber 1999) and the resulting rise in the number of Backward Class politicians in the Hindi belt (Table 4.1), tell only half the story. These figures do not show the political and social fragmentation that accompanies this development. By design, India's reservation policy is well equipped to address durable inequality on an aggregate level. Inequality between Scheduled Castes, Backward Classes, and Others,[21] is a well-documented structural characteristic of Indian society. Whether one looks at per capita consumption expenditure (a measure often used by the National Statistical Survey), years of education, wages, or occupational categories, the pattern is always the same: 'Hindu [upper castes] fare much better than the national average, Hindu Backward Classes are close to the average, and Muslims somewhat worse off, while Scheduled Castes and Scheduled Tribes are by far the worst off' (Weisskopf 2011, 48). However, these caste-based categories are administrative simplifications and, as Pradipta Chaudhury notes, reservation policy has long been based on the assumption 'that almost the entire population of each of the categories [OBC and SC] suffers from a uniformly high degree of deprivation' (1989, 2004). In the real world each of these target categories is made up of numerous distinct, separate, and unequally ranked castes and sub-castes, and reservation policy is not as well equipped to deal with that.

A party that commands the Backward Class vote would be a formidable political force, but as yet no party has succeeded in doing so. The paradox is that while the policy of reservations has contributed much to the political emancipation of the Backward Classes, it has also encouraged a process of social and political fragmentation that weakens their political clout. I call that process 'the logic of affirmative action'.

A group's inclusion in the list of Backward Classes entitles its members to reserved jobs and admissions in educational institutions. Elites from potentially eligible groups (the caste leaders who lobby Backward Class commissions) use the prospect of recognition to mobilize caste members and demand inclusion. If they succeed, if the group is recognized as a Backward Class, then all members of the group potentially benefit. However, the actual number of jobs and admissions in education to be distributed under reservation policy is much lower than the number of eligible people. The Backward

Classes comprise about half the population of India; reserved jobs and educational admissions, even under a 27 per cent quota, are but a very small fraction of that.

Who, then, profits from reservations? As a rule those sections of the eligible population who are ahead of others in terms of education, income, and organizational capacity are the first to profit (De Zwart 2000, 245–247). The others, those who are eligible but have not (yet) profited, face the problem that the benefits have been cornered by other groups. Their best option to also profit from the policy is to organize along a refined definition of the officially recognized division – caste – and claim a share of the quota for their own. The resulting fragmentation is sheer endless. As noted, the national list of Backward Classes currently holds over 5,000 *jatis*, but this classification is still a stark simplification of social reality.[22] Most of these five thousand recognized Backward Classes are regional- or state-level clusters of *jatis*, and whereas these clusters are treated as groups with similar status *by outsiders*, including the government, they are still highly stratified for insiders.

The subtleties of ritual ranking, and the economic and educational differences that often accompany it, within a caste cluster are often unknown or unrecognized by people outside it. However, the logic of affirmative action brings these differences to the fore. Better-off and relatively better educated sections of castes corner the benefits, which stimulates those who have not (yet) profited to organize, mobilize, and demand quota within quota.[23]

The resulting increase of caste and sub-caste claims, and the proliferation of beneficiary categories that accompanies it, is clearly visible in the work of Backward Classes Commissions. A 1992 Supreme Court ruling directs national and state governments to constitute permanent Backward Classes Commissions for 'entertaining, examining and recommending upon requests for inclusion and complaints of over-inclusion and under-inclusion in the list of OBCs'.[24] The National Backward Classes Commission holds public hearings across the country to consider requests from castes for inclusion in the central list of Backward Classes. The commission's annual reports give an idea of the magnitude of this task, for example the Annual Report 2008–2009 mentions fifteen hearings in thirteen states during which requests from 194 'castes/communities' were heard. The result was a series of 'advices' to the government regarding inclusion, and, rarely, exclusion of 132 castes (Government of India 2009). In principle the commission's advice is binding, and the government regularly announces additions to the national list of Backward Classes.

In a public lecture at the University of Hyderabad, the Chairman of the National Backward Classes commission commented on this trend: 'What is glaringly present in the contemporary scenario', he observes,

> is the consolidation of caste groups. . . . Upholding of the Mandal Commission's Report by which reservations were sanctioned by the government of

India has raised hopes in many sections of the population with the consequence that depending upon its popularity and power, each social group is trying to find a place in the list of Backward Classes for securing the benefits under Articles 15(4) and 16(4). (Rao 2012, 79–80)

The requests in commission hearings (national and state) mostly come from leaders of caste associations. There are hundreds of caste associations today, and making claims on reservations is an important *raison d'être* (Deshpande 2010; Gupta 2005, 419–420; Rudolph 2003). Deshpande who researches the rise and proliferation of caste associations in Maharashtra, notes that

> at the national as well as the State level the logic of Mandal inaugurated a new phase of caste politics – mainly a politics of presence – in which each small caste wanted to participate and be visible. . . . The small, backward sub-castes among Lingayats seek maximum benefits of the reservation policy [and] with the help of their caste-based mobilizations . . . these castes like many other backward castes keep demanding a separate quota within quota for themselves. (2010, 9, 15)

Backward Class leaders create a clientele by delivering or at least working on a claim to a sub-quota. If they succeed they are often incorporated in political parties, which partly explains the rise of Backward Class politicians after implementation of the Mandal report.

Given the limited number of political posts available in existing parties, centralized methods of elite incorporation which are common in the Congress Party and the BJP, promote 'splits and defections by elites from initially harmonious categories or even from the same ethnic category' (Chandra 2000, 837). This principle helps to explain the process of party fragmentation along caste and sub-caste lines. Today regional parties represent about half of the Indian voters in national elections, and many of those parties are associated with a single caste (Jaffrelot 2012).

To illustrate, look at Uttar Pradesh, India's most populous state, which returns 80 of the 543 MPs in the national parliament. In January 2012, newspapers reported that the Congress party in Uttar Pradesh would propose in its election manifesto a sub quota for the so-called Most Backward Castes (MBC's). In order not to exceed the 50 per cent ceiling, this quota would have to come from the 27 per cent quota for Backward Castes. There is no other way, Congress General Secretary Digvijaya Singh is quoted in the *Economic Times*, 'grievances of MBCs have to be addressed. . . . The party, if voted to power, will study the experience of reservation in the past two decades and ensure that the not-so-well-off among Backwards get the benefits of quota' (*Economic Times*, January 17, 2012).

This announcement by the Congress party followed after public protests protest in Uttar Pradesh by the two large caste clusters in the Backward Class category, the Yadavs and Kurmis, aggrieved by an earlier plan to create a 9 per cent (out of the 27 per cent) sub quota for Muslims.[25] Yadavs and Kurmis are the most forward caste clusters among Backward Classes in Uttar Pradesh, and they have cornered most of the reservation benefits. Kurmi votes were uncertain for Congress at the time, while Yadavs vote SP, a Backward Class party led by Mulayam Singh Yadav.[26] Congress' electoral strategy therefore was to attract votes from the so-called 'Most Backward Castes' – for example Kushwahas, Nishads, Nonias, Rajbhars, and Lodhs. The latter comprise about 70 per cent of the Backward Class population in the state, and they have long-standing grievances regarding monopolizing the benefits of reservations by Yadavs and Kurmis.

The process just sketched is not unique for Uttar Pradesh. We find similar pressure for quota within quota in most states (e.g., Panini 1996; Radhakrishnan 1996; Tripathi 2001; Zérini 2009).[27] Recently the National Commission for Backward Classes (NCBC) submitted a report on sub-categorization within the Other Backward Classes (Government of India 2015). The commission strongly recommends the national government makes a reasonable 'sub-classification' by differentiating 'Extremely Backward Classes', 'More Backward Classes', and 'Backward Classes' (14–15). The central government would then distribute the benefits of reservation to these sub-categories in 'proportion to their population within the 27%' (8). The NCBC researched current practices in the states where quota within quota are increasingly common, and discussed, as an example, the four-fold division currently used in Andhra Pradesh. In Andhra, Group A has castes whose 'traditional occupation is begging, pig-rearing, fishing, washing . . . watchmen at burial ground . . . bird catchers, snake charmers, drum beaters' (12). Group A now has fifty-two castes but, the commission stresses, 'still there is anomaly having the difference within the 52 castes\communities' (12). In short, a truly fair distribution of sub quota would require further division between more and less deprived castes within the category of Backward Classes.

Besides fragmentation within the beneficiary categories, a recent development in the logic of affirmative action is the growing pressure to include hitherto not included groups (forward castes) as beneficiary categories. 'The clamour for recognition as "backward" by the "forward" classes has been getting louder', as Radhika Kumar puts it (2016, 17). Several very large caste clusters in North and West Indian States – for example Jats, Marathas, and Patels – have recently organized demonstrations, which often became violent agitations (Jaffrelot 2016; Kumar 2016; Sen 2015), to support their claim to backward status. Jats are 30 per cent of the population of Haryana, Maratha's are 30 per cent of Maharashtra, and Patels comprise 12 per cent of Gujarat. These castes are not recognized as Backward Classes by the Mandal Commission, but given their size, it is hardly surprising that governments and political parties are inclined to accommodate their claims.

The most flagrant example of such accommodation occurred in March 2014, when, a day before the general election, the ruling UPA government in Delhi decided to include Jats nine different states in North and West India in the national list of Other Backward Classes. Protests from extant Backward Class groups and their political representatives followed, and a year later the Supreme Court stepped in and rejected the UPA government's decision to include Jats. The Jats are a relatively well educated and well organized caste cluster, so other Backward Classes feared that, should this go through, Jats would quickly corner all benefits within the 27 per cent quota. Reservations are a zero-sum game.

CONCLUSION

The logic of affirmative action predicts that the recent mobilization of large forward caste clusters that try to be recognized as 'backward' to receive quota, shall evolve in a similar way as that of the Backward Classes. Once the large cluster is recognized as eligible, fission follows.[28] Jats, Marathas, and Patels, like all caste clusters, are made up of numerous ranked sub-castes. In the case of Backward Classes, fission into sub-categories with their own sub quota brought 'backward', 'most backward', and 'extremely backward' levels, and the National Backward Classes Commission suggests argues that *justice demands further subclasssification*. The extent to which this logic shall materialize, however, depends on electoral considerations. The category Most Backward Clasts is now becoming prominent, as leaders from within its rank demand recognition and a fair share of the quota, while all political parties fight over the 'most backward vote' and therefore accommodate leaders from that category.

The demand to hold a Caste Census, after eighty years, was a radical step in the logic of affirmative action. It came primarily from politicians who belong to Backward Class parties. They face the problem that they cannot keep the 'most backward' sections from among their support base loyal without supporting sub-quota that would cut into the 27 per cent quota for the larger category Backward Classes. Raising that percentage would give these parties space to accommodate sub-categories, the 27 per cent follows from the Supreme Court's 50 per cent ceiling, which is hard to change. Holding a caste census is one way to pressurize the Supreme Court; many Backward Class leaders think that the number of Backward Classes is much higher than the official estimates, and that a caste census would therefore make it clear that 27 per cent quota is far too low to be just.

Other parties, including Congress and BJP, have supported the decision to hold a caste census because they cannot afford to alienate the Backward Class vote. Instead, their current strategy is to patronize an electorally interesting sub-category of the Backward Classes. The Congress Party's attempt to bring in the Jat vote just before the 2014 election by promising them Backward Class status, and the BJP's recent catering to the 'most backward classes' with Prime Minister Modi's decision to agree to national subcategorization of Backward Classes, are good examples (see Krishna 2017).

The kind of politics that is stimulated by the logic of affirmative action is hard to capture well with Stokes' rigid distinction between 'programmatic redistribution', 'pork barrel', and 'clientele politics' (2011). Quota politics in India is not pure clientele politics as Stokes pictures it, because the target categories are too large to ensure that only those who support the patron receive actual benefits. However, reservations cannot qualify as pork barrel, and in proper programmatic redistribution one would expect much less political interference and *ad hoc* categorization motivated by electoral prospects.

Stokes' ideal type is nevertheless helpful to characterize the political process described in this chapter. Over time, the logic of affirmative action turns reservations from the originally intended programmatic redistribution into a key resource for clientelist politics. Moreover, the social, political, and administrative fragmentation that is the primary outcome of this logic, also undermines the simple distinction between a cleavage and a catch-all system. Cleavages are not given with social structure; they form and reform with institutional context.

NOTES

1. I wish to thank participants in the workshop *Clientelism and Public Policy* at the 2014 ECPR *Joint Sessions of Workshops*, Salamanca, for their helpful comments on an early draft of this chapter. Jim Sadkovich helped me out with many language and editorial issues. I am grateful for that. All mistakes left in the chapter are mine.

2. The 'Congress system', which guaranteed the party's electoral success for decades depended on coopting local patrons – landlords, notables, big merchants, social workers, and moneylenders – whose dependents and clients then delivered the vote. Power effectively aggregated from the bottom up through patron-client networks (Rudolph and Rudolph 1967; Weiner 1967). The Congress system, however, started to decline in the 1980s (see Brass 1984, 105; Kohli 1990; Wilkinson 2014).

3. In this election the Congress Party could not to take a clear stance in the Mandal issue without risking the loss of either forward or backward caste supporters and therefore lost support among both (Chhibber 1999, 149–150).

4. In India affirmative action is commonly called 'reservations'.

5. 'Scheduled Castes' are India's former 'untouchables', 'Scheduled Tribes' are its indigenous tribal population, and the Backward Classes are the lower castes.

6. Candidates applying for a job or access to an educational institution have to prove eligibility for reserved positions by showing a 'Caste Certificate' which certifies that they were born into a caste that is scheduled or recognized and listed by the relevant Backward Classes Commission (state or national) for the Backward Classes.

7. 'Caste' is also used to refer to *Varna*. Varna's are the four categories into which the Hindu scriptures divide society at large: Brahmins (priests and scholars), Kshatriyas (rulers and soldiers), Vaishya's (traders and merchants) and Shudras (agriculturalists). The categories upper castes, intermediate castes, and backward castes that are common in the literature, correspond roughly to this scheme. But *Varna's* are not actual groups; they form an ideological scheme, used by people 'as a handy gross classification of others' (Mandelbaum 1970, 13).

8. Besides the Backward Classes, the constitution also lists 1,208 Scheduled Castes (Constitution Scheduled Castes Order of 2012) and 640 Scheduled Tribes (Scheduled Tribes Order of 1950), about 22,500 of the population, as eligible for quota.

9. The relevant constitutional provisions are section 4, article 46 in the Directive Principles of State Policy, and section 3, articles 15(4) and 16(4), on education and government jobs, in the Fundamental Principles. The latter articles are amendments added during the first round of Constitutional amendments in 1951.

10. Principle drafter of the Constitution.

11. Article 340 of the Constitution empowers the President of India to install such commissions.

12. There is debate about the motives for this. Some authors argue that there was a general idea that caste-based affirmative action did not befit the modernizing liberal agenda of India's political elite. Others argue that the Congress party was dominated by high-caste Hindu's who wanted primarily to avoid the emancipation of the lower castes in order to stay in power (see De Zwart 2000; Jaffrelot 2003, 48–136).

13. In states, especially in South India, and since the 1970s also in the North, reservation policy was already being implemented. The selection of beneficiaries and the precise quota to be reserved were left to state-level Backward Classes Commissions.

14. The United Front, a thirteen-party coalition, formed a minority government of nine parties that came to power in 1996 with support from the Congress party. The BJP-led National Democratic Alliance (NDA) government, formed in 1999, consisted of twenty-four parties. The Congress led UPA coalition that took power in 2009 had eight member parties and five supporting parties.

15. Table 4.1 represents MP's returned from Uttar Pradesh, parts of Punjab, Haryana, Chandigarh, Madhya Pradesh, Rajasthan, Bihar, and Delhi (see Jaffrelot & Kumar 2009, 6–11). The pattern in South India is different. The South had a strong backward class movement and backward class political parties opposing the Brahmin-dominated Congress party already before independence (Irshick 1969; Radhakrishnan 1996).

16. The percentage of Scheduled Caste MPs is steady ever since the first elections in 1952 because it remains close to the quota of parliamentary seats reserved

for them. Reservations for the Backward Classes do not entail a quota of seats in the national parliament or in state assemblies.

17. This chapter concentrates on 'substantial' redistributive measures. However, it is the combination of symbolic and substantial measures that underlies political emancipation of the Backward Classes. Symbolic measures relate to recognition of status, rights, and needs; 'substantial' relates to redistributive measures of which job and educational quota are the prime example (see Jaffrelot 2006, 2012).

18. Chandra (2013) makes a helpful distinction between ethnic structure and ethnic practice: '[S]tructure refers to the repertoire of descent based attributes and therefore the sets of "nominal" identities that all individuals in a population possess. . . . Ethnic "practice" refers to the set of "activated" identities that individuals actually employ in any given context' (18). The point is that the logic of affirmative action activates a particular selection (caste and sub-caste identities) from the total repertoire.

19. Many politicians in the early 1950s predicted this development and warned against it (De Zwart 2000, 238–240). For other examples of unintended but not unanticipated consequences see (De Zwart 2015).

20. *P. Rajendran versus State of Madras*, discussed in Galanter (1984, 197–198).

21. 'Others' or 'general castes' is often used in statistical analysis to refer to the upper and intermediate castes.

22. Note that the first national Backward Classes Commission had listed 'only' 2,392 castes.

23. In line with the logic of affirmative action, Huber and Suryanarayan (2016, 150) argue that "ethnification of party systems", that is, the degree to which parties in a particular system have unique ethnic bases of support, should increase as group identity and economic well-being become more strongly intertwined'. Their findings are consistent with this: 'In forty-one state-specific surveys across the two elections, subcaste [jati] produces the highest [party voting polarization] score twenty-four times (59 percent), caste produces the highest score fourteen times (34 percent), and religion produces the highest score three times (7 percent)' (2016, 164).

24. Supreme Court as quoted on the website of the National Backward Classes Commission: http://www.ncbc.nic.in/User_Panel/PresentCommissionView.aspx (last visited 30 November 2017). I use the work of the National Commission here to illustrate. State commissions operate in a similar way. Their list arranges access to the state services.

25. A large majority of Muslims are considered socially and educationally backward, but their inclusion in the list of Backward Classes is problematic because religious identities are not recognized constitutionally as eligible.

26. After the landslide victory for SP in the 2012 assembly elections, Mulayam Singh Yadav selected his son, Akhilesh Yadav as Chief Minister of UP.

27. Claims on sub quota do not come only from within the Backward Class category, but also from Dalit (Chandra 2000) and Muslim subgroups (Alam 2014, 219–221).

28. The political significance of subcategories depends on the level of politics. We have largely concentrated on the national level in this chapter, but at state and local levels much smaller subcategories are still electorally significant, encouraging further fission.

REFERENCES

Alam, M. (2014) 'Affirmative action for Muslims? Arguments, contentions and alternatives', *Studies in Indian Politics*, 2(2): 215–229.

Brass, P. (1984) 'National power and local politics in India: A twenty-year perspective', *Modern Asian Studies*, 18(1): 89–118.

Brass, P. (1991) *Ethnicity and nationalism: Theory and comparison*. New Delhi: Sage Publications.

Chandra, K. (2000) 'Elite incorporation in multiethnic societies', *Asian Survey*, 40(5): 836–865.

Chandra, K. (2004) *Why ethnic parties succeed: Patronage and ethnic head counts in India*. Cambridge: Cambridge University Press.

Chandra, K. (2005) 'Ethnic parties and democratic stability', *Perspectives on Politics*, 3(2): 235–252.

Chandra, K. (ed.) (2013) *Constructivist theories of ethnic politics*. Oxford: Oxford University Press.

Chhibber, P. (1999) *Democracy without associations: Transformation of the party system and social cleavages in India*. Ann Arbor: University of Michigan Press.

Chaudhury, P. (2004) 'The "creamy layer": Political economy of reservations', *Economic and Political Weekly*, 39(29): 1989–1991.

Deshpande, R. (2010) 'Caste associations in the post-mandal era: Notes from Maharashtra', *CAS Occasional Paper Series* no. 2. Pune University, Department of Politics & Public Administration, Pune.

De Zwart, F. (2000) 'The logic of affirmative action: Caste, class and quotas in India', *Acta Sociologica*, 43(3): 235–251.

De Zwart, F. (2015) 'Unintended but not unanticipated consequences', *Theory and Society*, 44(3): 283–297.

Galanter, M. (1984) *Competing equalities: Law and the backward classes in India*. Berkeley: University of California Press.

George, V. (2012) 'Mandalisation of the Congress', *Hindustan Times*, January 13, https://www.hindustantimes.com/india/mandalisation-of-the-congress/story-2aHVda4rKRCqG4l1ynsmHI.html (accessed 7 December 2017).

Glazer, N. and Moynihan, D. (eds.) (1975) *Ethnicity: Theory and experience*. Cambridge, MA: Harvard University Press,

Government of India (1956) *Report of the backward classes commission*. New Delhi: Government of India Press.

Government of India (1980) *Report of the backward classes commission*. New Delhi: Government of India Press.

Government of India (2009) 'National commission for backward classes', *21st Annual Report 2008–2009*. New Delhi.

Government of India (2011) *Socio-economic and caste census: Instruction manual for enumerators*. New Delhi: Government of India Press.

Government of India (2015) *Report relating to the proposal for the sub categorisation within the other backward classes*. New Delhi: National Commission for Backward Classes.

Gowda, R. and Sridharan, E. (2007) 'Parties and the party system 1947–2006', in S. Ganguly, L. Diamond and M.F. Plattner (eds.) *The state of India's democracy*. Baltimore: Johns Hopkins University Press, pp. 3–26.

Gupta, D. (2005) 'Caste and politics: Identity over system', *Annual Review of Anthropology*, 21: 409–427.

Horowitz, D. (1985) *Ethnic groups in conflict*. Berkeley: University of California Press.

Huber, J. and Suryanarayan, P. (2016) 'Ethnic inequality and the ethnification of political parties: Evidence from India', *World Politics*, 68(1): 149–188.

Irshick, E. (1969) *Politics and social conflict in South India: The non-Brahman movement and Tamil separatism, 1916–1929*. Berkeley: University of California Press.

Jaffrelot, C. (2003) *India's silent revolution: The rise of the low castes in North Indian politics*. New Delhi: Permanent Black.

Jaffrelot, C. (2006) 'The impact of affirmative action in India: More political than socioeconomic', *India Review*, 5(2): 173–189.

Jaffrelot, C. (2012) 'The caste based mosaic of Indian politics', *India Seminar*, http://www.india-seminar.com (accessed 7 December 2017).

Jaffrelot, C. (2016) 'Quota for Patels? The neo-middle-class syndrome and the (partial) return of caste politics in Gujarat', *Studies in Indian Politics*, 4(2): 218–232.

Jaffrelot, C. and Kumar, S. (eds.) (2009) *Rise of the plebeians? The changing face of Indian legislative assemblies*. London: Routledge.

Kohli, A. (1990) *Democracy and discontent: India's growing crisis of governability*. Cambridge: Cambridge University Press.

Kothari, R. (ed.) (1970) *Caste in Indian politics*. New Delhi: Sangam Books.

Krishna, S. (2017) 'OBC division boosts BJP in the South', *The Sunday Guardian*, http://www.sundayguardianlive.com/news/10642-obc-division-boosts-bjp-south (accessed 12 November 2017).

Kumar, R. (2016) 'Stooping to conquer: Jats and reservations in Haryana', *Economic and Political Weekly*, 51(16): 15–18.

Lijphart, A. (1996) 'The puzzle of Indian democracy', *American Political Science Review*, 90(2): 258–268.

Mandelbaum, D. (1970) *Society in India* (two volumes). Berkeley: University of California Press.

Mair, P. (2014) *On parties, party systems and democracy: Selected writings of Peter Mair*, edited by I. Van Biezen. Colchester: ECPR Press.

Nehru, J. (1994) *Selected works of Jawaharlal Nehru*, vol. 16(1). New Delhi: Teen Murti House.

Panini, M. (1996) 'The political economy of caste', in M. Srinivas (ed.) *Caste: Its twentieth century avatar*. New Delhi: Viking, pp. 28–68.

Radhakrishnan, P. (1996) 'Backward class movements in Tamil Nadu', in M. Srinivas (ed.) *Caste: Its twentieth century avatar*. New Delhi: Viking, pp. 110–134.

Rudolph, L. (2003) 'Book review: Pradeep K. Chhibber, democracy without associations: Transformation of the party system and social cleavages in India. Ann

Arbor: University of Michigan Press. 1999', *Comparative Political Studies*, 36(9): 1115–1119.

Rudolph, L. and Rudolph Hoeber, S. (1967) *The modernity of tradition: Political development in India*. Chicago: University of Chicago Press.

Rao, M. (2012) *Perspectives on social cohesion and social justice*. Lecture delivered on 23rd June at Osmania University, Hyderabad. Brookings Institution, Washington, DC.

Sen, R. (2015) 'The Patel agitation and the OBC puzzle', Working paper, Institute of South Asian Studies, National University of Singapore, *ISAS Insights*, 292, 21 September.

Sowell, T. (1990) *Preferential policies: An international perspective*. New York: William Morrow and Company, Inc.

Stokes, S. C. (2011) 'Political clientelism', in R. Goodin (ed.) *The Oxford handbook of political science*. Oxford: Oxford University Press, pp. 1–30.

Tripathi, P. (2001) 'Counting on quota', *Frontline*, 18(16): 1–4.

Varshney, A. (2000) 'Is India becoming more democratic?' *The Journal of Asian Studies*, 59(1): 3–25.

Weiner, M. (1967) *Party building in a new nation: The Indian national congress*. Chicago: University of Chicago Press.

Weiner, M. (2001) 'The struggle for equality: Caste in Indian politics', in A. Kohli (ed.) *The success of India's democracy*. Cambridge: Cambridge University Press, pp. 193–225.

Weisskopf, T. (2011) 'Why worry about inequality in the booming Indian economy?' *Economic and Political Weekly*, 46(47): 41–51.

Wilkinson, S. (2014) 'Patronage politics in post-independence India', in A. Piliavsky (ed.) *Patronage as politics in South Asia*. Cambridge: Cambridge University Press, pp. 259–280.

Zérinini, J. (2009) 'The marginalization of the savarnas in Uttar Pradesh?' in C. Jaffrelot and S. Kumar (eds.) *Rise of the plebeians? The changing face of Indian legislative assemblies*. London: Routledge, pp. 27–64.

Chapter Five

Democratic Regression and Clientelism

Evidence from Russia

Inga A.-L. Saikkonen[1]

INTRODUCTION

Electoral clientelism, that is, the distribution of targeted (material) benefits in return for electoral support, is a particularly prevalent electoral strategy in developing democracies and electoral authoritarian regimes. Clientelistic political machines are known to vary their strategies, such as vote buying and turnout buying, in response to different electoral contexts (Gans-Morse, Mazzuca and Nichter 2014; Mares and Young 2016). Political regime type also affects the choice of the clientelistic strategies. The dynamics of authoritarian elections make turnout buying – that is, mobilizing voters to the polls – a particularly attractive clientelistic strategy in electoral autocracies. Such regimes engage in *selective turnout buying* by mobilizing specific, state-dependent sectors of the population in elections. This clientelistic strategy both stabilizes authoritarian rule and exacerbates democratic regression by further disconnecting electoral results from popular preferences.

This chapter first outlines the theoretical framework on selective turnout buying in electoral autocracies. This theoretical setting leads to specific hypotheses about particular demographic sectors that are likely to be targeted in turnout mobilization in authoritarian elections. These hypotheses are tested with original local level data from one of the most prominent electoral authoritarian regimes of today, the Russian Federation. The chapter focuses on two research questions. First, it shows that localities with higher shares state-dependent populations report higher levels of electoral turnout in Russian presidential elections, in line with the expectations of dynamics of turnout buying in electoral autocracies. Second, the chapter studies these patterns over time, in Russian presidential elections between 2000 and 2012. The expectation is that the patterns would intensify in Russian presidential elections after 2000, as the Russian political regime becomes more hegemonic. The chapter finds that all of the indicators associated with selective turnout buying are systematically associated with higher electoral turnout rates in Russian presidential elections over the 2000s. However, the effects vary over time in interesting, and occasionally unexpected, ways. The results of multilevel models also suggest an increasingly negative association between opposition party-voter share and turnout over time. The results indicate that turnout buying is an important part of Russia's authoritarian development over the 2000s.

CLIENTELISM IN POST-COMMUNIST COUNTRIES

The former communist countries in Eastern Europe and Eurasia experienced a profound political and economic change with the break-up of the communist regimes in the late 1980s and the beginning of 1990s. The hierarchical nature of the former system, the legacies of state-controlled economies, and the weakness of political parties created a fertile ground for corruption, patronage politics and clientelism in the post-communist space (see Holmes 2006; Kopecký and Spirova 2011; Kostadinova and Spirova 2018). Former Soviet countries, such as Russia, experienced a longer time under communist rule, and the destruction of old autonomous societal institutions was arguably more thorough in these countries than in Eastern Europe. While most of the former communist regimes in East Central Europe have democratized (although with worrying democratic backsliding in, e.g., Hungary), many of the post-Soviet countries have developed into electoral authoritarian regimes. Recent literature has paid attention to the patrimonial and statist dynamics in the new authoritarian regimes in the post-Soviet space (see, esp., Darden 2008; Hale 2014; Ledeneva 2006). The subordination of the state into the service of the authoritarian regime is a particularly salient feature of post-Soviet authoritarianism, and a politicized state bureaucracy and other state-dependent sectors play a crucial role in coordinating machine politics in these regimes.

Electoral clientelism refers to the distribution of targeted (material) benefits in return for electoral support, and it entails a *quid pro quo* exchange in which getting benefits is dependent on voting, and the voting behaviour is being monitored. This *contingency* makes electoral clientelism different from programmatic politics or other types of particularistic politics, such as 'pork-barrel politics'[2] (Hicken 2011; Kitschelt and Wilkinson 2007; Stokes 2007; Stokes et al. 2013). Clientelistic machine politics also entail complex hierarchies which coordinate the monitoring and the rewards/punishments allocated to voters (Stokes 2005; Stokes et al. 2013).

Clientelistic machines use a variety of tactics to manage and enforce this exchange (Mares and Young 2016). In instances of 'vote buying' the clientelistic exchange is based on the distribution of targeted benefits (e.g. cash, food, or access to social services) to voters. Such exchanges have been prevalent in Latin America and India. However, clientelistic exchanges can also be based on a *threat* of losing material benefits (e.g., jobs or welfare services). Beatriz Magaloni et al. describe such a 'punishment mechanism' in Mexico, where opposition supporting districts were denied government transfers under the PRI regime (Magaloni, Diaz-Cayeros and Estevez 2007), and similar strategies have been reported in Taiwan, Argentina, and in Italy (Stokes 2007).

This kind of 'punishment mechanism' based electoral clientelism has been well-documented in electoral authoritarian regimes in the post-Soviet space (Allina-Pisano 2010; Buzin and Lyubarev 2008; Darden 2008; Frye, Reuter and Szakonyi 2014; Golosov 2013). What is typical for these regimes is the use of 'administrative resources', that is, the politicization of state bureaucracy, and the recruitment/intimidation of state-connected actors, such as electoral commission members, directors of (state-connected) firms, heads of (state-connected) agricultural enterprises, and even teachers and doctors, to act as vote brokers (see Allina-Pisano 2010; Forrat 2015; Frye, Reuter and Szakonyi 2014). Most of the literature on clientelism in Russia identifies this type of 'voter intimidation' as the primary mechanism by which non-voluntary voter mobilization takes place (see Allina-Pisano 2010; Frye, Reuter and Szakonyi 2014; Saikkonen 2017).[3] Several accounts describe the *contingent* nature of these exchanges, where voters have been threatened by the loss of a benefit, such as employment and tuition, for the failure to turn out to vote (e.g. Buzin and Lyubarev 2008). These sanctions are considerable, which increases the likelihood of compliance with voter intimidation (Frye, Reuter and Szakonyi 2014). Recent literature has also documented the emergence of voter intimidation tactics in some of the former communist regimes in East Central European countries, such as Bulgaria and Romania (Mares, Muntean and Petrova 2016).

CLIENTELISTIC STRATEGIES IN AUTOCRACIES

Clientelistic machines vary their strategies depending on the electoral context. Recent research has distinguished between at least four strategies that clientelistic machines employ during elections: vote buying (mobilizing votes for a particular party or candidate), turnout buying (mobilizing voters to the polls), abstention buying (aiming to discourage/prevent people from voting) and 'double persuasion' (aiming both at increasing electoral participation and votes for a particular party) (Gans-Morse, Mazzuca and Nichter 2014). The strategic electoral context, such as the existence of compulsory voting, and/or the secret ballot, affects the likelihood of the employment of these strategies within electoral democracies (Gans-Morse, Mazzuca and Nichter 2014). Likewise, it is important to note that regime type, too, affects the optimal choice of the clientelistic strategy. Electoral democracies and electoral autocracies represent different kind of strategic settings. The dynamics of authoritarian elections makes turnout buying an especially attractive strategy in electoral autocracies.

In electoral autocracies elections are only nominally contested, and the ruling party usually wins them with a considerable margin. While the incumbents do not normally have to worry about losing elections, non-contested elections still pose several strategic dilemmas to autocrats. Autocracies benefit from general political apathy – especially among the opposition supporters. Yet, turning elections into empty rituals can have problematic consequences: it can lower the voters' incentives to participate in the elections voluntarily. Yet, autocracies need to maintain 'decent' participation levels in elections, as a low turnout may delegitimize and even invalidate elections, and signal regime unpopularity (Magaloni 2006; Simpser 2013). However, turnout mobilization through means used in democracies – via the media and political parties (see Powell 1986; Rosenstone and Hansen 2003) – can be 'dangerous' in electoral authoritarian regimes, as this kind of mobilization can also mobilize 'sleeping' opposition supporters to the polls (for a similar argument, see e.g., Kynev and Lyubarev 2016; Reuter 2016). Under these conditions, keeping the elections as non-programmatic as possible, while simultaneously engaging in (punishment mechanism based) turnout mobilization among state-dependent 'supporters', becomes an optimal strategy. Authoritarian machine politics is thus likely to target electoral mobilization efforts at particular, state-dependent voter groups to achieve the 'necessary' turnout levels in otherwise non-contested elections.

It is important to note that the effectiveness of this strategy should increase as the regime becomes more hegemonic. For voter intimidation to be effective, voters need to believe that the regime will be in power after the elections (so that the potential punishment for 'wrong' electoral behaviour can be realized). Thus, voter intimidation should be more effective in non-contested elections in which the outcome is not in any doubt. These expectations will be further tested below.

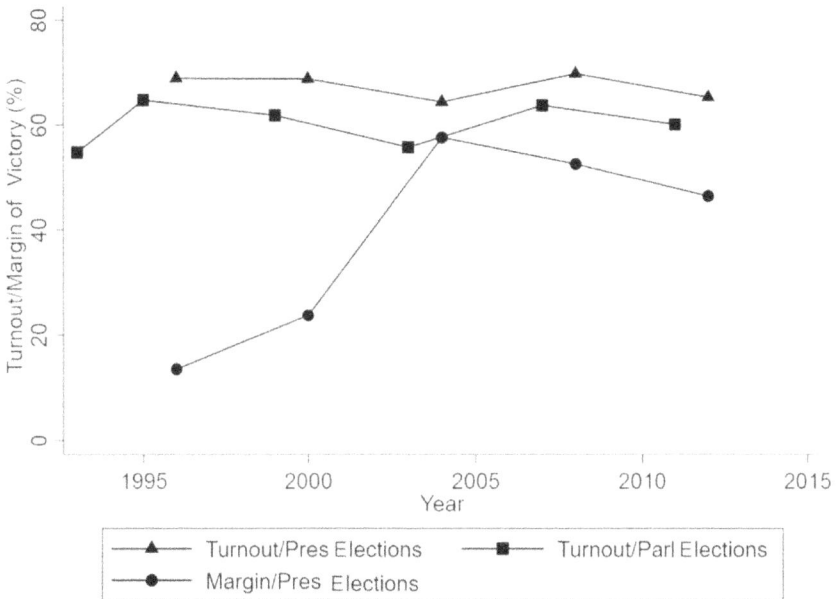

Figure 5.1 Turnout and the Margin of Victory in Russian National Elections, 1993–2012
Source: Data sources: Central Electoral Commission of Russia, and the CD-Rom Rossi-iskie vybory v tsifrakh i kartakh (2007), calculations by the author.

RUSSIAN ELECTIONS IN THE 2000s: FROM COMPETITION TO HEGEMONIC OUTCOMES

Elections in Russia have become increasingly non-competitive over the 2000s. The incumbent president Vladimir Putin's considerable personal popularity and Russian economic growth combined with the increasing repression of the opposition parties (including barring opposition candidates from the elections) has made the Russian presidential elections virtually non-contested after 2000. Figure 5.1 shows both the margin of victory of the winning candidate, and electoral turnout in Russian presidential and parliamentary elections between 1993 and 2012. Although electoral competition levels have dramatically decreased in the Russian presidential elections, turnout levels have not declined, and aggregate turnout even increased in the 2008 presidential elections. Thus electoral participation rates have increased even when the elections have become increasingly predictable, which runs counter to the evidence found in many established democracies (see Blais 2000). This suggests that turnout mobilization is indeed an important part of the story of

Russian presidential elections, and the section below outlines the dynamics of selective turnout mobilization in Russian elections.

SELECTIVE TURNOUT MOBILIZATION IN RUSSIA

As argued above, the dynamics of authoritarian elections can make autocracies focus on turnout buying. To avoid mobilizing passive opposition supporters, authoritarian regimes focus on *selective turnout mobilization*, targeting state-dependent sectors of the population. This theoretical framework leads to expectations on specific sectors of the population that would be targeted in electoral mobilization in Russian elections. As outlined above, clientelism in post-Soviet Russia typically takes the form of voter intimidation, where voters are threatened with the loss of certain benefits if they fail to turn out to vote. The sections below test specific hypotheses on turnout intimidation among state-dependent voter groups in Russia.

The panel dataset covering the presidential elections between 2000 and 2012 also allows us to test hypotheses regarding the effectiveness of this strategy over time. The effectiveness of voter intimidation as an electoral strategy should increase as the regime becomes more hegemonic. For the intimidation strategy to be effective, voters need to expect that the regime will be in power after elections (so that the potential punishment will be realized). In Russia the political regime became increasingly stable after the 2003 legislative elections, and there has been very little uncertainty over the electoral outcomes after that. The last (somewhat) contested presidential elections were the ones held in 2000. According to these theoretical expectations we should see stronger mobilization effects in the presidential elections held from 2004 onwards.

Mobilization in Rural and State-Dependent Localities

We thus expect turnout mobilization in Russian elections to be focused on localities with higher concentrations of state-dependent populations. Instances of voter intimidation focusing on rural localities have long been reported in post-Soviet countries (see Allina-Pisano 2008, 2010). An urban-rural voting difference, where opposition voters are concentrated in urban areas, and the regime draws support from the rural areas, has been found in many developing democracies and electoral autocracies (see, e.g., Gandhi and Lust-Okar 2009). Voter turnout is easily monitored in small, rural communities, especially as the polling stations have often been located in the former collective farms themselves (Allina-Pisano 2010). Rural areas are also known to be targeted by so-called 'mobile voting', where electoral commission members travel around rural locations with a mobile ballot box, under conditions in which voluntary nature of electoral participation cannot always be guaranteed (Buzin et al. 2012; Saikkonen and White 2017; White 2011). While many studies have examined the association between rurality and higher rates of electoral turnout (Clem and Craumer 1998; Goodnow, Moser and Smith 2014; Reisinger and Moraski 2008; Saikkonen 2017; White and Moser 2014), less is known about how these patterns would vary over time. We are therefore particularly interested in the strength of this association over time in line with the theoretical expectations that clientelistic mobilization becomes more effective as the Russian regime becomes more hegemonic by 2004. Thus, we test the following two hypotheses:

H1a: Localities with a greater proportion of rural population should report higher electoral turnout levels

H1b: This association should be stronger in Russian presidential elections after 2000

Another state-dependent sector often targeted in voter mobilization in Russia includes pensioners. Pensioners can be vulnerable to voter intimidation for two reasons. First, pensioners are often economically dependent on state transfers, and can be easily targeted for 'reward or punishment, making this risk-averse population even less likely to challenge local authorities' (Hale 2003, 246). Second, pensioners often vote via assisted voting, whereby local electoral commission members visit their homes with a portable ballot box ('mobile voting') (Buzin et al. 2012; White 2011). These circumstances make electoral abstention difficult, especially as several reports have suggested that people have been placed on these 'mobile voting' lists without their knowledge (Buzin and Lyubarev 2008; ODIHR 2012).We would thus expect electoral turnout levels to be especially high in localities with higher proportion of pension-age population, and that the intensity of this mobilization to increase in elections after 2000. Therefore we expect that:

H2a: Localities with a greater proportion of pension-age population should report higher electoral turnout levels

H2b: This association should be stronger in Russian presidential elections after 2000

Poverty and Clientelistic Mobilization

As noted in the Introduction to this volume, clientelistic parties are known to target both poor voter groups and ethnic voter groups in voter mobilization. Poor voters are through to be more receptive to vote buying or voter intimidation, as they value the clientelistic benefits more highly than wealthy voters (e.g., Calvo and Murillo 2004; Dixit and Londregan 1996; Stokes 2005).

Russia is a modernized, middle-income country, with high levels of education, full literacy levels and little abject poverty (on these and other Soviet modernization legacies, see, e.g., Fish 2005). However, levels of income inequality have diverged substantially after the fall of the Soviet Union (for a thorough exploration, see Remington 2011), and there are considerable differences in the levels of people dependent on state transfers, both between and within the Russian regions. As poverty, dependency on state transfers can make people highly vulnerable to vote buying or voter intimidation.[4] Economically more autonomous groups, such as the urban middle classes or private sector workers should be more predisposed not to vote or to support the opposition (see, e.g., Gandhi and Lust-Okar 2009; Magaloni 2006). Thus we could expect dependency on government transfers to be associated with more effective turnout buying. As before, we also expect turnout buying to be more effective in the more hegemonic presidential elections held between 2004 and 2012, than in the more contested 2000 elections. We would thus hypothesize that:

H3a: Localities with a greater proportion of people dependent on government transfers should report higher electoral turnout levels

H3b: This association should be stronger in Russian presidential elections after 2000

Ethnicity and Machine Politics

Ethnicity and ethnic ties have also long been associated with clientelism in the comparative literature, as ethnicity provides means of identifying and targeting certain groups, and this enables ethnic parties to mobilize and reward co-ethnics in elections (see, e.g., Chandra 2007, also the Introduction to this volume). The mechanism identified in the extant literature on Russia rests on a similar logic, but is modified by the Soviet ethno-federal legacies. The Soviet Union had a peculiar, hierarchical ethno-federal structure, which targeted 'affirmative action' type privileges (such as access to jobs and education) at specific ethnic minority groups (Gorenburg 2003). This ethnic minority privileging intensified after the Soviet collapse (Hale 2003). Henry Hale has argued that this has created a 'clientelistic exchange', whereby votes from ethnic minority areas were 'exchanged' in return for these benefits (Hale 2003, 2007). However, there is also evidence of outright voter fraud in some ethnic republics (e.g., Goodnow, Moser and Smith 2014; Moser and White 2013; Myagkov, Ordeshook and Shakin 2005). While many studies have examined the association between ethnic minority status and voting in Russia (Clem and Craumer 1998; Goodnow, Moser and Smith 2014; Reisinger and Moraski 2008; Saikkonen 2017; White and Moser 2014; White and Saikkonen 2016), we know very little on how these patterns would vary over time. Thus, here we are particularly interested in seeing if the patterns intensify after the 2000 Russian presidential elections, in line with the theoretical expectations. We therefore test two hypotheses:

H4a: Localities with a greater proportion of ethnic minorities should report higher electoral turnout levels

H4b: This association should be stronger in Russian presidential elections after 2000

EMPIRICAL STRATEGY AND CONTROLS

This chapter investigates these linkages and their change over time with an original panel dataset that includes demographic and federal presidential electoral data aggregated at both region and rayon ('county') level from the Russian Federation between 2000 and 2012. The rayons are the smallest units for which both electoral and demographic data is available in Russia (Clem 2006), and are roughly equivalent to US counties. As the rayon data is nested within the regions, the empirical analysis here is conducted by estimating hierarchical linear (random intercepts) models of turnout clustered in regions. Likelihood ratio tests also suggest that the hierarchical models are a significant improvement over single level models.[5]

The models control for a host of socio-economic characteristics drawn from the comparative turnout and clientelism literatures, as well as the extant literature on voting in Russia. In line with the 'resource model' of political participation (see Dalton 2008), age and higher education have been found to be related to electoral participation in Russia (Colton 2000; McAllister and White 1998; White and McAllister 2007), and these characteristics are also often included in the battery of controls in studies of clientelism (e.g., Nichter 2014). While the share of pensioners per rayon already proxies older age in the models, they include a control for the share of people with higher education per rayon. Comparative literature has long associated community size with propensity for electoral clientelism (Remmer 2010; Stokes 2005), and thus the models control for rayon size. A plausible alternative explanation would expect partisan mobilization to affect electoral turnout levels, as networks of political recruitment are shown to play a role in political participation in comparative studies (see Carreras and

Castaneda-Angarita 2014). While the reach of political parties in Russia has traditionally been weak outside of Moscow, the Communist Party (CPRF) has retained the strongest partisan network at the local level (e.g., Clem and Craumer 1998), and therefore the models include a measure for CPRF support in the elections.

An extensive literature has demonstrated the existence of electoral fraud in Russian elections (Goodnow, Moser and Smith 2014; Mebane Jr. and Kalinin 2009; Myagkov, Ordeshook and Shakin 2005, 2009). Studies on electoral fraud have shown that patterns of fraud tend to be geographically concentrated in some ethnic republics (Goodnow, Moser and Smith 2014; Myagkov, Ordeshook and Shakin 2009) and the North Caucasus (Goodnow, Moser and Smith 2014; Reisinger and Moraski 2010). Therefore the models below include dummy variables denoting whether the region is an ethnic republic or a republic located in the North Caucasus. Additionally, the models also account for the size of the region by the number of rayons per region. The data sources are detailed in the appendix.

EMPIRICAL RESULTS

The results are presented in Table 5.1. In general, the hypotheses regarding the selective turnout mobilization in state-dependent localities are confirmed, but the results over time vary in unexpected ways. As previous studies have shown, turnout mobilization is more effective in rural rayons, but the effects show interesting variation over time. The coefficient for the proportion of rural population grows in 2004, when compared with the coefficient in 2000, and then drops in 2008 and 2012. On the basis of Model 2 (2004) in can be estimated that once the share of rural population increases from approximately the mean to the maximum value, electoral participation increases with almost 17 percentage points. The growth in the size of the effect from 2000 to 2004 is in line with the expectation that the effectiveness of turnout mobilization would increase as the presidential electoral setting becomes more hegemonic. However, the drop in the size of the effect after the 2004 elections is more unexpected. In 2008, an increase from the mean to the maximum level in rural population per rayon results in just over 9 percentage point increase in turnout. There could be several explanations for this that are related to the structural changes in the Russian agriculture. In the 2000s the Russian agricultural sector experienced significant restructuring which led to both the improvement of material conditions in the Russian rural areas, as well as to demographic shifts as workers moved to other sectors of the economy (see

O'Brien and Patsiorkovskiy 2008; Wegren 2008). These factors – decreasing rural poverty as well as a smaller population base – could have plausibly made the rural areas less 'attractive' targets for electoral mobilization in the late 2000s.

The statistical results also support the expectation that electoral mobilization in Russia would be more effective in localities with a higher concentration of pensioners. The share of pensioners per rayon is consistently associated with higher turnout, and the coefficients stay rather similar and highly statistically significant throughout. The effects are also substantive: an increase from the mean to the maximum value in the share of pensioners per rayon is associated with a 3.54 percentage point increase in turnout in the 2012 elections.

The results regarding the association between economic dependency on the state and the turnout patterns are in line with the theoretical expectations. In contrast with established democracies, where, for example high unemployment is often associated with lower electoral turnout, in the Russian presidential elections the rayons with higher shares of people dependent on government transfers show consistently high turnout rates. This effect is substantial, too. For example, in 2004, the increase from the mean to the maximum value in the share of people receiving benefits in 2004 is associated with 8.54 percentage point increase in rayon level turnout. However, the effect of socio-economic dependency on the state on voting seems to decline somewhat over time, and in the 2012 elections the coefficient is statistically significant only at the 0.05 level. A plausible explanation for this could be that poverty levels in Russia have consistently declined during the 2000s.

In contrast, the coefficients for share of non-Russian population per rayon do not vary so dramatically over time. There is a slight increase in the effect of non-Russian population on turnout between 2000 and 2004, suggesting that turnout mobilization became more effective in these rayons by the 2004 elections. However, the magnitude of the effects stays rather similar in the 2004, 2008 and 2012 elections. This suggests that electoral mobilization in the Russian ethnic areas continued to be effective throughout the 2000s.

Regarding the control variables, the models do not support the alternative explanation regarding partisan electoral mobilization, at least by the CPRF. In fact, the coefficients for CPRF support are negative, and highly statistically significant throughout the various years. Also, interestingly, this negative effect grows markedly by 2008 and 2012. These findings are in line with previous studies on Russian electoral geography and electoral fraud (Clem and Craumer 2004; Myagkov, Ordeshook and Shakin 2005), which suggest

94 *Inga A.-L. Saikkonen*

Table 5.1 Determinants of Turnout in Russian Presidential Elections, 2000–2012

	Model 1	Model 2	Model 3	Model 4
	Turnout 00	Turnout 04	Turnout 08	Turnout 12
Rural	1.079***	1.272***	0.684***	0.536***
	(0.0779)	(0.111)	(0.111)	(0.0993)
Pensioners	0.277***	0.220***	0.156***	0.233***
	(0.0306)	(0.0439)	(0.0438)	(0.0392)
State Dependent	0.129***	0.111***	0.0866**	0.0689*
	(0.0235)	(0.0333)	(0.0336)	(0.0299)
Non Russ	0.0595***	0.0637***	0.0617***	0.0624***
	(0.00760)	(0.0108)	(0.0109)	(0.00974)
High Ed	0.368***	0.211***	0.156**	0.559***
	(0.0412)	(0.0585)	(0.0588)	(0.0524)
Rayon Size00	−2.790***			
	(0.144)			
CPRF00	−0.144***			
	(0.0128)			
Republic	0.0767	4.051	1.191	4.534*
	(1.375)	(2.463)	(2.155)	(2.001)
NorthCauc	8.813***	17.79***	5.976	7.390*
	(2.401)	(4.292)	(3.756)	(3.489)
Region Size	0.143***	0.176*	0.142*	0.177**
	(0.0390)	(0.0705)	(0.0613)	(0.0571)
Rayon Size04		−3.967***		
		(0.201)		
CPRF04		−0.256***		
		(0.0290)		
Rayon Size08			−2.728***	
			(0.205)	
CPRF08			−0.756***	
			(0.0297)	
Rayon Size12				−1.779***
				(0.180)
CPRF12				−0.744***
				(0.0315)
Constant	85.22***	93.70***	100.9***	77.58***
	(2.245)	(3.513)	(3.304)	(3.004)
sigma_u				
Constant	4.392***	8.010***	6.936***	6.465***
	(0.378)	(0.670)	(0.585)	(0.545)
sigma_e				
Constant	4.022***	5.685***	5.748***	5.128***
	(0.0630)	(0.0890)	(0.0900)	(0.0803)
Observations	2114	2114	2114	2114
BIC	12239.3	13739.4	13763.7	13287.7

Note: Standard errors in parentheses. * $p < 0.05$, ** $p < 0.01$, *** $p < 0.001$.

that turnout increases in Russia appear to benefit the regime candidates at the expense of the opposition parties. Rayon size is consistently negatively associated with turnout, and the coefficients are highly statistically significant. This, too, is in line with the expectations from the clientelism literature, which has long linked smaller community size with vulnerability to clientelistic targeting. Again, the effect is largest in 2004, suggesting greatest mobilization efforts in those elections.

Regarding the other control variables, higher education has a consistently positive and statistically significant association with turnout, which is in contrast to some findings from electoral autocracies[6] but in line with previous individual level studies on voting in Russia (Colton 2000; McAllister and White 1998). Turning to the region level controls, the coefficient for ethnic republic is positive, as expected, but reaches statistical significance only in 2012. (When the North Caucasus dummy is omitted from the models, the coefficient for ethnic republics remains positive and reaches statistical significance in 2004 and 2012.) In contrast, a republic's location in the North Caucasus appears to have a strong effect on turnout – according to the 2004 model turnout would be over 17.8 percentage points higher in a republic located in the North Caucasus. However, the coefficient is not significant in 2008, and size of the coefficient and the significance level drops in 2012, which may suggest that the rayon share of non-Russian population may have absorbed some of these effects already. Region size has consistently positive and significant association with turnout, suggesting that turnout would be higher in larger regions.

All in all, the results strongly support the expectations from the clientelism literature. While previous studies have shown that electoral mobilization is more prevalent in rural settings and non-Russian minority ethnic areas, these results also show that socio-economic dependency on the authorities and a smaller community size are associated with electoral mobilization in Russia. These results are also in line with the findings from several comparative studies on clientelism. Overall, the pressures for mobilization seem to have been the greatest in the 2004 Russian presidential elections, in which Vladimir Putin 'cemented' his rule. Yet, there is interesting variation in these effects over time. While it seems that turnout mobilization declined in Russian rural areas over time, ethnic minority areas show continuously high turnout rates throughout the 2000s. Also, the negative association between the vote share for the main Russian opposition party, CPRF, and turnout increase markedly over time, corroborating previous findings from the literature on Russian voting and electoral fraud.

We cannot fully rule out all other possible alternative explanations with the current data. For example, some of the very high turnout figures, especially in the North Caucasus, may reflect ballot box stuffing as well as clientelistic electoral strategies (see, e.g., Myagkov, Ordeshook and Shakin 2009). However, electoral reports by both domestic and foreign observers include a lot of evidence of voter intimidation and other clientelistic electoral strategies (see, e.g., Buzin et al. 2012; ODIHR 2012). This suggests these tactics are a prevalent strategy to increase official turnout figures in Russia. Future studies should employ more fine-grained data to fully disentangle the different mechanisms used to inflate turnout figures in Russian elections.

CONCLUSIONS

This chapter has argued that autocracies focus on selective turnout buying, and mobilize certain state-dependent demographic sectors to achieve the 'needed' turnout levels in otherwise non-contested elections. As such, turnout buying is a central part of the stabilization of electoral authoritarian regimes. Selective turnout buying can be less noticeable than outright repression of the opposition, but can be an even more effective tactic in authoritarian electoral management. All in all, it is plausible to expect that clientelism based electoral mobilization becomes more prevalent in Russia in future elections, as egregious use of 'pure' electoral fraud can provide a focal point for post-electoral protests, as happened in Russia in 2011/12 (on this, see Tucker 2007). In contrast, clientelism and machine politics involve coordination dilemmas on behalf of the clients (e.g., Hicken 2011), and thus may be less likely to trigger mass mobilization than grossly fraudulent electoral results.

Turnout buying can have equally grave effects for democratic regression as electoral fraud. In electoral authoritarian regimes elections have lost their democratic function, and do not provide a means of people to signal their political preferences. Turnout intimidation deprives the voters even the right to signal their preference by *not* voting in such democratically meaningless elections. If vote buying 'make[s] a mockery of democratic accountability' (Stokes 2005, 316), turnout buying through voter intimidation makes a mockery of electoral participation, and consequentially, a mockery of the democratic process itself.

APPENDIX

Data Sources

The dataset used here combines *rayon* (TIK) level electoral results with rayon-level socio-economic data from the Russian 2002 census.[7] The 2000 and 2004 presidential electoral results come from the CD-rom *Rossiiskie vybory v tsifrakh i kartakh* (Mercator and IGRAN 2007) and the 2008 and 2012 electoral results come from the Russian Central Electoral Commission website.

Most of the demographic data comes from the 2002 Russian census. The 'ruralness' of the rayon is operationalized by the percentage of agrarian employees per rayon (*Rural*), and the variable 'non-Russian' measures the percentage of the rayon's population that is not ethnically Russian[8] (*Non Russ*). Socio-economic dependency on the state is operationalized by two variables, the percentage of people receiving government benefits per rayon (*State Dependent*), and the percentage of pensioners in *rayon* (*Pensioners*).

In terms of the control variables, community size is operationalized by the number of registered voters per *rayon* (logged) (*Rayon size*). The percentage people with higher education in *rayon* (*High Ed*) is drawn from the census data. There are no direct measures of the strength of party organization available at the Russian municipal level. To proxy CPRF party mobilization and strong grassroots organization (Clem and Craumer 1998) the rayon level vote share for CPRF party candidate in each election[9] was used (*CPRF*). The models also include a dummy variable measuring ethnic republic status (*Republic*), and whether the republic is located in the North Caucasus (*NorthCauc*).[10] The models also account for the size of the region by the number of *rayon*s per region (*Region size*).

Elections in Russia

Russia has a semi-presidential system, with an exceptionally powerful presidency. The president is elected by a two-round majority system in a single nation-wide constituency. The presidential electoral system has undergone fewer revisions than the national legislative (Duma) electoral system. The only major recent reform was the lengthening of the presidential term of office from four to six years in 2008.

Russians vote in federal presidential, parliamentary (Duma), sub-national gubernatorial (1996–2005, 2012–), sub-national parliamentary and municipal elections. Voting is non-compulsory, and there is no separate registration procedure 'beyond the Stalinist system of compulsory registration (propiska) of one's place of residence with the police' (Colton 2000, 36). Everyone over the age of eighteen are eligible to vote, apart from the incarcerated and those judged incapable by court (Lounev 2002).

For elections, the regions are further divided into administrative subdivisions, TIKs and UIKs. TIKs are based on existing administrative units (rayons), and hence change little from one election to the next. TIK is an abbreviation of 'territorial electoral commission' (territorialnaya izbiratel'naya komissiya), which denotes both the local electoral commission personnel administering the elections and the geographical unit (based on rayons). Rayons are roughly equivalent to counties in the United States. Rayons/TIKs vary considerably in size and population.

Rayons are further divided into UIKs (equivalent to precincts). Voter registration is conducted automatically on the basis of the local registration (propiska) information from the heads of local municipalities twice a year (Lounev 2002). Citizens are notified of their UIK (often a school) by lists in apartment block hallways or notices to post boxes.[11] Voters can ask their registration to be amended prior to the elections.

NOTES

1. Research for this paper was conducted at the Social Science Research Institute, Åbo Akademi University and the MacMillan Center, Yale University. Research funding from the Academy of Finland (project number 258190) and A. Kordelin Foundation is gratefully acknowledged. I thank Ralph Clem and the editors of this book for excellent comments and suggestions. All errors are naturally my own.

2. In general, it is the terms of how goods or benefits are being distributed, not the goods per se that make exchanges clientelistic (e.g., Hicken 2011). While pork barrel politics (e.g., public spending targeted at particular districts) can be considered a non-optimal way of public resource allocation, it does not fulfil the criteria that most scholars consider central in clientelistic exchanges: that the receipt of the benefits is contingent on voting behaviour, and that this voting behaviour would be monitored.

3. This is not to say that cash or small goods would not be distributed to voters during election time, but the extant literature generally treats this as a secondary mechanism.

4. Unemployment levels are often used to proxy poverty in comparative studies (see Remmer 2010). Yet, in the Russian context, the official unemployment statistics can mask high rates of hidden unemployment, and the measurement validity of the indicator is questionable. Instead of redundancies, Russian firms use shorter working hours and lower wages to adjust labour costs (e.g., Gimpelson, Vladimir and Rostislav Kapeliushnikov 2011. 'Labor Market Adjustment: Is Russia Different?' in *Working Paper WP3/2011/04, Labour Markets in Transition*. Higher School of Economics, Moscow). In addition, few unemployed register for state benefits (see Crowley 2015). Therefore the official unemployment statistics are not likely to capture the extent of 'real' unemployment in Russia, and thus this measure is not used here.

5. Empty models (without explanatory variables, not presented here) show that the region level variance (i.e., the differences between the regions) is statistically highly significant for each year.

6. See Blaydes on the linkage between illiteracy and turnout in the Egyptian elections under Mubarak (Blaydes 2006).

7. Data from all of the elections was merged first to allow for observing the same TIKs over time (thus only the TIKs which stayed the same over the years could be matched, and a small number of TIKs had to be excluded due to redistricting). This data was then combined with the 2002 census data (a small number of observations could not be matched). The census data has only one observation per city, and so mean city electoral results (from the sub-city TIKs) were calculated prior to the merge. The dataset includes all the 'normal' federation subjects, that is twenty ethnic republics, six krays, and forty-nine oblasts. The dataset does not include the Chechen Republic (due to the effects of the two Chechen wars and their aftermath on data availability), nor the two federal cities, Moscow and St Petersburg. The AOs (ten autonomous okrugs and one autonomous oblast) are also excluded, as most of them were merged to the adjacent regions after 2005.

8. That is, the share of the rayon population coded ethnically Russian in the census was subtracted from 100.

9. Gennadiy Zyuganov in 2000, 2008 and 2012 and Nikolay Kharitonov in 2004.

10. This includes the following ethnic republics: Dagestan, Ingushetiya, Kabardino Balkaria, Karachaevo Cherkessiya, North Ossetiya.

11. I thank Dr Arkadiy Lyubarev for clarifying this and other details about the Russian electoral system.

REFERENCES

Allina-Pisano, J. (2008) *The Post-Soviet Potemkin Village, Politics and Property Rights in the Black Earth*. New York: Cambridge University Press.
Allina-Pisano, J. (2010) 'Social Contracts and Authoritarian Projects in Post-Soviet Space: The Use of Administrative Resource', *Communist and Post-Communist Studies* 43: 373–82.
Blais, A. (2000) *To Vote or Not to Vote, the Merits and Limits of Rational Choice Theory*. Pittsburgh: University of Pittsburgh Press.
Blaydes, L. (2006) 'Who Votes in Authoritarian Elections and Why? Determinants of Voter Turnout in Contemporary Egypt', Paper presented at the APSA, Philadelphia, PA.
Buzin, A. Y. and Lyubarev, A. E. (2008) *Prestupleniye Bez Nakazaniya, Adminsitrativnye Tekhnologiifederal'nykh Vyborov 2007–2008 Godov*. Moscow: Nikkolo-M.
Buzin, A. Y., Vakhshtain, V. S., Kynev, A. V. and Lyubarev, A. E. (2012) *Federal'nye, Regional'nye I Mestnye Vybory V Rossii 4 Dekabrya 2011 Goda, Analiticheskiy Doklad*. Moscow: Golos.
Calvo, E. and Murillo, M. V. (2004) 'Who Delivers? Partisan Clients in the Argentine Electoral Market', *American Journal of Political Science* 48(4): 742–57.

Carreras, M. and Castaneda-Angarita, N. (2014) 'Who Votes in Latin America? A Test of Three Theoretical Perspectives', *Comparative Political Studies* 47(8): 1079–104.

Central Electoral Commission of Russia. Available at www.vybory.izbirkom.ru

Chandra, K. (2007) 'Counting Heads: A Theory of Voter and Elite Behaviour in Patronage Democracies', in H. Kitschelt and S. I. Wilkinson (Eds.), *Patrons, Clients, and Policies, Patterns of Democratic Accountability and Political Competition*. New York: Cambridge University Press, pp. 84–109.

Clem, R. C. (2006) 'Russia's Electoral Geography: A Review', *Eurasian Geography and Economics* 47(4): 381–406.

Clem, R. C. and Craumer, P. R. (1998) 'Regional Patters of Voter Turnout in Russian Elections, 1993–96', in M. Wyman, S. White and S. Oates (Eds.), *Elections and Voters in Post-Communist Russia*. Cheltenham: Edward Elgar Publishing Ltd.

Clem, R. C. and Craumer, P. R. (2004) 'Redrawing the Political Map of Russia: The Duma Election of December 2003', *Eurasian Geography and Economics* 45(4): 241–61.

Colton, T. (2000) *Transitional Citizens, Voters and What Influences Them in the New Russia*. Cambridge, MA: Harvard University Press.

Crowley, S. (2015) 'Monotowns and the Political Economy of Industrial Restructuring in Russia', *Post-Soviet Affairs*, published online 22 June.

Dalton, R. J. (2008) *Citizen Politics, Public Opinion and Political Parties in Advanced Industrial Democracies*. Washington, DC: QC Press.

Darden, K. (2008) 'The Integrity of Corrupt States: Graft as an Informal State Institution', *Politics & Society* 36(1): 35–60.

Dixit, A. and Londregan, J. (1996) 'The Determinants of Success of Special Interests in Redistributive Politics', *Journal of Politics* 58(4): 1132–55.

Fish, M. S. (2005) *Democracy Derailed in Russia: The Failure of Open Politics*. Cambridge: Cambridge University Press.

Forrat, N. (2015) 'Shock-Resistant Authoritarianism: Teachers and Regime's Support in Putin's Russia', Paper presented at the ASEEES, Philadelphia.

Frye, T., Reuter, O. J. and Szakonyi, D. (2014) 'Political Machines at Work: Voter Mobilization and Electoral Subversion in the Workplace', *World Politics* 66(2): 195–228.

Gandhi, J. and Lust-Okar, E. (2009) 'Elections Under Authoritarianism', *Annual Review of Political Science* 12: 403–22.

Gans-Morse, J., Mazzuca, S. and Nichter, S. (2014) 'Varieties of Clientelism: Machine Politics During Elections', *American Journal of Political Science* 58(2): 415–32.

Gimpelson, V. and Kapeliushnikov, R. (2011) 'Labor Market Adjustment: Is Russia Different?' in Working Paper WP3/2011/04, Labour Markets in Transition. Higher School of Economics, Moscow.

Golosov, G. V. (2013) 'Machine Politics: The Concept and Its Implications for Post-Soviet Studies', *Demokratizatsiya: The Journal of Post-Soviet Democratization* 21(4): 459–80.

Goodnow, R., Moser, R. G. and Smith, T. (2014) 'Ethnicity and Electoral Manipulation in Russia', *Electoral Studies* 36: 15–27.

Gorenburg, D. (2003) *Minority Ethnic Mobilization in the Russian Federation.* Cambridge: Cambridge University Press.

Hale, H. E. (2003) 'Explaining Machine Politics in Russia's Regions: Economy, Ethnicity, and Legacy', *Post-Soviet Affairs* 19(3): 228–63.

Hale, H. E. (2007), 'Correlates of Clientelism: Political Economy, Politicized Ethnicity, and Post-Communist Transition', in H. Kitschelt and S. I. Wilkinson (Eds.), *Patrons, Clients, and Policies, Patterns of Democratic Accountability and Political Competition* (Cambridge: Cambridge University Press): 227–50.

Hale, H. E. (2014) *Patronal Politics: Eurasian Regime Dynamics in Comparative Perspective.* New York: Cambridge University Press.

Hicken, A. (2011) 'Clientelism', *Annual Review of Political Science* 14: 289–310.

Holmes, L. (2006) *Rotten States? Corruption, Post-Communism and Neo-Liberalism.* Durham, NC: Duke University Press.

Kitschelt, H. and Wilkinson, S. I. (2007) 'Citizen Politician Linkages: An Introduction', in H. Kitschelt and S. I. Wilkinson (Eds.), *Patrons, Clients, and Policies, Patterns of Democratic Accountability and Political Competition.* New York: Cambridge University Press.

Kopecký, P. and Spirova, M. (2011) ' "Jobs for the Boys"? Patterns of Party Patronage in Post-Communist Europe', *West European Politics* 34(5): 897–921.

Kostadinova, T. and Spirova, M. (2018) 'Combatting Corruption', in A. Fagan and P. Kopecký (Eds) *The Routledge Handbook of East European Politics.* Oxon: Routledge.

Kynev, A. V. and Lyubarev, A. E. (2016) 'Osobennosti Predvybornoy Agitatsii, Izmeneniya V Sostave Zaregistrirovannyks Kandidatov I Partiynykh Spiskov Na Regional'nykh I Federal'nykh Vyborakh 18 Sentyabrya 2016', Komitet grazhdanskykh initsiativ, Analiticheskiy doklad.

Ledeneva, A. V. (2006) *How Russia Really Works.* Ithaca, NY: Cornell University Press.

Lounev, S. (2002) 'Russia, Voter Registration', in IDEA (Eds.), *Voter Turnout Since 1945,* A Global Report.

Magaloni, B. (2006) *Voting for Autocracy, Hegemonic Party Survival and Its Demise in Mexico.* New York: Cambridge University Press.

Magaloni, B., Diaz-Cayeros, A. and Estevez, F. (2007) 'Clientelism and Portfolio Diversification: A Model of Electoral Investment with Application to Mexico', in H. Kitschelt and S. I. Wilkinson (Eds.), *Patrons, Clients, and Policies, Patterns of Democratic Accountability and Political Competition.* New York: Cambridge University Press.

Mares, I., Muntean, A. and Petrova, T. (2016) 'The Incidence of Economic Intimidation at Times of Elections: Evidence from Romania and Bulgaria', *Government and Opposition,* published online 5 December, doi:10.1017/gov.2016.39

Mares, I. and Young, L. (2016) 'Buying, Expropriating, and Stealing Votes', *Annual Review of Political Science* 19: 267–88.

McAllister, I. and White, S. (1998) 'To Vote or Not to Vote: Election Turnout in Post-Communist Russia', in M. Wyman, S. White and S. Oates (Eds.), *Elections and Voters in Post-Communist Russia.* Cheltenham: Edward Elgar Publishing Ltd.

Mebane Jr., W. R. and Kalinin, K. (2009) 'Electoral Fraud in Russia: Vote Counts Analysis Using Second-Digit Mean Tests', Paper presented at the MPSA, Chicago.

Mercator and IGRAN (2007) 'Elektoral'nyi Spravochnik 'Rossiiskie Vybory V Tsi-
    frakh I Kartakh'. 1995–2007 (CD-rom)'.
Moser, R. G. and White, A. C. (2013) 'The Expansion of Electoral Fraud in Russia:
    Comparing Electoral Manipulation in the 1990s and 2000s', Paper presented at
    APSA, Chicago.
Myagkov, M., Ordeshook, P. C. and Shakin, D. (2005) 'Fraud or Fairytales: Russia
    and Ukraine's Electoral Experience', *Post-Soviet Affairs* 21(2): 91–131.
Myagkov, M., Ordeshook, P. C. and Shakin, D. (2009) *The Forensics of Election
    Fraud*. Cambridge: Cambridge University Press.
Nichter, S. (2014) 'Conceptualizing Vote Buying', *Electoral Studies* 35: 315–27.
O'Brien, D. J. and Patsiorkovskiy, V. (2008) 'Changing Social and Economic Condi-
    tions in Russian Villages, 1991–2008', *Russian Analytical Digest* 52, 16 December.
ODIHR. (2012) 'Russian Federation, Elections to the State Duma 4 December 2011,
    OSCE/ODIHR Election Observation Mission Final Report', Warsaw.
Powell, G. B. (1986) 'American Voter Turnout in Comparative Perspective', *Ameri-
    can Political Science Review* 80(1): 17–43.
Reisinger, W. M. and Moraski, B. J. (2008) 'The Relationship Between Turnout and
    Competition Levels in Russia', *University of Iowa, Iowa Research Online* 4(5):
    1–38.
Reisinger, W. M. and Moraski, B. J. (2010) 'Regional Changes and Changing
    Regional Relations with the Centre', in V. Gel'man and C. Ross (Eds.), *The Politics
    of Sub-National Authoritarianism in Russia*. Farnham: Ashgate.
Remington, T. F. (2011) *The Politics of Inequality in Russia*. Cambridge: Cambridge
    University Press.
Remmer, K. L. (2010) 'Political Scale and Electoral Turnout: Evidence from the Less
    Industrialised World', *Comparative Political Studies* 43(3): 275–303.
Reuter, O. J. (2016) '2016 State Duma Elections: United Russia After 15 Years', *Rus-
    sian Analytical Digest* 189.
Rosenstone, S. J. and Hansen, J. M. (2003) *Mobilization, Participation, and Democ-
    racy in America*. New York: Longman.
Saikkonen, I. A.-L. (2017) 'Electoral Mobilization and Authoritarian Elections: Evi-
    dence from Post-Soviet Russia', *Government and Opposition* 52(1): 51–74.
Saikkonen, I. A.-L. and White, A. (2017) 'Strategic Targeting: Authoritarian Capac-
    ity, State Dependent Populations, and Electoral Manipulation', Paper presented at
    APSA, San Francisco, CA.
Simpser, A. (2013) *Why Governments and Parties Manipulate Elections, Theory,
    Practice and Implications*. New York: Cambridge University Press.
Stokes, S. C. (2005) 'Perverse Accountability: A Formal Model of Machine Politics
    with Evidence from Argentina'. *American Political Science Review* 99(3): 315–25.
Stokes, S. C. (2007) 'Political Clientelism', in C. Boix and S. C. Stokes (Eds.), *Oxford
    Handbook on Comparative Politics*. Oxford: Oxford University Press.
Stokes, S. C., Dunning, T., Nazareno, M. and Brusco, V. (2013) *Brokers, Voters, and
    Clientelism, the Puzzle of Distributive Politics*. New York: Cambridge University
    Press.

Tucker, J. (2007) 'Enough! Electoral Fraud, Collective Action Problems, and Post-Communist Colored Revolutions', *Perspectives on Politics* 5(3): 535–51.

Wegren, S. K. (2008) 'The Food Problem in Russian Agriculture', *Russian Analytical Digest* 52, 16 December.

White, S. and McAllister, I. (2007) 'Turnout and Representation Bias in Post-Communist Europe', *Political Studies* 55 (3): 586–606.

White, A. C. and Moser, R. G. (2014) 'Voter Turnout in Russia: A Tale of Two Elections – 1999 and 2011', Paper presented at the MPSA, Chicago.

White, A. C. and Saikkonen, I. A.-L. (2016) 'More Than a Name? Variation in Voter Mobilization of Titular and Non-Titular Ethnic Minorities in Russian National Elections', *Ethnopolitics* 16 (5): 450–470.

White, S. (2011) 'Elections Russian-Style', *Europe-Asia Studies* 63(4): 531–56.

Chapter Six

A New Model of Clientelism
Political Parties, Public Resources, and Private Contributors

Sergiu Gherghina and Clara Volintiru[1]

INTRODUCTION

Political clientelism has been traditionally defined as the distribution of selective benefits to individuals or groups in exchange for political support (Katz 1986; Piattoni 2001; Hopkin 2001; 2006b; Kitschelt and Wilkinson 2007). Earlier studies have shown that many contemporary clientelistic linkages take the form of a pyramid structure. This assumes the existence of exchanges between patrons (i.e., parties) and clients (i.e., voters) with the help of brokers (i.e., intermediaries from within or outside party organizations). In this scheme, the exchange takes the form of resource allocation or access (from parties to voters) and of electoral support (from voters to parties). Although useful, this structure raises two troubling questions. The first is a theoretical concern and refers to its one-dimensional character. While aimed to enhance electoral mobilization, clientelism relies on resources that have been treated until now as endogenous to the political system. Second, it is unclear what happens in those settings where brokers have low capacity because party membership organizations are minimal.

This chapter[2] tries to provide an answer to both questions by proposing a bi-dimensional model of clientelism that emphasizes the role of exogenous resources. The vertical linkage between political parties and electorate is complemented by a horizontal nexus between parties and private contributors (i.e., economic agents). In an environment characterized by low internal resources, parties involve external actors to get the necessary money. The central argument of this new model is that public resources are no longer used in systematically targeting electoral groups, but focused primarily at private campaign donors. The latter benefit from public procurement procedures and supply financial support to political parties. Political parties can then employ the formal and informal financial support thus obtained to deploy the electoral mobilization strategy based on the distribution of selective benefits (e.g., vote buying), which is what clientelism essentially does (see Kitschelt 2000; Kitschelt and Wilkinson 2007). To illustrate how this bi-dimensional mechanism works we focus on Romania between 2008 and 2012, a crucial case for the study of clientelism due to the high number of references to this process in the media and international reports. Our empirical study uses qualitative content analysis of official public records, media reports and legislation regarding private donations and public procurement. Party histories and secondary data are also used to assess the extent of membership organizations.

The major contribution brought by this study to the existing literature lies in the identification of a new analytical layer. By exploring the link between political parties and economic actors, the bi-dimensional clientelistic model explains how a new category of clients emerges and how this linkage reinforces the mechanism of classic clientelism through redistribution of resources. Thus, unlike earlier studies that accounted for systemic explanation for the perpetuation of clientelism, our analysis brings in the picture the resources outside the political system. The clientelistic mechanism presented in this chapter is a paradigm shift in how clientelistic parties focus on resource accumulation for political consolidation. Clientelistic parties have always been dependent on the preservation of a continuous flow of discretionary resources, but the literature has never before engaged with the strains institutional reforms might place on the availability of such resources.

Clientelistic engagement with private contractors to ensure electoral funding falls in line with the business-firm model of contemporary party organizations (Hopkin and Paolucci 1999). This has implications to the role clientelism can play on the output side of democratic governance (e.g., policy formulation and implementation). Generally, clientelistic parties have week incentives to reform and exercise bureaucratic oversight (Cruz and Keefer 2015). But, at the same time, politicians seem to be able to survive longer in office if they develop merit-based institutional procedures (Lapuente and Nistotskaya 2009). Whether it is through contextual imposition, or self-interest maximization, it is much easier to 'externalize' such services to private contractors and informal intermediaries.

The following section reviews the literature on clientelism and criticizes the shortcomings of the pyramid structure. Next, we briefly discuss the issue of private funding and emphasize the elements favouring a close connection between private contributors and political parties. The third section presents in detail the new model of clientelism and explains its theoretical mechanisms. The fourth section brings empirical evidence from the Romanian case to illustrate how this new model functions in real-life. The conclusions summarize the main findings and discuss the implications of our analysis.

THE CLIENTELISTIC PHENOMENON: STRUCTURAL CHANGES AND ADAPTATION

The studies concerned with the clientelistic phenomenon can be seen as having a similar evolution with the changes and adaptations of the clientelistic manifestations themselves. Most of the relevant literature is structured around the model of exchanges between a patron and a client, but there are significant variations in how this relationship is further framed and contextualized across different countries and political settings. As such, most of the first comprehensive studies on this topic looked at clientelistic exchanges either as a phenomenon embedded in the political practice (Weingrod 1968; Scott 1972), or as a broader cultural and societal issue (Gellner and Waterbury 1977, Eisenstadt and Roniger 1984).

Given the opportunity of regime changes in many of the most frequently covered cases of clientelism spread across Latin America and Southern Europe, the literature gradually focused on the connection between political transformations and the adaptive reactions of agents involved in clientelistic practices (Lyrintzis 1984; Caciagli 2006). Consequently, political scientists were able to provide much more structured perspectives on this phenomenon, linking the participants within coherent schemes of electoral mobilization (Piattoni 2001; Hopkin 2006a; Kitschelt and Wilkinson 2007).

From very early on the literature has revealed the concept of machine politics and the corrupt connections with business groups and private interests (Chubb 1981, 1983; Stokes 2005). While in practice, we often see pervasive corruption as intrinsically connected to clientelistic networks, the two should be treated separately from a theoretical point of view. This disentanglement of clientelistic transactions and corruption is useful in distinguishing the structural changes suffered by the clientelistic system itself. In this sense, given its network deployment, political relevance and consequence, and interpersonal normative function, clientelism presents a wealth of avenues to explore and assess. In this sense, our assessment of the political parties' reliance on public contractors is directly addressing the aforementioned lineage, in the existent literature, which targets the clientelistic phenomenon.

The Pyramid Structure and Its Shortcomings

Given this phenomenon's survival and entrenchment within the context of democratic politics, clientelism can be analysed as a multi-layered system, with complex structures. Gradually, the dyadic ties described above have evolved into a more 'complex pyramid exchange network of client-broker-patron exchange' (Kitschelt and Wilkinson 2007, 8). Clientelism becomes the object of market exchanges between supply provided by the political parties and candidates, on one side, and the demand of clients willing to exchange their votes for goods and favours, on the other side. Within this approach, the clients' leverage is high as they are no longer forced into a relationship of asymmetrical power but voluntary participants into a transaction (Hopkin 2006a). In other words, 'democracy strengthens the clients' bargaining leverage vis-à-vis brokers and patrons' (Piattoni 2001).

Following these developments, clientelism can be visualized in the form of a pyramid structure with clients at the base, brokers in the middle and suppliers at the top. Referring to politics, this pyramid approach includes three categories of participants: (1) the electorate (clients) as a general group and the party supporters or voters as specific groups of beneficiaries, (2) party organizations (brokers) including members or local leaders acting as intermediaries between the electorate and the supply side, and (3) political leaders or party in the central office (patrons) able to control and distribute goods and services to the clients (Figure 6.1). The 'broker-mediated distribution' (Stokes et al. 2013) is probably the most important addition to the clientelistic phenomenon in the transition from personal patronage to the new large scale, electorally driven system.

Second, there are the vote-buying strategies in which money and goods are offered – during the electoral campaign or Election Day – usually on a

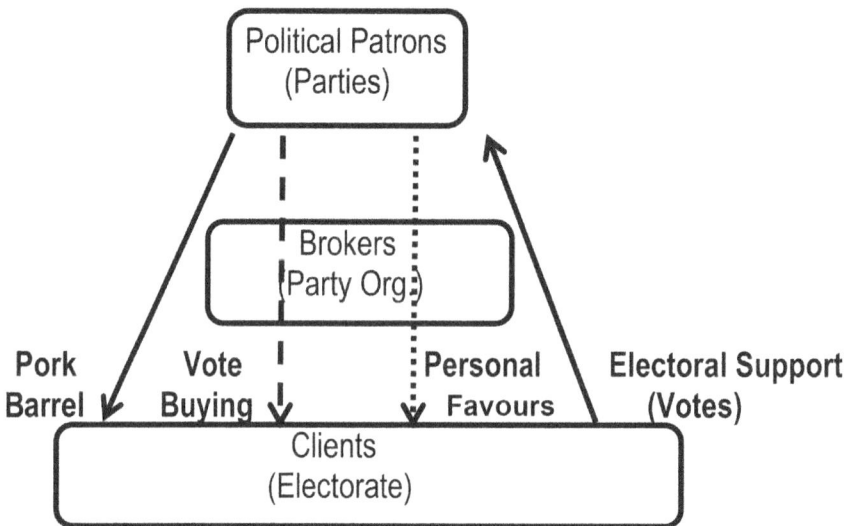

Figure 6.1 The Pyramid Clientelistic Structure

non-iterative basis. Brokers are necessary intermediaries, but their influence is considerably diminished compared to the previous case of personal favours, because they are no longer required to provide the functions of selection and oversight. Furthermore, the clients can be both the loyal supporters and the undecided voters. Stokes et al. (2013) bring evidence to show that loyal supporters that are usually the target of non-iterative exchanges from parties. Gherghina (2013) illustrates that, in addition to targeting their own supporters, parties use vote-buying strategies to persuade the undecided. As a result, it is not so much about persuading votes, as much as mobilizing turnout.

Third, there is a formal exchange of targeted public spending in return for political support. This process of channelling public resources or material benefits to selected districts or particular categories of voters is generally referred to as pork-barrel spending (Ferejohn 1974; Shepsle and Weingast 1994; Case 2001; Ashworth and de Mesquita 2006). While serving to strengthen the electoral support for the ruling party, pork-barrel politics follows to a certain extent the logic of programmatic mechanisms, and as such it is a formal process of rewarding loyal supporters, that bypasses the party organizations. Examples include targeting spending on wages or pensions for certain categories of people, or localized programs of infrastructure development.

In spite of its useful structuring of linkages, this pyramid conceptualization of clientelism has several flaws. To begin with, it assumes that all selectively distributed goods and services are public resources controlled by the political patron and deployed according to an electoral strategy of survival. This assumption is problematic for two reasons: (1) certain favours such as public contracts usually require more than just political support in exchange, and (2) to control substantial resources, patrons need electoral victories; this leads to a vicious circle in which only ruling parties can employ clientelistic practices. While the first assumption will be addressed by the present research, the latter has already been contradicted by evidence from earlier studies, showing that it is not only the ruling parties that deploy clientelistic tactics (Piattoni 2001; Schaffer 2007; Gherghina 2013).

Furthermore, the pyramid structure assumes the existence of an effective territorial deployment of party organizational capacity. Accordingly, it takes for granted the existence of brokers (i.e., intermediary level) in the clientelistic pyramid. Since party membership is shrinking in many West European countries (Mair and van Biezen 2001; van Biezen et al. 2012) and has been minimal in Eastern Europe (Webb and White 2007; Gherghina 2014), one can easily argue that political parties face significant challenges in terms of their brokering capacity. Consequently, their capacity to engage in several clientelistic linkages is fairly limited.

In light of these shortcomings, we argue that clientelism can be better understood – at least in Eastern Europe – as a composite of horizontal and vertical linkages. In doing so, we bring in the picture the role of private donors. While the issue of private party financing has been extensively discussed in the literature, to our knowledge there is no prior linkage with the clientelistic system of resource distribution. Private funding becomes important when vote buying prevails over the other two forms of clientelistic exchanges, that is personal favours and pork-barrel. This happens because the latter rely more on state resources, while vote buying can make efficient use of private contributions. In our model state resources are not used to reach the clients (as in the pyramid structure) but are directed towards private contractors in exchange for money. The following section explains in detail how private funding creates the nexus with political parties in our modified model of political clientelism.

THE NEXUS WITH PRIVATE FUNDING

Almost one century ago political parties were considered the pillars of representative democracies (Bryce 1921; Schattschneider 1942). Since then, their importance remained unchanged but their functions diversified. Parties are the transmission belt between society and the state being the channel through which individuals and groups in society are integrated into the political system. Parties articulate, aggregate and represent interests, mobilizing the general public during elections (van Biezen and Kopecký 2007; Katz 2011). Since politics consists of complex and sophisticated processes the choice among initial alternatives is not often accessible to ordinary voters. Parties simplify choices and generate symbols of identification and loyalty (Neumann 1956; Dalton and Wattenberg 2000). Following elections, parties are essential for government through political decisions and implementation, that is policy-making. To fulfil these functions and exercise their core activities parties need substantial resources.

Costs related to administration and election campaigns are high – and have increased over time – and parties use a mix of private and public sources of income. Since internal party funding (e.g., membership fees, profits of party-owned businesses) is fairly limited, political parties have to rely on external means of financing such as contributions or donations from private individuals and companies.[3] In this context, the major risk lies in the misuse of these resources to influence specific political decisions. To partly diminish these risks and to ensure multi-party competition, many countries have adopted regulations on public funding. These provisions bring some disadvantages since public money may lead to dependence on the state and inhibit parties' connections with the electorate (van Biezen 2004). Under these circumstances, private finances can be healthy for a political system if it is strictly regulated to allow for transparency (of revenues and expenditures) and if there is a balance between the two types of funding.

The debate on private funding has been built around three inter-connected topics: illicit contributions, inequalities, and corruption. First, the illicit contributions refer to the private donations that contravene existing laws of political financing. Illegal donations cast major doubts on the morality of the political competitors accepting them and often translate into non-transparent handling. Parties do not keep reliable records of private contributions and avoid or falsify public disclosure. Consequently, illicit donations are considered scandalous independent of their effect. This is the case even when the contributor does not expect any benefit in return for the donation (Pinto-Duschinsky 2002) especially if the donors are contested sources such as mafias or drug cartels (Freidenberg and Levitsky 2006). Second, private resources often lead to unequal competition for public office. Political parties or candidates with wealthy supporters are in a better position than their competitors. They can spend more in electoral campaigns, increase their visibility, reach more voters, and thus gain greater political influence (Ewing 1992; Johnston and Pattie 1995; Fisher 2002).

Third, and by far the most discussed problem associated with private funding, there is a risk of corruption. Although a contested concept, corruption essentially rests on the distinction between formal obligations to pursue the public good and behaviours or practices that undermine the public good. Corruption takes several forms when private funding is involved, and they can refer either to sources or to mechanisms through which political decisions are influenced and distorted. To begin with the sources, one of the most obvious situations is the use of money originating from corrupt transactions. In this case the donation may not be illicit, but remains highly problematic because the receiving party overlooks misconduct of the donor. Related to the latter, corruption scandals surround the acceptance of money from disreputable sources (Pinto-Duschinsky 2002). Apart from the overlap with their illicit character (see above), tainted donors are usually associated with tainted practices by the electorate and media.

Private money often comes with strings attached. Contributors and parties are likely to enter a relationship of reciprocity in which money are offered in exchange for specific political decisions. In extreme situations, when the sponsorship is high, the party is effectively bought and abandons its initial purposes. As a result, it delivers policies to the donors and partly or completely fails delivering them to society (Nassmacher 1993; Williams 2000). Simply put, political parties make use of state resources to favour or to promise favours to their benefactors. The corrupt practices include also the spending for unfair or illegal purposes such as vote buying. Parties and provide voters gifts of various kinds (see the empirical section of this chapter) aiming at securing their electoral support. Empirical evidence shows that vote buying remains a component of many election campaigns around the world. While in theory the usual suspects are the impoverished countries or poor voters where 'the politics of the belly' prevails, vote buying occurs in countries with various degrees of economic development and democracy (Pinto-Duschinsky 2002; Brusco et al. 2004; Schaffer 2007; Bratton 2008).

The policy distortion and illegal spending fuelled by private financing lie at the core of the horizontal linkage in our model (Figure 6.2). In this respect, political parties make massive use of private contributions to buy electoral support. In doing so, they do not allocate state resources to directly buy votes but channel them towards the private contractors as rewards them for their generous contributions. The horizontal clientelistic loop created between parties and private donors is reinforced by their mutual benefits: the former retain power, while the latter increase their economic profits. According to the data from the Democratic Accountability Linkage Project (Kitschelt 2000), Romanian parties have indeed been traditionally more inclined to the distribution of consumer goods or preferential public benefits than more narrow and complex mechanisms like favourable regulatory proceedings or public employment.

A NEW MODEL OF CLIENTELISM

As preciously explained, the new model of clientelism works best when the resource allocation is narrowed to one major strategy, that is vote buying. These are the circumstances under which the involvement of private contributors brings large benefits to parties, that is more money to buy electoral support. These two changes lead to a bi-dimensional clientelistic structure (Figure 6.2) with two types of exchanges: vertical (between parties and voters) and horizontal (between parties and private contractors).

One characteristic of this model is the minor role played by brokers leading to fewer clientelist means used to reach the electorate. This is consistent with empirical realities of the most recent decades in which party membership has decreased considerably. Small party organizations mean few available brokers and thus large-scale distribution of personal favours is unlikely to happen. At the same time, in the context of a decreasing turnout (Cassel and Luskin 1988; Flickinger and Studlar 1992; Gray and Caul 2000) the strategy of continuously fuelling the loyal voters through personal favours becomes less effective that the one-off exchanges in the electoral periods such as vote buying. In brief, both dimensions of decreasing participation – involvement in parties and voting – determine a shift in the clientelistic paradigm. The discretionary distribution of benefits is partly deprived of party brokers and

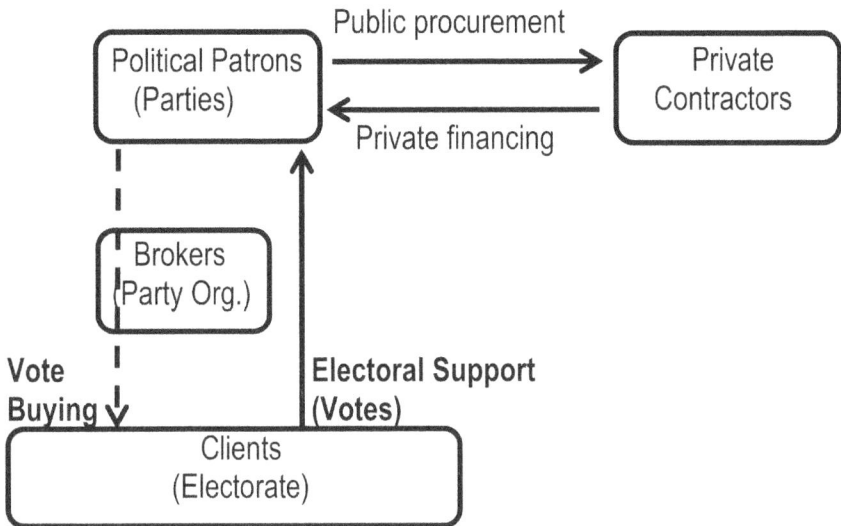

Figure 6.2   The Bi-Dimensional Clientelistic Structure

permanent clients. As such, it becomes significantly more focused on accumulating resources, and deploying such funds within the specific electoral periods.

Another characteristic is the limited role of pork-barrel. It is an effective mean of mobilizing the electorate both by distributing benefits and by showing loyalty to the electoral base. In addition, it is entirely legal if not necessarily legitimate, to support the interests of the party voters more intensely than those of the rest of the electorate. In spite of these advantages, it is less used in comparison to other clientelistic strategies for at least two reasons. First, it is costly and thus harder to use in an environment of budgetary constraints. Second, it is limited to the relationship between the ruling party and core voters and thus not helpful in mobilizing undecided voters.

Following these changes, the strategy of vote buying becomes the key element for resource distribution. Its efficiency does not rely on pyramid informal structures maintained over time but on the level of allocated resources. It bypasses the selection and oversight functions of the long-term clientelistic linkages. Reversely, it is particularly conditioned by the patrons' availability of resources. This creates the need of the clientelistic system to extend its mechanisms of resources accumulation. This is the moment when private contractors become vectors of resource accumulation in the clientelistic scheme. In light of the potential profit they can make, private contractors working on public contracts are likely to be highly involved in the horizontal linkage depicted in Figure 6.2. They engage in a closed circuit with political patrons exchanging private funds for public resources. Private contractors receive public funds through public procurement contracts, which lead back to the political parties in government through legal private donations. While this exchange may involve secondary processes (e.g., illegal donations) it sheds light on the preferential resource allocations and indicates that the accumulation of resources is a priority for political parties. These contractors lack incentives to target electoral mobilization (clients) or to enhance party organizations (brokers) and that is why they are unlikely to engage in the horizontal clientelism. With one exception, the situation in which private contractors electorally mobilize their employees, there is a clear distinction between the horizontal and vertical clientelism: one is mobilizing resources, and the other is mobilizing voters.

Through the development of a horizontal layer, the clientelistic system is not only a principal vehicle of electoral mobilization but also one of resource accumulation. It no longer serves as a continuous platform of patronage, but works as a 'buy-off' system limited in time and value. This new survival strategy provides two advantages to the political parties. First, the clientelistic networks are more easily manageable as they comprise fewer participants, clearly separated. On the horizontal linkage the interactions usually involve political patrons and private contractors. On the vertical linkage, the structure includes patrons, brokers, and clients, but it is much narrower than in the pyramid structure. Second, this clientelistic arrangement allows more resources to be accumulated by the patrons. Accordingly, it ensures the convergence of party elites' interests and thus improves the possibilities of remaining in power. On the background of a general party cartelization tendency, political parties can become even further intertwined as they benefit from the same distributional paths.

In contrast, the electorate loses. While the pyramid clientelistic model brings some benefits to the clients through the preferential distribution of public resources, the bi-dimensional clientelistic system deprives voters from their share of public resources; it goes instead to private contractors. In this new setting, the clientelistic linkages have also an exploitative function in addition to that of electoral mobilization. The importance electoral competition is matched by resource accumulation, and they reinforce each other.

So far, we have built a theoretical model of clientelism meant to better capture the types of exchanges in which political parties may engage in contemporary times. To show how it works we use the case study of Romania between 2008 and 2012 (the most recent legislative elections). This is the most likely case where the new model of clientelism can be observed. As illustrated in the following section, the Romanian politics has features of cartelization, the parties have small organizations, and there is extensive evidence of vote buying. All these features contribute to the emergence of a solid horizontal linkage between parties and private contractors.

THE FUNCTIONING OF THE BI-DIMENSIONAL CLIENTELISM

This section starts with the brief presentation of the Romanian parties' features in terms of cartelization and limited party organization. The second subsection brings evidence about the vertical clientelism, while the third presents in detail the horizontal linkage.

Cartel Politics

Until the legislative elections of December 2012 Romania was the only East European country where no new political parties have entered the parliamentary arena for two decades.[4] Since 1992 only a handful of political competitors have secured parliamentary seats and thus participated in coalition governments. Among these parties, some failed to gain parliamentary seats and have never managed to return to the legislature since then, for example the Christian Democratic National Peasants Party in 2000, the Greater Romania Party (PRM) in 2008. There were many failures of other political competitors to gain parliamentary representation, for example the Alliance for Romania and the Union of Right Forces in 2000, the Socialist Alliance Party in consecutive elections, the New Generation Party (PNG) in 2004 and 2008 etc.

The four parties with a continuous presence in parliament that have shaped the Romanian political scene over the last two decades are the Social Democratic Party (PSD), Democratic Liberal Party (PDL), National Liberal Party (PNL) and the Democratic Alliance of Hungarians in Romania (UDMR).[5] These parties display inclusive coalition formation patterns in the sense that each party joined a coalition with every other party. In addition, the elite is very homogenous and rarely changes: a large amount of the members of parliament (MPs) are re-nominated and re-elected in consecutive terms (Stefan et al. 2012). Even when new parties emerge, like the case of the People's Party Dan Diaconescu (PPDD), a part of the elite promoted to parliament belonged in the past to some of the major political parties (Gherghina and Soare 2013).

In addition to this cartelization of politics, the alternation in government makes every party subject of clientelism (both vertical and horizontal). A brief history of parties' electoral performances will provide a better understanding of their dynamic over the last two decades, in general, and of the situation in the two most recent elections in particular. The PSD is a successor communist party, being the largest in the Romanian party system. Its origins go back to the 1992 split of the National Salvation Front (FSN), the winner of the 1990 elections. Following an internal dispute between the first two men from the party elite, the party split in two: the FDSN (later PDSR and PSD) and FSN (later PD and PDL). Since its formation, the PSD won five out of six legislative elections and took part in four coalition governments (three times as the *formateur*). Since 2000 the party enjoys a stable electoral support situated around 33 per cent of the votes. The other successor party, the PDL, is the second-largest party in Romania throughout the post-communist period. It got second in the 1996, 2004 (in two different electoral alliances), 2008, and 2012 legislative elections. It was part of three coalition governments, in one of them (2008–2012) as the main governing party. Unlike the PSD, the PDL is not characterized by constantly high electoral results across the entire post-communist period. Its electoral support is quite oscillating with high levels of volatility.

The PNL is the third largest party in post-communist Romania. In the most recent legislative elections (2012) it ran into an alliance with the PSD (the Social Liberal Union – USL), registering a landslide win. It has participated in two other coalition governments (1996 and 2004, once as the leading party). Its average share of votes is around 15 per cent with a tendency to stabilize in the most recent decade. The UDMR has a very stable electorate and has enjoyed a pivotal role several times. It has participated four times in government coalitions being partner with each of the previous three parties. Apart from these four political parties, this analysis will also refer to the PPDD because it has engaged in clientelism to secure a position in the parliamentary arena. It came third in the 2012 elections (approximately 14 per cent of the votes) but soon after the vast majority of its parliamentary elite left the party.

Small Membership Organizations

Membership organizations act as brokers on which the patrons (i.e., political parties) can rely for vertical clientelism. The argument in the literature can be summarized as follows: when membership organizations are large, political parties have more possibilities to use clientelism. This happens for two reasons. On the one hand, large membership can provide the financial resources to distribute to voters since members contribute to the party coffers. On the other hand, established membership means that brokers are more stable, they establish long-term contacts with more voters, that is broader networks in society (Gherghina 2014), and are also reliable. In the absence of large membership organizations political parties are likely to complement the vertical clientelism with the horizontal nexus with private donors. This linkage offers them resources to distribute and strengthens their position in office; by office we do not mean exclusively in government, but also in parliamentary opposition since in many countries this is not a permanent status and opposition parties in one term can be in government at the next elections.

An extensive body of literature has illustrated that political parties in Eastern Europe have very small membership organizations (Mair and van Biezen 2001; Szczerbiak 2001; van Biezen 2003; Weldon 2006; Spirova 2007; Webb and White 2007; Lewis 2008; van Biezen et al. 2012; Gherghina 2014). In Romania, with the exception of the PSD, the Romanian parties have membership organizations smaller than 1 per cent in the electorate. Among these, the youngest party (PPDD) has less than 0.3 per cent. In addition to these low levels, the PDL has lost members between the two elections. The same trend can be observed at country level. The PSD is the only party that has significantly augmented its membership organization from approximately 1.6 per cent to more than 2.2 per cent. Figure 6.3 depicts the evolution of membership percentages at country and party level in the 2008 and 2012 legislative elections.[6]

These numbers indicate that Romanian political parties do not have strong membership organizations that would allow them to engage in multiple clientelistic linkages with the electorate. Governmental programmes such as conditional cash transfers in Latin America (for Oportunidades in Mexico see De La O 2013, for Panes in Uruguay see Manacorda et al. 2011) have been successful in mobilizing turnout and support for national party incumbents, but in the Romanian setting such programmes have only yielded support to local incumbents (see Pop-Eleches 2009). When engaging in vote buying, political parties could use a broad territorial coverage of their local organizations. The three major parties investigated in this chapter (PSD, PDL, and PNL)

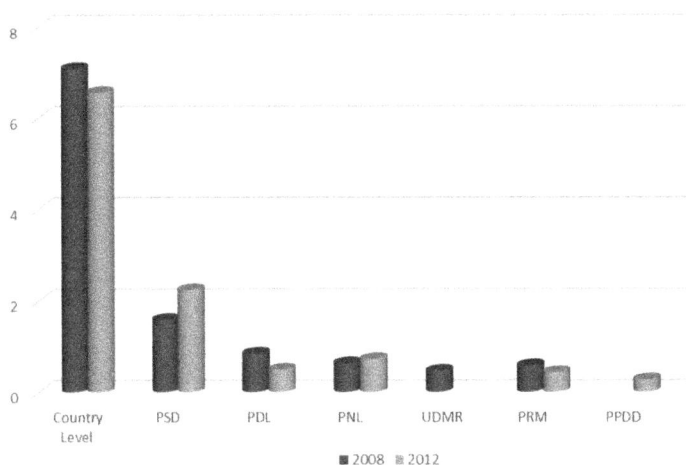

Figure 6.3   Party Membership as Percentage in the Electorate in Romania
Source: Official Party Registry in Romania (2012); Gherghina (2014)

established local organizations in every commune (several villages together), thus ensuring an exhaustive coverage throughout the country.

Vote Buying and Private Donations

This section focuses on the most popular three forms of vote buying: (1) outright vote buying is the payment of money from candidates or parties to the voters in return for votes; (2) treating is the provision of food or alcohol in exchange for votes but can also refer to feasts put on for voters, and (3) conveyance is the transport of voters to polling venues. Combinations between these three forms are likely to occur, for example conveyance is usually accompanied by outright vote buying or treating. To show the incidence of vote-buying practices in Romania we use two sources: media reports and the official number of criminal case files registered at the High Court of Cassation and Justice (Romania's Supreme Court of Justice).

The media reports were used to collect data on vote buying in electoral campaigns and during Election Day for 2008–2012. We used the online and printed versions of five national daily newspapers, considered the most important in terms of subscribers: *Adevarul*, *Cotidianul*, *Evenimentul zilei*, *Gandul*, and *Jurnalul National*.[7] In addition to these newspapers, reports from the Romanian Press Agency (*Mediafax*) were also taken into consideration. Many articles included vote-buying allegations without substantial documentation. We have considered only those cases in which vote buying was either well documented by journalists (i.e. interviews with bribe receivers, photos or videos) or the situation ended up with a criminal case record. As a result, the final dataset includes a total number of 581 articles reporting on various types of vote buying. The articles refer to 136 cases of vote buying with considerable overlap in terms of coverage. Table 6.1 summarizes the vote-buying practices reported in the media indicating the number of practices and the county (territorial administrative division corresponding to constituencies in the previous PR list system) where they took place. Sometimes, more vote-buying activities occurred in the same county and that is why the number of practices does not always coincide with the number of counties in brackets.

Treating appears to be the most popular vote-buying practice among the Romanian parties during electoral campaigns or during election days. It takes various forms from concerts (where food is provided) and feasts thrown for the electorate to bags with gluttony or clothes, free one-day excursions, and services provided for free such as medical consultations or car washing. There are two reasons behind its extensive use. First, parties can argue that these are not vote-buying actions but charity events or treating matching the legal requirements. The legislation allowed until 2012 the distribution of symbolic

Table 6.1   Vote-Buying Practices in the Romanian Elections, 2008–2012

		Treating	Outright Vote Buying	Conveyance
2008 Local	PDL	1 (Bacau)		
	PSD	2 (Bucharest)	1 (Arges)	
2008 Legislative	PDL	4 (Bistrita-Nasaud, Neamt, Prahova, Vrancea)	1 (Constanta)	
	PNL	4 (Calarasi, Ilfov, Ialomita)	3 (Bucharest, Constanta)	1 (Bucharest)
	PSD	8 (Arges, Bacau, Bucharest, Calarasi, Gorj, Ialomita)		
2009 EU	PDL	1 (Bucharest)		3 (Bucharest, Dambovita, Prahova)
	PNL			1 (Bucharest)
	PSD	5 (Bucharest, Dolj, Giurgiu, Ialomita, Iasi)	5 (Bucharest, Ilfov, Vrancea, Galati)	7 (Bistrita-Nasaud, Bucharest, Giurgiu, Ilfov, Olt, Teleorman)
2009 Presidential	PDL	6 (Bucharest, Gorj, Iasi, Prahova, Timis)	2 (Giurgiu, Vrancea)	3 (Bucharest, Dambovita, Suceava)
	PNL	1 (Bucharest)		
	PSD	4 (Arges, Constanta, Maramures, Vrancea)	1 (Constanta)	3 (Bucharest, Ialomita, Ilfov)
2012 Local	PDL	12 (Arad, Bucharest, Constanta, Dambovita, Gorj, Prahova, Sibiu, Valcea)	2 (Bacau, Cluj)	
	PNL + PSD	11 (Arad, Buzau, Olt, Constanta, Galati, Gorj, Hunedoara, Iasi, Prahova)	3 (Constanta, Dolj, Vrancea)	
	PPDD	2 (Arges, Caras-Severin)		
2012 Legislative	PDL	7 (Timis, Vaslui, Neamt, Brasov, Olt, Iasi)	1 (Neamt)	
	PNL + PSD	12 (Cluj, Dolj, Iasi, Prahova, Neamt, Severin, Suceava, Valcea, Vaslui)	1 (Dolj)	2 (Cluj, Teleorman)
	PPDD	3 (Gorj, Iasi)		
2012 Referendum	PNL + PSD	2 (Suceava, Timis)	6 (Alba, Cluj, Bistrita-Nasaud, Bihor)	8 (Bucharest, Dolj, Olt, Severin, Teleorman)

Source: *Adevarul, Cotidianul, Evenimentul zilei, Gandul, Jurnalul National,* and *Mediafax.*

goods with the party logo on them (e.g., T-shirts, lighters, pens) (Gherghina 2013). The new law, adopted several weeks before the 2012 elections, allows parties to distribute goods with a maximum value of 2.5 €. Second, treating is likely to reach more voters at a lower cost than outright vote buying. For example, the costs of a feast thrown for a few hundred voters are significantly lower than money given to each individual voter. Based on media reports, when bought separately, a vote costs on average 12 €.

The numbers in Table 6.1 indicate widespread vote buying throughout the entire territory of the country – there are quite a few counties (out of a total of 41) listed in brackets. When comparing the three major parties, the PNL uses the least vote buying but its activity intensifies as soon as it gets into electoral alliance with the PSD (where + appears in the table). The PNL appears to use more vote buying when in government, for example in 2008 and 2012, compared with the situations when it is in opposition. For the other two parties, the propensity of vote buying is not connected with their government or opposition status. They use this clientelistic linkage in almost every instance. For example, before the 2009 presidential elections the PDL was incumbent and the PSD in the opposition and the intensity of their vote-buying activities does not differ significantly. Similarly, the vote buying does not change when the party gets into opposition. For example, the PSD was in government before the 2004 legislative elections and in opposition before the 2008 general elections and 2009 presidential and EU elections. However, there is no decrease in terms of bribery.

The number of criminal case files registered at the High Court of Cassation and Justice substantiate the empirical evidence from media reports. For all elections and referendums in 2008 and 2009, the Court has analysed a total number of 7,956 Police documented cases of vote buying. For the 2012 local elections there are 2,052 cases, while in the 2012 referendum there were 632 cases (Agerpress 2012).

The money used for vote buying come from private sources and they take two forms: super-fees and donations. A super-fee refers to supersized party membership fees paid by specific members. The average value of a regular fee/month is 2 € and all fees that exceed the value of ten minimum wages should be declared (super-fees). Donations are money coming from private individuals and firms. Our analysis lumps them because quite often CEO's make individual donations in addition to their firm's contribution. This procedure masks the real donation made by a private firm. Table 6.2 summarizes the amounts received by each party between 2008 and 2012; the figures are those reported by parties. It can be easily observed that the amount of both super-fees and donations is considerably high in election years (2008, 2009, and 2012) compared to non-election years. In light of our argument, these hikes in funding during electoral years can be linked to the costs during

Table 6.2 Private Donations Received by the Romanian Political Parties (million €)

	2008		2009		2010		2011		2012	
	Super-Fees	*Donations*	*Super-Fees*	*Donations*	*Super-Fees*	*Donations*	*Super-Fees*	*Donations*	*Super-Fees*	*Donations*
PDL	5.35	8.35	3.30	7.00	0.05	1.10	0.02	1.30	0.21	6.70
PNL	2.15	6.85	0.85	1.50	0.005	0.45	0.002	0.28	0.30	1.30
PSD	4.50	5.90	2.50	2.90	0.07	1.85	0.13	0.16	1.20	4.50
UDMR					0.003	0.10	0.006	0.20	0.001	1.00
PPDD										1.10

Note: In 2012, there is an additional 4.10 million € for the USL (PSD+PNL).
Source: Official Gazette (2009–2013).

campaign and elections. As the three major parties have had relatively good chances to end up in the government coalition (with the exception of 2012), the received amounts are substantial.

The collected data have allowed us to check where the top donors are located. Their territorial dispersion brings evidence linking them to vote buying. Each of the three major parties counts on extensive private contributions in those counties where many vote-buying activities take place (Table 6.1). The PDL has a large amount of donations in Bucharest (around 30 per cent of top donations) and Cluj (10–20 per cent of top donations). The PNL benefits from substantial contributions of private companies based in Bucharest (around 27 per cent of top donations). The PSD has substantial donations from companies in Teleorman (40–51 per cent of top donations) and Constanta (17–97 per cent of top donations).

The Horizontal Linkage: Parties and Private Contractors

Our argument is that some of the private money from Table 6.2 follows the horizontal linkage presented in Figure 6.2. This linkage means that political parties allocate public resources to private contractors through public procurement in exchange for formal or informal contributions. Let us take a close look at this exchange in Romania between 2008 and 2012.

The size and problems of public procurement make it efficient in transforming public funds into private funds. The European Commission estimates the average value of public procurements in the EU Member States at 18 per cent of the country's GDP, while Romania allocates approximately 10 per cent of its GDP (Eurostat, 26.03.2012). The procurement budget is not included in the annual national budget as a stand-alone category, but as part of each public authority's budget making it extremely difficult to investigate it rigorously.

There are two major categories of problems regarding public procurement procedures in Romania. First, there is the issue of proper control mechanisms. Although the Electronic System for Public Procurement (SEAP) is active since 2006, in 2011 only 16 per cent of enterprises in Romania opted to access tender documents and specifications in the electronic procurement system, compared to the EU average of 21 per cent. It is common practice for the open advertisements on SEAP to be discussed or negotiated in person between a representative of the contracting authority and the winning economic operator. While official standards have been set to establish the framework for each contracting authority throughout the year, there are large difference between these principles and what happens in practice. Most of these refer to the allocated budget for different procedures, and to the disregard for the initial inventory of necessities (Romanian Court of Accounts 2008; Ministry of Public Finance 2010). Second, there are preferential criteria set in the tender book with the purpose of favouring certain contractors, in contradiction to legal provisions (Government Decree 34/2006). Another way to exert positive discrimination for certain economic operators is to change the selection criteria during the procedure, leaving 'unwanted' applicants with insufficient time to comply.

To illustrate how the horizontal linkage functions, we have matched the donations of private contractors with their benefits from private procurement. In this case, the benefits come from direct allocation of public contracts, or from open contest public procurement procedures. Table 6.3 includes ten examples for each major party whose activity is mostly based on the direct allocation of public contracts, that is the fastest and safest procedure of employing private contractors by public institutions. The final list of matches between public contracts and party financing is considerably longer. In addition, many donors have indirect benefits from public policy choices that do not necessarily involve the direct transactions, like in the case of public procurement contracts. A special interest in favourable regulation and policies is found in the case of companies from sectors such as energy distribution, agriculture, or cargo activities.

The activity profiles of these companies indicate the extent to which their revenues are based on public procurement contracts. All three parties have many top donors with business activities in the fields of constructions, infrastructure, and energy distribution. It must be noted that the companies made efforts. Some top donors divide their contributions into several payments so that without a proper analysis of the data, the donations would appear modest or of marginal value.

Table 6.3 Top Donors with Public Procurement Contracts (amounts in €)

Party	Company	Value of Donation	Year of Donation	Nature of Activity
PDL	Grup Salubrizare Urbana SA	90,000	2008	Cleaning Services
PDL	Transilvania Construct	65,000	2008	Constructions
PDL	Proserv	60,000	2008	Constructions
PDL	SC Victor Construct	25,000	2008	Constructions
PDL	Industrial Montaj Grup	25,000	2008	Infrastructure
PDL	Transilvania Construct	110,000	2009	Constructions
PDL	Criseni SRL	25,000	2009	Constructions
PDL	SC Victor Construct	25,000	2009	Constructions
PDL	Conrec SA	5,000	2010	Constructions
PDL	Euro Grup DG Transport	6,000	2011	Constructions
PDL	Compact Industrial SA	5,000	2011	Labor Protection
PDL	Pro-Consul Prod SRL	25,000	2012	Constructions
PNL	Carpati Proiect SRL	12,500	2008	Constructions
PNL	SC Universal SA	12,000	2008	Constructions
PNL	M&D Cons Investitii SRL	9, 000	2008	Financial Services
PNL	International SA	40,000	2009	Constructions
PNL	SC Electrosistem SRL	10,500	2009	Electrical Components
PNL	Elita Construct	12,500	2010	Constructions
PNL	M&D Cons Investitii SRL	12,500	2010	Financial Services
PNL	SC Simultan SRL	25,000	2012	Food Delivery
PSD	Modul Proiect SA	125,000	2008	Engineering and Infrastructure
PSD	SC Simca SA	125,000	2008	Constructions
PSD	General Concrete SRL	40,000	2008	Constructions
PSD	Deep Serv 2000 SRL	9,000	2008	Cleaning Services
PSD	SC Artego SA	12,500	2008	Rubber Products
PSD	SC Proinvest SRL	50,000	2009	Constructions
PSD	Argenta SRL	10,000	2010	Infrastructure
PSD	SC Simultan SRL	25,000	2012	Food Delivery
PSD	SC Victor Construct	16,000	2012	Constructions
PSD	SC Tehnodomus	9,300	2012	Constructions

Source: Official Gazette (2009–2013) and Public Procurement announcements.

At the same time, amongst the top donors who benefit from public procurement contracts, some of the private firms contribute to the campaign of more parties (e.g., SC Victor Construct in Table 6.3). When comparing party donations to our main competing political parties, we can see a pattern of multiple donations for 65 out of 1,430 donors, in the period 2007–2013. While the percentage of such multiple donors is relatively small – 4.6 per cent, we see that their total donation value is substantially higher – 14.03 per cent.[8] Taking into consideration that many of these donations are proxies for larger exchange based mechanisms, we can detach a tendency of cartelization, for top donors. Still, as the figures show, this is not a mainstream element of the clientelistic relationships presented here, and the vast majority of donations remain politically focused on a single beneficiary.

The evidence suggests that most of the public procurement problems can be traced to the construction and infrastructure sectors, where the value of the awarded contracts is substantially bigger than in other sectors (Doroftei and Dimulescu 2015). These are also sectors where most of the public works would necessitate agreeable relations with the political awarding authorities across several mandates, and would constitute a strong incentive for political engagement through funding, on behalf of the private contractors.

Our bi-dimensional model of clientelism in which the horizontal level focuses only on resource accumulation shows congruence with the contextual evidence mentioned in the previous paragraphs. Since firms bear little interest in vertical clientelism, that is electoral mobilization, they supply more parties with resources to maximize their chances of getting public procurement. In addition, this procedure is consistent with the earlier discussed cartelization of political parties in Romania. There is high likelihood of inter-party coop- eration at county levels – the place where most public procurement activity is deployed. As a final detail regarding the donors' profile, the PNL receives donations from investment companies. Apart from their direct interest in public procurement, these companies may be a facade for other firms. Public companies might prefer to reroute their donations so that they are not directly linked to the party.

A close look at these donors' economic activity over time reveals two rel- evant aspects for the clientelistic nexus. Many top donors record significant hikes in their activity during electoral years. For example, most donors of the PDL have a turnover increase by ten-fold in the electoral years of 2008–2009 (when the PDL was in government next to the PSD or alone). Also, in the case of the PNL), turnovers of top donors expand significantly during elec- tion years and some of the companies seize to exist after these years. The latter may suggest an instrumental use of private companies with the purpose to channel public funds into party organizations.

CONCLUSIONS

This chapter developed a bi-dimensional model of clientelism that empha- sized the existence of a horizontal linkage between political parties and pri- vate contributors. The core argument was that political parties with minimal organizations reduced the spectrum of clientelistic exchanges to vote buying and engaged in cooperation with external actors to secure the necessary resources. Accordingly, public resources were no longer used in relationship with the electorate, but with private campaign donors. The latter benefited from public procurement procedures and continued to supply financial support to political parties.

This study presented evidence on the relationship between political parties and private contractors, and as such it developed a framework for analysis that moves beyond fragmented relations (i.e., rich donors – political parties, politicians – corrupt contractors, informal electoral exchanges based exclusively on public resources). While the literature has recognized both axes it has never before attempted to correlate all three components, and to trace informal sources of funding with informal electoral exchanges, in an empirical, systematic analysis.

The analysis of Romanian parties between 2008 and 2012 illustrates the functioning of this clientelistic model. Empirical evidence showed how parties rely on a relatively small percentage of members and gradually abandon the idea of personal favours and pork-barrel as clientelistic exchanges. Instead, they focus extensively on vote-buying practices – in the form of outright vote buying, treating, and conveyance – and they require financial resources. Such resources are provided by private firms that receive in exchange preferential access to public procurement. As Romanian politics is cartelized, these exchanges take place at large scale (i.e., the most important political parties) and on iterative basis. In theory, all parties are likely to target these links with private donors to augment their resources. In practice, private donors are likely to establish connections with parties who have governing potential, which are likely to be in a government coalition in the foreseeable future.

Since the investigated case study is only illustrative, the applicability of the model is likely to be broader. We expect it to be testable in settings with (partial) features of cartel politics and limited party organizations. The most important implication of this study is the inclusion in the clientelistic model of a clear linkage between political parties and private contributors. Along these lines, the theoretical contribution lies in the identification of a second clientelistic dimension that deserves further investigation. While we have identified some empirical mechanisms in the Romanian case, future research can focus on the diversity and challenges of horizontal clientelistic linkages in different settings. Furthermore, it can explore the way in which these horizontal connections between parties and private companies shape the vertical linkage between political parties and voters.

NOTES

1. We are grateful to Julia Fleischer, Laurenz Ensser-Jedenastik, Maria Spirova, Saskia Ruth, and Frank de Zwart for their useful comments and constructive criticism on earlier drafts of this chapter.

2. This book chapter has been previously published, in a slightly modified version as Sergiu Gherghina and Clara Volintiru. 2015. 'A new model of clientelism: political parties, public resources, and private contributors', *European Political Science Review*, online first.

3. We see parties as voluntary private associations that perform public roles and thus our argument considers internal party funding as a component of private financing. There are some authors who have differentiated between the two, one of the first being von Beyme (von Beyme 1985) who suggested a typology with three forms of party financing: internal, external, and public.

4. The partial exception to this rule is the Conservative Party (formerly Romanian Humanist Party) that gained parliamentary seats always in alliance with the social democrats.

5. For reasons of simplicity, this chapter uses the current names of the parties.

6. The data for UDMR in 2012 is not available and the PPDD has been created in September 2011. The percentage for the PDL in 2012 is calculated on the basis of twenty-eight out of forty-one territorial organizations, the party did not supply the rest of data.

7. Tabloids were not included in the analysis. Over time, only one of the selected newspapers was biased in reporting vote buying practices: *Jurnalul National* favoured PSD and reported considerably less on its deeds.

8. Based on triangulated information from the author's data base on party donations, and recently collected data by Madalina Doroftei and Valentina Dimulescu, from the Romanian Academic Society.

REFERENCES

Agerpress, 2012. *Procurorii au în lucru peste 2.000 de dosare privind desfășurarea referendumului și a alegerilor locale din 2012 (The Prosecutors Work on more than 2,000 Case Files for the 2012 Local Elections and Referendum).* Available at: http://www.agerpres.ro/justitie/2012/09/10/procurorii-au-in-lucru-peste-2-000-de-dosare-privind-desfasurarea-referendumului-si-a-alegerilor-locale-din-2012-17-00-15.

Ashworth, S. & de Mesquita, B. E., 2006. Delivering the Goods: Legislative Particularism in Different Electoral and Institutional Settings. *Journal of Politics*, 68(1), pp. 168–179.

Bratton, M., 2008. Vote Buying and Violence in Nigerian Election Campaigns. *Electoral Studies*, 27(4), pp. 621–632.

Brusco, V., Nazareno, M. & Stokes, S. C., 2004. Vote Buying in Argentina. *Latin American Research Review*, 39(2), pp. 66–88.

Bryce, J., 1921. *Modern Democracies.* New York: Palgrave Macmillan.

Case, A., 2001. Election Goals and Income Redistribution: Recent Evidence from Albania. *European Economic Review*, 45(3), pp. 405–423.

Chubb, Judith. 1981. "The Social Bases of an Urbino Political Machine: The Case of Palermo." *Political Science Quarterly* 96(1): 107–25.

Chubb, Judith. 1983. *Patronage, Power and Poverty in Southern Italy: A Tale of Two Cities*. Cambridge: Cambridge University Press.

Caciagli, Mario. 2006. "The Long Life of Clientelism in Southern Italy." In *Comparing Political Corruption and Clientelism*, edited by Junichi Kawata, 157–70. London: Routledge.

Cassel, C. A. & Luskin, R. C., 1988. Simple Explanations of Turnout Decline. *The American Political Science Review*, 82(4), pp. 1321–1330.

Cruz, Cesi, and Philip Keefer. 2015. "Political Parties, Clientelism, and Bureaucratic Reform." *Comparative Political Studies* 48(14): 1942–1973.

Dalton, R. J. & Wattenberg, M. P., 2000. Unthinkable Democracy: Political Change in Advanced Industrial Democracies. In R. J. Dalton & M. P. Wattenberg, eds. *Parties without Partisans: Political Change in Advanced Industrial Democracies*. Oxford: Oxford University Press, pp. 3–16.

Eisenstadt, S. N., and Luis Roniger. 1984. *Patrons, Clients and Friends Relations and the Structure of Trust in Society*. Cambridge: Cambridge University Press.

Ewing, K., 1992. *Money, Politics and Law*. Oxford: Clarendon Press.

Ferejohn, J., 1974. *Pork Barrel Politics*. Stanford, CA: Stanford University Press.

Fisher, J., 2002. Next Step: State Funding for the Parties? *Political Quarterly*, 73(4), pp. 392–399.

Flickinger, R. S. & Studlar, D. T., 1992. The Disappearing Voters? Exploring Declining Turnout in Western European Elections. *West European Politics*, 15(2), pp. 1–16.

Freidenberg, F. & Levitsky, S., 2006. Informal Party Organizations in Latin America. In G. Helmke & S. Levitsky, eds. *Informal Institutions and Democracy in Latin America: Understanding the Rules of the Game*. Washington, DC: Johns Hopkins University Press, pp. 178–197.

Gellner, Ernest, and John Waterbury. 1977. *Patrons and Clients in Mediterranean Societies*. London: Duckworth.

Gherghina, S., 2013. Going for a Safe Vote: Electoral Bribes in Post-Communist Romania. *Debatte: Journal of Contemporary Central and Eastern Europe*, 21(2–3), pp. 143–164.

Gherghina, S., 2014. *Party Organization and Electoral Volatility in Central and Eastern Europe: Enhancing Voter Loyalty*. London: Routledge.

Gherghina, S. & Soare, S., 2013. From TV to Parliament: Populism and Communication in the Romanian 2012 Elections. *SSRN Electronic Journal*. Available at: http://papers.ssrn.com/abstract=2370006 [Accessed February 4, 2014].

Gray, M. & Caul, M., 2000. Declining Voter Turnout in Advanced Industrial Democracies, 1950 to 1997: The Effects of Declining Group Mobilization. *Comparative Political Studies*, 33(9), pp. 1091–1122.

Hopkin, J., 2001. A 'Southern Model' of Electoral Mobilisation?: Clientelism and Electoral Politics in Post-Franco Spain. *West European Politics*, 24(1), pp. 115–136.

Hopkin, J., 2006a. Clientelism and Party Politics. In R.S. Katz & W. Crotty, eds. *Handbook of Party Politics*. London: Sage Publications Ltd., pp. 406–412.

Hopkin, J., 2006b. *Conceptualizing Political Clientelism: Political Exchange and Democratic Theory*. Paper prepared for the APSA Annual Meeting, Philadelphia.

Hopkin, Jonathan, and Caterina Paolucci. 1999. "The Party as Business Firm: Cases From Spain and Italy." *European Journal of Political Research* 35(2): 307–39.

Johnston, R. & Pattie, C., 1995. The Impact of Spending on Party Constituency Campaigns in Recent British General Elections. *Party Politics*, 1(2), pp. 261–273.

Katz, R. S., 1986. Preference Voting in Italy: Votes of Opinion, Belonging or Exchange. *Comparative Political Studies*, 18(2), pp. 229–249.

Katz, R. S., 2011. Political Parties. In *Comparative Politics*. Oxford: Oxford University Press, pp. 219–236.

Kitschelt, Herbert. 2000. "Linkages between Citizens and Politicians in Democratic Polities." *Comparative Political Studies* 33(6–7): 845–79.

Kitschelt, H. & Wilkinson, S. I. eds., 2007. Patrons, Clients, and Policies: *Patterns of Democratic Accountability and Political Competition*. Cambridge: Cambridge University Press.

Lapuente, Victor, and Marina Nistotskaya. 2009. "To the Short-Sighted Victor Belong the Spoils: Politics and Merit Adoption in Comparative Perspective." *Governance* 22(3): 431–58.

Lewis, P. G., 2008. Political Parties. In S. White, J. Batt, & P. G. Lewis, eds. *Developments in Central and Eastern European Politics 4*. Houndmills: Palgrave Macmillan, pp. 174–192.

Lyrintzis, Christos. 1987. "The Power of Populism: The Greek Case." *European Journal of Political Research* 15(6): 667–86.

Mair, P. & van Biezen, I., 2001. Party Membership in Twenty European Democracies, 1980–2000. *Party Politics*, 7(1), pp. 5–21.

Manacorda, Marco, Edward Miguel, and Andrea Vigorito. 2011. "Government Transfers and Political Support." *American Economic Journal: Applied Economics* 3 (3): 1–28.

Ministry of Public Finance, 2010. *Raport Privind Activitatea de Audit Intern Din Sectorul Public (Report about the Activity of Internal Audit in the Public Sector)*. Available at: http://discutii.mfinante.ro/static/10/Mfp/audit/Rap_anual_audit2010. pdf.

Nassmacher, K.-H., 1993. Comparing Party and Campaign Finance in Western Democracies. In A. B. Gunlicks, ed. *Campaign and Party Finance in North America and Western Europe*. Boulder, CO: Westview Press, pp. 233–267.

Neumann, S. ed., 1956. *Modern Political Parties*. Chicago: University of Chicago Press.

Piattoni, S. ed., 2001. *Clientelism, Interests, and Democratic Representation: The European Experience in Historical and Comparative Perspective*. Cambridge: Cambridge University Press.

Pinto-Duschinsky, M., 2002. Financing Politics: A Global View. *Journal of Democracy*, 13(4), pp. 69–86.

Romanian Court of Accounts, 2008. *Raportul Public Anual (Annual Public Report)*. Available at: www.curteadeconturi.ro/sites/ccr/RO/default.aspx.

Schaffer, F. C. ed., 2007. *Elections for Sale: The Causes and Consequences of Vote Buying*. Boulder, CO: Lynne Rienner Publishers.

Schattschneider, E. E., 1942. *Political Parties*. New York: Holt, Riehart, and Winston.

Shepsle, K. A. & Weingast, B. R., 1994. Positive Theories of Congressional Institutions. *Legislative Studies Quarterly*, 19(2), pp. 149–179.

Spirova, M., 2007. *Political Parties in Post-Communist Societies: Formation, Persistence, and Change*. Houndmills: Palgrave Macmillan.

Stefan, L., Gherghina, S. & Chiru, M., 2012. We All Agree that We Disagree Too Much: Attitudes of Romanian MPs Towards Party Discipline. *East European Politics*, 28(2), pp. 180–192.

Stokes, Susan C. 2005. "Perverse Accountability: A Formal Model of Machine Politics with Evidence from Argentina." *American Political Science Review* 99(03): 315–25.

Stokes, S. C. et al., 2013. *Brokers, Voters, and Clientelism: The Puzzle of Distributive Politics*. Cambridge: Cambridge University Press.

Scott, James C. 1972. "Patron-Client Politics and Political Change in Southeast Asia." *American Political Science Review* 66(1): 91–113.

Szczerbiak, A., 2001. *Poles Together? Emergence and Development of Political parties in Post-Communist Poland*. Budapest: CEU Press.

van Biezen, I., 2003. *Political Parties in New Democracies*. Houndmills: Palgrave Macmillan.

van Biezen, I., 2004. Political Parties as Public Utilities. *Party Politics*, 10(6), pp. 701–722.

van Biezen, I. & Kopecký, P., 2007. The State and the Parties: Public Funding, Public Regulation and Rent-Seeking in Contemporary Democracies. *Party Politics*, 13(2), pp. 235–254. Available at: http://ppq.sagepub.com/content/13/2/235.short [Accessed February 12, 2014].

van Biezen, I., Mair, P. & Poguntke, T., 2012. Going, Going, . . . Gone? The Decline of Party Membership in Contemporary Europe. *European Journal of Political Research*, 51(1), pp. 24–56.

von Beyme, K., 1985. *Political Parties in Western Democracies*. New York: St. Martin's Press.

Webb, P. & White, S. eds., 2007. *Party Politics in New Democracies*. Oxford: Oxford University Press.

Weingrod, Alex. 1968. "Patrons, Patronage, and Political Parties." *Comparative Studies in Society and History* 10(4): 377–400.

Weldon, S., 2006. Downsize My Polity? The Impact of Size on Party Membership and Member Activism. *Party Politics*, 12(4), pp. 467–481.

Williams, R., 2000. Aspects of Party Finance and Political Corruption. In R. Williams, ed. *Party Finance and Political Corruption*. New York: Palgrave Macmillan, pp. 1–13.

Chapter Seven

Managing the Budgetary Commons by Programmatic and Clientelist Parties

Evidence from the European Union

Juha Ylisalo

INTRODUCTION

The effects of fragmented decision-making on economic policy outcomes have become a prominent topic in contemporary works on public finance, distributive politics, and party systems. The concept of fragmentation has often been the starting point in analyses of the origins of the fiscal problems. Consider the following setting. A number of actors, for example political parties, make a decision on the allocation of tax funds. Decision-makers seek to serve their target populations by channelling funds to policies those populations prioritize while letting others bear most of the costs. An increased number of decision-makers implies that more target groups are being served and a larger fraction of the costs are externalized, the amounts of resources being channelled to targeted spending becoming increasingly large. Hence the concept of the budgetary or fiscal common-pool problem: like natural resources may be destroyed when too many vessels are brought to a fishery or too many animals are brought to a pasture (Hardin 1968), political decision-makers may end up overburdening the tax base when each of them seeks to satisfy demands arising from narrow segments of the society.

One of the alleged manifestations of the commons problem is the growth of the public sector. As spending decisions are made with group interests in mind and without internalizing costs in full, the public economy becomes larger relative to the national economy, the process becoming more pronounced as the number of actors at the decision-making table grows. The emphasis in this literature has been on the interactions between parties as well as on formal rules whereas the linkages between parties and the rest of the society have scarcely received attention. In what follows, it is argued that the types of political linkages that are prevalent in a society affect the degree to

131

which this process characterizes a political system (see also Fukuyama 2014). Specifically, the relationship between the number of government parties, indicating the number of 'appropriators' in the budgetary commons, and changes in the level of public spending is at its strongest when clientelist linkages are prevalent. Conversely, changes in public spending are explained by the programmatic pledges that government parties have presented before elections, rather than by the number of parties, where clientelist practices are rare.

An analysis of data from European Union member states from 1990 to 2012 shows that clientelist practices, operationalized as the extent of vote buying in elections, condition the effects that both the number of government parties and the programmatic 'colour' of the cabinet have on changes in the level of government spending. However, analysing two sub-groups of countries, those with and without communist past, reveals differences in the political determinants of spending. There is very weak evidence of the number of government parties affecting spending in the countries with no communist legacy. However, even in those countries vote buying, where and when it exists, tends to dampen the spending consequences of party programmes. In the post-communist countries, in turn, the number of government parties does partially explain changes in spending levels alongside party programmes. An examination of interaction effects shows that the effect of coalition size disappears when clientelism does not characterize party-society linkages.

'FRAGMENTED' DECISION-MAKING

Weingast et al.'s (1981) model of pork-barrel politics in an American-style legislature is often cited as the first formalization of the budgetary common-pool problem, albeit Weingast et al. did not use the concept themselves. In Weingast et al.'s model, a legislature consisting of representatives from single-member districts decides on the allocation of 'projects' to geographical units. While each legislator internalizes the full benefit of spending targeted at his or her district, he or she only internalizes a fraction of the cost; most of the cost is borne by other districts due to general taxation. Therefore, the amount of district-specific spending each legislator perceives as optimal exceeds the socially optimal level. Weingast et al. assume that what they call the norm of universalism applies in the legislature so that each district is entitled to projects. As a result, total spending exceeds the spending that would maximize the net benefit of the society. Moreover, this inefficiency increases with the number of geographical units represented.

Weingast et al.'s argument has been applied to parliamentary systems as well. Scartascini and Crain (2002) assume that the norm of universalism also applies in the legislatures of parliamentary countries and that parties seek to channel funds to the groups that support them. They accordingly argue that the level of public spending tends to increase with the partisan fragmentation of parliaments. Bawn and Rosenbluth (2006; see also Persson et al. 2007) argue that electoral accountability encourages parties to prioritize certain issues and group interests and that these priorities become narrower as the number of parties increases. This makes parties' target populations smaller relative to the total population and consequently parties seek to externalize a larger share of the costs of spending targeted at their constituencies. These costs are not fully internalized in inter-party bargaining and therefore they are reflected in the level of government spending, the mismatch between the internalized benefits and costs being the larger the more parties take part in the bargaining process. Consequently, public spending increases with the number of parties in government.

Recent work has started to look at factors that may condition this relationship (e.g., Bäck et al. 2017). Especially rules governing the budgetary process have received attention in this respect (Martin and Vanberg 2013), and formal rules more generally have been extensively studied as possible solutions to budgetary common-pool problems (Hallerberg et al. 2009; de Haan et al. 2013). Others have argued that restrictions of electoral competitiveness and barriers to entry to the political arena can be justified on efficiency grounds (Lizzeri and Persico 2005). Although the aforementioned studies are concerned with the consequences of representative politics, they have very little to say about the context in which representation takes place. Instead, the relevant variation is assumed to be in formal institutions, explicit rules, and procedural norms. One of the few exceptions is Elgie and McMenamin (2008) who argue that party system fragmentation affects the occurrence of deficits – another alleged manifestation of the common-pool problem (Velasco 2000) – in established democracies but not in new ones. Elgie and McMenamin claim that this is so because in established democracies linkages between parties and the society are institutionalized and therefore the measurable characteristics of the party system are relevant in the first place. This argument also presupposes that it is electoral accountability that drives the relationship between party system fragmentation and apparently adverse fiscal policy outcomes. However, the assumption of a single kind of electoral accountability, applying in all political systems, will be relaxed in the following sections.

WHY CLIENTELISM AFFECTS THE MANAGEMENT OF THE BUDGETARY COMMONS

Formal rules have gained considerable attention and according to the literature they also appear to perform largely as expected, albeit their truly exogenous effects have been called into question (Heinemann et al. 2018; Rommerskirchen 2015). However, all variation in the dynamics of joint decision-making by multiple parties need not go back to formal rules and institutions. The relationships of decision-makers with actors and groups that are not directly involved in decision-making may also be relevant. A basic distinction can be drawn between programmatic linkages and clientelism (Kitschelt 2000), the latter referring to the exchange of selective favours controlled by politicians for political support. In short, the prevalence of clientelistic linkages is an important feature of an environment where joint decision-making by multiple parties is likely to have properties of common-pool problems that manifest themselves as spending increases.

Existing works on fragmented decision-making tend to give little weight to ideological and programmatic motivations, and they typically enter regression equations in the form of control variables that are not discussed at any length. However, functioning programmatic linkages may provide an effective antidote to overspending problems emerging from joint decision-making. It is sensible to assume that people are interested in having collective goods (infrastructure, education, health care, welfare services, etc.) provided by the state, goods that because of their nature as public goods (such as national defence) are not provided by the market or goods that have properties of 'merit goods' (Musgrave 1957) that should be consumed by everyone independently of purchasing power (such as basic education). Given the problems of aggregating individual preferences into collective ones, one need not maintain that even under the best feasible circumstances representative politics would lead to the optimal or efficient provision of such goods. But if the linkages between political parties, the main players of representative politics in virtually any contemporary democracy, and the public are based on programmatic competition, parties fulfil their task as partial solutions to problems of social choice by offering a limited number of relatively coherent alternatives (Kitschelt 2000).

If this is the case, the appeal of parties' publicized programmatic goals among the public should determine which parties gain decision-making power, and those goals should furthermore be reflected in actual policy outputs. In multi-party systems, policy outputs are not usually determined by one single party as policies are more typically formulated in an inter-party bargaining process, such as in negotiations on government formation and in within-cabinet negotiations during the government term (Powell 2000). In so far as programmatic competition reduces the dimensionality of the policy space so that it can be approximated by the conventional left-right dimension, the bargaining outcome should be some combination of parties' positions on that dimension. In other words, as parties have to take stances in a shared policy space, the likely outcome of their interactions is a weighted average of their stances, rather than a summation of bids made on different dimensions (a conclusion suggested by well-known bargaining models, e.g., Baron and Ferejohn 1989). Hence, it is less plausible that the number of parties or the dispersion of programmatic stances affect the level of spending, as programmatic stances represented by different points in the policy space draw the bargaining outcome in opposing directions. This can be contrasted with the inherently multi-dimensional bargaining process that Bawn and Rosenbluth (2006) identify as the source of inefficiencies.

This is more likely to correspond to empirical reality when parties seek to attract support not by offering programmatic packages that can be more or less neatly arranged along a limited number of policy dimensions but instead by engaging in conditional exchanges with certain groups. While programmatic parties may also seek to channel benefits to certain groups, they cannot make benefits conditional on electoral behaviour as policies need to apply to everyone satisfying certain preconditions. Clientelist parties, in turn, target their efforts more narrowly and exclusively (Kitschelt and Wilkinson 2007). If public expenditure and employment are used as means of voter mobilization, the provision of services and the use of government funds are likely to become increasingly inefficient. By concentrating their efforts on certain groups, the behaviour of political parties more readily corresponds to the assumptions that underlie models of fragmented decision-making, which in turn is translated into greater inefficiencies in inter-party bargaining. Distributive aspects that become visible in the connection between coalition sizes and spending may be present when political linkages are largely programmatic, but that effect is likely to be much stronger when clientelist practices are used.

Creating and upholding clientelist networks may be expensive, but this need not be the only source of inefficiencies related to multi-party decision-making in an environment characterized by clientelist exchanges. As the basis of keeping parties accountable on programmatic grounds is weakened, non-programmatic distributive spending going to special interests not directly involved in clientelist electoral mobilization may increase as well. In so far as clientelism is related to partial, low-quality state institutions and their correlates, such as bribery and nepotism (Rothstein 2011), special interests are plausibly able to intrude into the political system and extract resources to their own benefit. The feasibility of rent-seeking practices combined with the diffusion of responsibility in multi-party decision-making is another source of inefficiencies that may drive distributive spending upwards with the number of parties. When power is shared by a number of parties, they have more possibilities to utilize the information asymmetries between themselves and the public when making decisions that imply the waste of resources or are otherwise harmful to the society (Kiss 2009; see also O'Dwyer 2004).

One might ask how relevant clientelist exchanges are when the aim is to explain fiscal policy outcomes in the member states of the European Union. Clientelist practices are often argued to fade away with economic development (Stokes et al. 2013), and in this sense modern-day Europe should not provide them with fertile ground. However, there is evidence that such practices still thrive in some parts of the continent (e.g., Gherghina and Volintiru 2017), especially in the post-communist area. As will be shown in the next section, new data based on expert surveys suggests that the western and eastern parts of the union indeed differ from each other in this respect, but also that there is variation among the countries within the post-communist area as well as among the rest of the countries. However, in the post-communist area distributive aspects of politics can be assumed to be generally stronger, not all of these pressures going back to clientelist exchanges. Those countries arguably inherited dense networks of special interests from the communist era (Olson 2000), and in new democracies incentives and possibilities for rent-seeking tend to be more abundant than in established democracies (van Biezen and Kopecký 2007).

We can now summarize our expectations about the spending consequences of the number of government parties, cabinets' programmatic outlooks, and clientelism. The number of government parties is expected to be positively associated with spending, but the effect should be stronger in the post-communist area. Moreover, the effect should be the stronger the more prevalent clientelist practices are. The programmatic outlook of the cabinet, defined as its location on the left-right dimension, is expected to affect spending so that leftist cabinets spend more than rightist ones. However, this effect is expected to become weaker as clientelist exchanges become more common.

DATA AND METHODS

The data covers most of the countries that were members of the European Union at the time of writing, Luxembourg and Malta being excluded due to the lack of data (see below). This means that the data includes mature Western European capitalist democracies as well as post-communist countries whose democratic regimes were very young at the start of the time series. To account for this difference in historical legacies, three datasets are analysed: one that consists of twenty-six countries from 1990 or 1995 to 2012, one that covers the 'old' member states that joined the EU in 1995 or earlier as well as Cyprus, and one that is composed of countries that were ruled by communist regimes until the late 1980s or early 1990s. The time series end in 2012, when most EU countries adopted the so-called Fiscal Compact that contains new regulations on allowable fiscal policy outcomes.

Data on almost all of the economic variables are available for the post-communist countries only from 1995 onwards, and therefore this is the earliest year when any of the countries in the area enter the analysis. The countries are listed in Table 7.1, alongside the years for which data on all variables are available. Table 7.1 also reports the average number of parties in government per country as well as the average vote buying and government left-right scores (defined later). To form an impression about differences in vote buying across countries, it suffices to know that smaller values indicate that vote buying is more prevalent. As for the left-right score, larger values indicate that programmatic outlooks are more rightist. As for coalition sizes, there are no

Table 7.1 Countries, Years, and the Average Values of Key Variables in the Dataset

Country	Years	Average Number of Government Parties	Average Left-Right Location of the Cabinet	Average Level of Vote Buying
Non-Post-Communist Countries				
Austria	1990–2012	1.95	4.37	2.76
Belgium	1990–2012	4.24	−9.02	2.50
Cyprus	1997–2012	3.04	−4.61	1.35
Denmark	1990–2012	2.15	9.60	3.05
Finland	1990–2012	4.20	−9.24	2.68
France	1990–2012	2.10	−9.57	2.59
Germany	1990–2012	2.01	5.68	3.46
Greece	1990–2012	0.98	−7.96	1.55
Ireland	1990–2012	2.27	−3.99	2.58
Italy	1990–2012	3.40	9.98	0.85
The Netherlands	1990–2012	2.41	−0.86	2.75
Portugal	1990–2012	1.19	−5.36	2.42
Spain	1990–2012	1.00	−9.61	2.69
Sweden	1990–2012	2.21	2.71	2.58
The United Kingdom	1990–2012	1.11	12.65	3.24
Post-Communist Countries				
Bulgaria	1995–2012	1.91	2.80	−0.40
Croatia	2002–2012	3.04	2.25	1.73
Czech Republic	1995–2012	2.30	6.29	2.24
Estonia	1995–2012	2.40	4.92	2.38
Hungary	1995–2012	2.10	1.81	1.43
Latvia	1995–2010	4.19	3.06	1.70
Lithuania	1995–2012	2.82	8.08	1.23
Poland	1995–2012	1.96	4.16	1.65
Romania	1995–2012	3.09	1.84	−0.35
Slovakia	1995–2012	3.32	1.98	2.04
Slovenia	1995–2012	3.42	1.92	1.86

great differences between the country groups. When it comes to the programmatic orientation of cabinets, the variation between countries is smaller in the post-communist area where country averages tend to be relatively close to the centrist zero position. The rest of the countries show greater variation, and there are countries where governments have on average been clearly to the right or to the left of the centre. Lastly, vote buying tends to be more prevalent in the post-communist area, albeit there is notable variation. In the rest of the countries, vote buying appears to be rare although even in this group some countries exhibit quite low vote-buying scores.

The dependent variable is the *annual change of government spending* defined as the total outlays of general government measured as a percentage of gross domestic product. The data is obtained from the OECD and Eurostat databases via Armingeon et al. (2015). Total spending which includes all spending categories is used because we have no *a priori* expectation about how different spending categories are treated in political decision-making. For example, non-programmatic distribution can take the form of recruitments in the production of government services but it can also be based on transfers to certain groups of citizens or on subsidies to businesses.

The *lagged level of spending* is included in the set of regressors with the assumption that as the level gets higher, the cost of already existing programmes makes it more difficult to adopt new ones. Moreover, a higher spending level means that a larger number of demands for spending are already satisfied, and demands for new spending are fewer. It can thus be expected that spending at $t-1$ has a negative effect on the change of spending between $t-1$ and t.

The variable measuring the extent of clientelist practices is obtained from the Varieties of Democracy dataset (version 6; Coppedge et al. 2016). The variable used is *election vote buying* which measures the extent to which money or gifts were distributed to influence the vote choices of individuals, families, or small groups. The variable is constructed so that smaller values indicate the prevalence of vote buying whereas larger values indicate that such practices are less common. The vote-buying variable is available for election years. For other years, the value referring to the previous election year is used. The variable is suitable for the present purposes as it explicitly does not measure the prevalence of pork-barrel politics and other distributive policies that belong to the set of phenomena to be explained (Coppedge et al. 2016). The variable is time-variant, albeit the amount of variation differs across countries. As the variable is not available for two EU countries, Luxembourg and Malta, these countries are not included in the analysis.

The *number of government parties* is the number of parties that Döring and Manow (2015) identify as cabinet parties. The expected sign of the variable is positive, provided that vote buying is prevalent. The *left-right* orientation of the cabinet, which can also be called its programmatic centre of masses, is the weighted mean of cabinet parties' left-right scores where parties' shares of the total number of parliamentary seats held by cabinet parties are used as weights. This corresponds to the expectation that when politics is programmatic, the bargaining outcome is a weighted combination of parties' stances, as highlighted above. Left-right scores are obtained from the Comparative Manifesto Project data (Volkens et al. 2015), which is especially suitable for the present purposes as it is based on material that parties publicize prior to elections and therefore reflects what parties say they will do when they are in office. Specifically, Comparative Manifesto Project data seeks to measure the priorities parties give to a number of issues, the left-right score being a composite score that covers several issues. Expert surveys are another way of assessing party positions. However, scores so obtained may be more influenced by what parties actually do and therefore they are not as good at operationalizing the theoretical concept of interest, parties' programmatic statements. The theoretical maximum and minimum values of the left-right score are –100 and 100, larger values indicating a more rightist programme. Parties that prioritize in their programmes 'rightist' issues, such as economic orthodoxy and the limitation of social services, are likely to restrict spending while the opposite applies to parties that prioritize 'leftist' issues like the expansion of education and social services. Hence, the expected sign of the variable is negative provided that it is significant in the first place, that is when vote buying is not prevalent.

Left-right scores are not available for all cabinet parties. Most often such parties are small, and they would have negligible effect on the weighted average of all government parties in any case and therefore they have been omitted in the calculations. In particular, the Manifesto data only includes parties that have won seats in the parliament, and as parties that have no parliamentary representation sometimes participate in the cabinet, their weight would be zero in any case. When calculating the centre of masses, the most recent left-right score is used for each party. In most cases, this is the score of the party in the previous election. If a given party is not assigned a score, the score from the election preceding the previous election is used instead, if available. Sometimes the instabilities of the party system lead to a situation where left-right scores cannot be assigned to any cabinet party or a considerable subset of them even after looking at past elections. Such country-years had to be omitted entirely.

Caretaker cabinets lack the mandate to enact major policy changes, and for such cabinets both cabinet-related variables are set to zero: there are zero parties in government and the programmatic centre of masses is exactly centrist. *Caretaker time,* the fraction of a year such a cabinet was in office, is controlled for. The *effective number of parliamentary parties* is included to control for the partisan fragmentation of the parliament. The variable is the familiar Laakso-Taagepera (1979) index $1/\sum_{i=1}^{n} s_i^2$ where s_i is the seat share of party i. The index was calculated based on election results reported in Döring and Manow (2015).

The values of political variables often change during the year, typically following an election. When the partisan composition of the cabinet changes, all cabinet-related variables are weighted by the fraction of the year the cabinet was in office, the weights being obtained from Döring and Manow (2015). The same applies to the effective number of parliamentary parties, where weights are the fractions of the year that different parliaments were in office. As the budget of a given year is typically passed the year before, in the analyses all political variables are lagged by one year.

The regression models contain a set of variables that are likely to affect government spending. The fluctuation of the business cycle may make spending change because of both so-called automatic stabilizers and governments' deliberate efforts to smooth the cycle. Therefore, the *real GDP change* is controlled for. Also controlled for is the annual *change of the unemployment rate* which reflects business cycle effects but also structural changes in the economy. The lagged level of *government debt* is controlled as existing debt can put downward pressure on new spending and encourage governments to balance the budget by cutting tax-financed programmes. *Inflation* is included because it may affect public finances in various ways. It can decrease the real value of government debt and increase nominal tax revenue, both of which increase the government's room for manoeuvre, but it may also make it more difficult to provide programmes on conventional levels as their costs increase. These variables are obtained from the OECD Economic Outlook database, Eurostat, and AMECO via Armingeon et al. (2015).

Countries have adopted several kinds of rules that set targets and limits on fiscal policy and regulate the decision-making process with the intention of improving the sustainability of public finances. To capture the effects of such rules, two variables are included in the regressions. One is the dummy variable *Maastricht* whose value is one from 1992 or the year of EU accession onwards and zero otherwise. The variable captures the effects of the fiscal policy rules contained in the Maastricht Treaty, or more formally the Treaty on European Union signed in 1992, the most notable rules being the 3 per cent deficit ceiling and the 60 per cent debt ceiling. Another variable is the *fiscal rule index* produced by the European Commission (2015). The index assigns to each country annually a numerical value indicating the stringency of the numerical budgetary rules in place, larger values indicating more comprehensive and stringent rules. The index is available for all countries included in the analysis from 1990 onward.

Descriptive statistics are reported in Table 7.2. Preliminary diagnostic tests reveal that a number of complications that often arise in the analysis of time-series cross-sectional data cannot be ruled out. In order to account for panel heteroscedasticity and contemporaneous correlation, panel-corrected standard errors are used in tests of statistical significance (Beck and Katz 1995). The data also exhibits significant unit effects, and therefore fixed country effects are included in all models by using within-unit transformation.

The regression models contain the annual change of spending as the dependent variable and the lagged level of spending as one of the explanatory variables. Combined with unit effects, this may give rise to bias (Achen 2000). However, in the present case this risk is not considered too large when compared with the risk of omitted variable bias following the exclusion of the lagged level variable whose inclusion has a theoretical justification. Moreover, preliminary Wooldridge tests suggest that the exclusion of the lagged level variable introduces serial correlation. However, to make sure that the results are not forged by bias caused by the lagged level variable, a series of Prais-Winsten regressions with an AR1 error structure were estimated whereby the lagged level of spending was excluded. The results are substantively in line with those reported below. They are not included due to space considerations but are available from the author upon request.

As the hypotheses presented at the end of the previous section are conditional, of the type that the effect of one variable depends on the value of another, interaction models need to be estimated. To make the results more informative, the marginal effects of the variables of interest are estimated across empirically relevant values of the conditioning variable and presented in the form of marginal-effect plots (Brambor et al. 2006).

Table 7.2 Descriptive Statistics

Variable	Mean	Std. Dev.	Min.	Max.
Number of Government Parties	2.47	1.31	0.00	8.35
Left-Right	0.70	12.83	−36.67	37.66
Vote Buying	2.03	0.95	−0.79	3.73
Caretaker	0.02	0.11	0.00	1.00
Effective Number of Parliamentary Parties	4.00	1.46	2.07	9.05
Spending	45.76	7.03	30.50	70.21
GDP Change	2.59	3.46	−14.81	11.74
Unemployment	8.84	4.08	1.60	24.80
Debt	60.37	32.82	4.30	166.01
Inflation	7.08	46.31	−4.48	1058.37
Fiscal Rule Index	0.06	0.95	−1.01	3.05

RESULTS

Regression results are reported in Table 7.3. The table contains six models, that is an additive and interaction model for three groups of countries: all twenty-six EU countries for which data is available, the group of fifteen countries consisting of the so-called old member states and Cyprus, and the group of eleven post-communist member states.

The general impression from Table 7.3 is such that the existing level of spending, changes in the gross domestic product, inflation, and the fiscal rules countries have adopted are the most consistent predictors of changes in the spending level. Unemployment and the Maastricht treaty also affect spending in the member states that have no communist heritage. As expected, the effects of political variables differ across the sets of countries. In the additive model that includes all twenty-six countries (column I), the coefficient on the number of government parties has a positive sign, suggesting that spending indeed increases with the number of parties in government, but the coefficient is statistically insignificant. The programmatic centre of masses also has the expected effect which is furthermore statistically significant so that more rightist governments tend to reduce spending. Contrary to what could be expected, the effective number of parliamentary parties has a statistically significant effect with a negative sign, indicating that increased partisan fragmentation in the parliament puts downward pressure on spending. When the number of government parties is interacted with vote buying (column II), its coefficient increases in size and becomes statistically significant. However, as this coefficient only tells the effect when the value of the vote-buying variable is zero and the interaction term, despite having the expected negative sign, lacks statistical significance, it is premature to conclude that the two interact or condition the effects of each other. The coefficient on the programmatic centre of masses also performs as expected as its sign becomes statistically indiscernible from zero when vote buying is prevalent (i.e., when the value of the respective variable is zero). However, the coefficient on the interaction term composed of the left-right variable and vote buying is practically zero, so there is no evidence of an interaction effect.

When the set of non-post-communist countries is considered, none of the political variables have effects that would be statistically indiscernible from zero in the additive model (column III), albeit the coefficients on the number of government parties and the left-right centre of masses have the expected signs. In the interaction model (column IV), only the left-right variable is statistically significant, but now with a positive sign. This indicates that when vote buying is pervasive (i.e., the value of the vote-buying variable is zero), the effect of the programmatic orientation of the cabinet is outright contrary to what should be expected. However, the negative coefficient on the interaction

Table 7.3   Regression Results

	All Countries		Old Member States and Cyprus		Post-Communist Countries	
	I	*II*	*III*	*IV*	*V*	*VI*
Number of Government Parties	0.184 (0.142)	0.442 (0.238)*	0.056 (0.159)	0.146 (0.313)	0.507 (0.230)**	0.945 (0.329)***
Left-Right	-0.030 (0.009)***	-0.030 (0.024)	-0.010 (0.008)	0.070 (0.032)**	-0.052 (0.022)**	-0.037 (0.030)
Vote Buying	-0.166 (0.407)	0.445 (0.621)	-0.435 (0.424)	-0.563 (0.721)	-0.182 (0.704)	0.905 (0.806)
Caretaker	1.330 (1.385)	1.118 (1.400)	0.956 (1.656)	1.412 (1.666)	0.968 (1.912)	-0.207 (2.052)
Effective Number of Parliamentary Parties	-0.298 (0.162)*	-0.313 (0.161)*	-0.196 (0.191)	-0.227 (0.186)	-0.786 (0.285)***	-0.859 (0.277)***
Number of Government Parties × Vote Buying		-0.173 (0.124)		-0.027 (0.148)		-0.381 (0.181)**
Left-Right × Vote Buying		0.001 (0.010)		-0.032 (0.013)**		-0.007 (0.021)
Lagged Spending Level	-0.374 (0.035)***	-0.371 (0.035)***	-0.293 (0.042)***	-0.305 (0.041)***	-0.597 (0.052)***	-0.587 (0.051)***
GDP Change	-0.351 (0.038)***	-0.350 (0.037)***	-0.397 (0.064)***	-0.392 (0.063)***	-0.329 (0.044)***	-0.331 (0.043)***
Unemployment Change	0.085 (0.093)	0.091 (0.094)	0.258 (0.144)*	0.269 (0.141)*	-0.051 (0.101)	-0.067 (0.102)
Debt	0.006 (0.009)	0.006 (0.009)	-0.005 (0.011)	-0.003 (0.010)	-0.010 (0.019)	-0.012 (0.019)
Inflation	-0.014 (0.003)***	-0.014 (0.003)***	-0.173 (0.059)***	-0.220 (0.061)***	-0.011 (0.005)**	-0.010 (0.005)**
Fiscal Rule Index	-0.791 (0.166)***	-0.790 (0.166)***	-0.515 (0.170)***	-0.590 (1.723)***	-1.192 (0.297)***	-1.175 (0.300)***
Maastricht	-0.492 (0.233)*	-0.439 (0.230)*	-1.263 (0.324)***	-1.311 (0.332)***	-0.404 (0.305)	-0.266 (0.322)
N	516	516	337	337	179	179
Adjusted R^2	0.416	0.417	0.419	0.415	0.525	0.553

Note: Dependent variable: annual change in total general government spending, % of GDP. Results obtained using within-unit transformation. Panel corrected standard errors in parentheses. Significance levels: *** $p < 0.01$, ** $p < 0.05$, * $p < 0.10$.

term means that the marginal effect becomes smaller as vote buying becomes less prevalent. Given our theoretical claim that programmatic goals become more relevant to policy outputs as vote buying decreases, the marginal effect should at some point acquire the 'correct' negative sign.

Figure 7.1 shows that this is indeed the case. In the figure, the marginal effect of the number of government parties is plotted against the values of the vote-buying variable that are empirically relevant in this group of countries. The plot is accompanied by the boundaries of the 90 per cent confidence interval. As both boundaries are above the horizontal zero line in the left-hand end of the figure, the marginal effect is statistically significant with a positive sign when vote buying is prevalent. However, on high levels of the vote-buying variable, the marginal effect plot as well as the boundaries of the confidence interval are below the zero line. This indicates a negative effect whereby spending decreases as the programmatic outlook of the cabinet moves to the right.

The last two columns in Table 7.3 suggest that political variables are generally more relevant with respect to spending changes in the post-communist countries. In the additive model (column V), both the number of government parties and the programmatic centre of masses are statistically significant

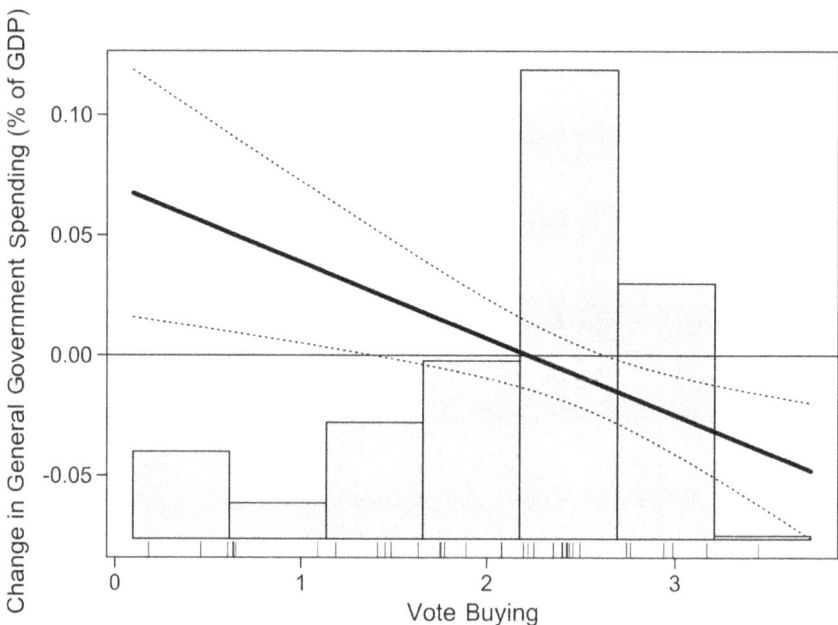

Figure 7.1 **The Marginal Effect of Government Left-Right Orientation on Spending in the Old Member States and Cyprus**

with the expected signs: spending tends to increase with coalition size and decrease when rightist governments are in office. Unlike in the other country group, the effective number of parliamentary parties has a negative effect. In the interaction model (column VI), only the interaction term composed of the number of government parties and vote buying is statistically significant, the one containing the left-right variable being very close to zero. The coefficient on the number of government parties indicates that when the value of the vote-buying variable is zero, the effect of coalition size on spending is not only statistically but also substantively significant, close to 1 per cent of GDP. However, the negative coefficient on the interaction term suggests that the effect becomes weaker as vote buying becomes less prevalent.

This is illustrated in Figure 7.2 where the marginal effect of the number of coalition parties is plotted as a function of the prevalence of vote buying. On the lowest values of the vote-buying variable, the point estimate of the marginal effect is more than 1 per cent of GDP, which is a substantial cost for the addition of one government party. The boundaries of the 90 per cent confidence interval range from about 0.5 to almost 2 per cent of GDP in the left-hand end of the figure, so even the lower boundary marks an economically significant spending increase. The marginal effect plot slopes

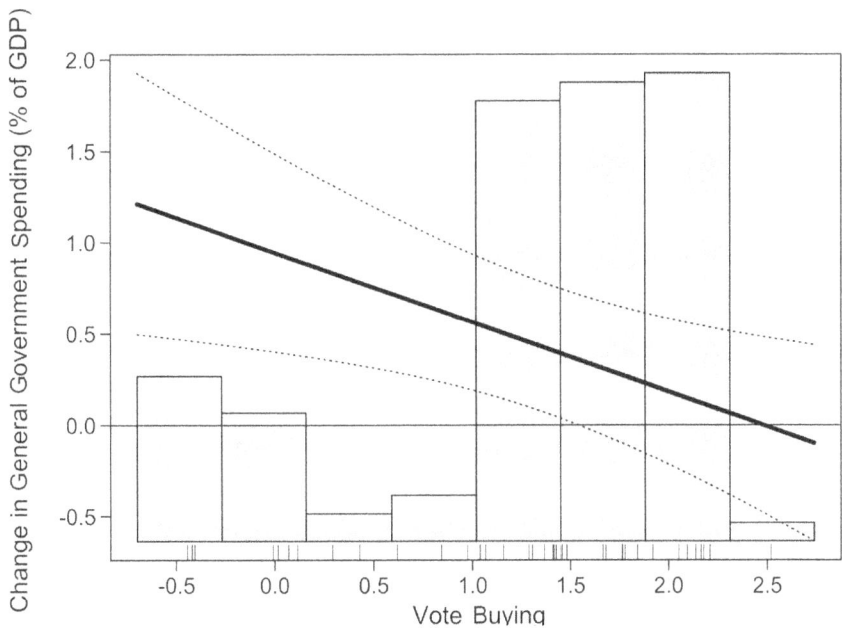

Figure 7.2   **The Marginal Effect of the Number of Government Parties on Spending in the Post-Communist Countries**

downward, and the effect becomes indiscernible from zero when vote buying is rare.

The number of parties in government thus never seems to have a negative effect on spending. In contrast, the fragmentation of the party system at the parliamentary level does suppress spending at least in the post-communist countries, as seen in columns V and VI of Table 7.3. The substantial effect in these countries also appears to be responsible for the somewhat weaker yet statistically significant effect observable in the entire set of twenty-six countries (columns I and II), as no effect is discernible in the other sub-group of countries. The negative effect is anomalous given the established view about the fiscal consequences of party system fragmentation, and its occurrence in the post-communist countries is contrary to our expectation that spending tends to increase with the number of parties exactly in this set of countries.

The spending consequences of the number of parties cannot therefore be established without being explicit about the organs of state one is referring to. A possible explanation for the opposite effects of the two measures of the number of parties starts from the proposition that the government consists of the 'appropriators' of the budgetary commons that may over-exploit the tax pool if clientelist practices encourage them to do so. The parliament, whose consent is needed to pass the budget, is however able to challenge and monitor government policies more efficiently as the number of parties in the parliament increases (see Pettersson-Lidbom 2012). It is also possible that a more fragmented parliament introduces inertia into the budgetary process, so that a cabinet that would like to increase spending finds it more difficult to have its preferences implemented. Some earlier studies (e.g., Bäck et al. 2017; Martin and Vanberg 2013) have also found that at least in some model specifications a large effective number of parliamentary parties tends to suppress spending while a large number of government parties tends to increase it. Others (e.g., Bawn and Rosenbluth 2006) have not found the effective number of parliamentary parties to have any statistically significant effect on spending. Further research on why opposing effects sometimes emerge is therefore needed.

To summarize, the effects that the number of government parties and the programmatic centre of masses of the cabinet have on spending depend on whether one looks at a set of countries consisting primarily of mature capitalist democracies where the level of spending is already high or a group of relatively new post-communist democracies. In the former, in so far as political variables have discernible effects, it is the programmatic statements of the government parties that affect spending, and where vote buying is an issue, that effect tends to disappear. In the latter group of countries, also the number of parties has spending consequences. However, this seems to depend on the prevalence of clientelist linkages: when party-society linkages have sufficient programmatic content, operationalized here as the low prevalence of vote buying, the effect is statistically indiscernible.

CONCLUSION

At the beginning of this chapter, it was argued that studies on the connections between the number of decision-makers and fiscal policy outputs have for the most part failed to explicitly account for the possibility that linkages between political parties and the rest of the society vary for reasons that do not go back to formal rules and institutions. Another issue that was argued to affect the relationship between the number of 'appropriators' in the fiscal commons and policy outcomes was whether or not the regime has a communist past.

An analysis of European data reported in this chapter suggests that with respect to spending increases, the explanatory force of a simple but important measure of party system fragmentation, the number of government parties, effectively disappears when clientelist linkages are sufficiently weak and is not discernible when one looks at a group of countries that primarily consists of established capitalist democracies. The location of the cabinet on the left-right dimension, in turn, turned out to affect government spending only when clientelist practices are rare. While the latter finding may appear self-evident, together with the ones concerning the effects of coalition size, it suggests that the metaphor of the budgetary common-pool problem does not apply equally well in all circumstances and the literature on fragmented decision-making should go beyond formal rules and institutions (see also Raudla 2010). This is not to deny the fiscal problems that numerous countries face. However, the number of parties taking part in decision-making is not always credible even as a partial explanation.

The notion of the common-pool problem leads one not only to think about possible connections between the number of decision-makers and policy outcomes in empirical terms but also to interpret the normative implications of the results in a certain way. The problem is the inefficiency of spending, but finding an empirical relationship between the number of parties and spending is by no means direct evidence of such inefficiency (Ylisalo 2015). However, as the phenomenon seems to characterize relatively clientelist political systems, this information gives some additional albeit still indirect support for the claim that spending increases that follow from an increased number of parties taking part in decision-making signify the waste of resources.

An important limitation of this chapter is the fact that it only considered spending as such, not what society gets out of spending in terms of human well-being or economic prosperity. There are some arguments (e.g., Tanzi 2011) according to which the efficiency of spending tends to decrease after a certain level has been reached. An important topic for future research would be finding out whether and how forms of political linkages condition the consequences of spending increases in this respect. After all, if spending increases that follow from multi-party decision-making as such led to significant welfare gains, there would be little reason to be concerned about such spending. This is, however, unlikely the case given the vast possibilities for unproductive distribution of resources that accompany pervasive clientelist networks.

ACKNOWLEDGEMENTS

This work has been supported by the Academy of Finland via the Strategic Research Council project 'Participation in Long-Term Decision-Making' (312671) and the academy project 'Democratic Reasoning: Deliberation, Accountability and Trust in Representative Democracies' (274305).

REFERENCES

Achen, C. H. 2000. Why Lagged Dependent Variables Can Suppress the Explanatory Power of Other Independent Variables. Paper prepared for the Annual Meeting of the Political Methodology Section of the American Political Science Association, UCLA, July 20–22.

Armingeon, K., Isler, C., Knöpfel, L., Weisstannter, D. and Engler, S. 2015. *Comparative Political Data Set 1960–2013*. Bern: Institute of Political Science, University of Berne. Available at www.cpds-data.org.

Bäck, H., Müller, W. C. and Nyblade, B. 2017. Multiparty government and economic policy-making: Coalition agreements, prime ministerial power and spending in Western European Cabinets. *Public Choice* 170:1, 33–62.

Baron, D. P. and Ferejohn, J. A. 1989. Bargaining in legislatures. *American Political Science Review* 83:4, 1181–1206.

Bawn, K. and Rosenbluth, F. 2006. Short versus long coalitions: Electoral accountability and the size of the public sector. *American Journal of Political Science* 50, 251–265.

Beck, N. and Katz, J. N. 1995. What to do (and not to do) with time-series cross-section data. *American Political Science Review* 89:3, 634–647.

Brambor, T., Clark, W. R. and Golder, M. 2006. Understanding interaction models: Improving empirical analyses. *Political Analysis* 14, 63–82.

Coppedge, M., Gerring, J., Lindberg, S. I., Skaaning, S. E., Teorell, J., Altman, D., Andersson, F., Bernhard, M., Fish, M. S., Glynn, A., Hicken, A., Knutsen, C. H., McMann, K., Mechkova, V., Miri, F., Paxton, P., Pemstein, D., Sigman, R., Staton, J. and Zimmerman, B. 2016. *V-Dem Codebook v6*. Gothenburg: Varieties of Democracy (V-Dem) Project.

de Haan, J., Jong-A-Pin, R. and Mierau, J. O. 2013. Do budgetary institutions mitigate the common pool problem? New empirical evidence for the EU. *Public Choice* 156, 423–441.

Döring, H. and Manow, P. 2015. *Parliaments and governments database (ParlGov): Information on parties, elections and cabinets in modern democracies.* Development Version. Available at www.parlgov.org.

Elgie, R. and McMenamin, I. 2008. Political fragmentation, fiscal deficits and political institutionalisation. *Public Choice* 136, 255–267.

European Commission. 2015. *Numerical fiscal rules in the EU Member States.* Available at http://ec.europa.eu/economy_finance/db_indicators/fiscal_governance/fiscal_rules/index_en.htm.

Fukuyama, Francis. 2014. *Political Order and Political Decay: From Industrial Revolution to the Globalisation of Democracy.* London: Profile Books.

Gherghina, S. and Volintiru, C. 2017. A new model of clientelism: Political parties, public resources, and private contributors. *European Political Science Review* 9:1, 115–137.

Hallerberg, M., Strauch, R. R. and von Hagen, J. 2009. *Fiscal Governance in Europe.* New York: Cambridge University Press.

Hardin, G. 1968. The tragedy of the commons. *Science* 162, 1243–1248.

Heinemann, F., Moessinger, M.-D. and Yeter, M. 2018. Do fiscal rules constrain fiscal policy? A meta-regression-analysis. *European Journal of Political Economy* 51, 69–92.

Kiss, A. 2009. Coalition politics and accountability. *Public Choice* 139, 413–428.

Kitschelt, H. 2000. Linkages between citizens and politicians in democratic polities. *Comparative Political Studies* 33:6/7, 845–879.

Kitschelt, H. and Wilkinson, S. I. 2007. Citizen-politician linkages: An introduction. In H. Kitschelt and S. I. Wilkinson (eds.), *Patrons, Clients and Policies: Patterns of Democratic Accountability and Political Competition.* Cambridge: Cambridge University Press, 1–49.

Laakso, M. and Taagepera, R. 1979. 'Effective' number of parties: A measure with application to West Europe. *Comparative Political Studies* 12:1, 3–27.

Lizzeri, A. and Persico, N. 2005. A drawback of electoral competition. *Journal of the European Economic Association* 3:6, 1318–1348.

Martin, L. W. and Vanberg, G. 2013. Multiparty government, fiscal institutions, and public spending. *The Journal of Politics* 75:4, 953–967.

Musgrave, R. A. 1957. A multiple theory of budget determination. *Finanzarchiv/ Public Finance Analysis* 17 (new series), 333–343.

O'Dwyer, C. 2004. Runaway state building: How political parties shape states in postcommunist Eastern Europe. *World Politics* 56:4, 520–553.

Olson, M. 2000. *Power and Prosperity: Outgrowing Communist and Capitalist Dictatorships.* New York: Basic Books.

Persson, T., Roland, G. and Tabellini, G. 2007. Electoral rules and government spending in parliamentary democracies. *Quarterly Journal of Political Science* 2, 155–188.

Pettersson-Lidbom, P. 2012. Does the size of the legislature affect the size of government? Evidence from two natural experiments. *Journal of Public Economics* 96, 269–278.

Powell, G. B. 2000. *Elections as Instruments of Democracy: Majoritarian and Proportional Visions*. New Haven, CT: Yale University Press.

Raudla, R. 2010. Governing budgetary commons: What can we learn from Elinor Ostrom? *European Journal of Law and Economics* 30:3, 201–221.

Rommerskirchen, C. 2015. Fiscal rules, fiscal outcomes and financial market behaviour. *European Journal of Political Research* 54:4, 836–847.

Rothstein, B. 2011. *The Quality of Government: Corruption, Social Trust, and Inequality in International Perspective*. Chicago: University of Chicago Press.

Scartascini, C. G. and Crain, W. M. 2002. *The size and composition of government spending in multi-party systems*. Available at SSRN: http://ssrn.com/abstract=1353462.

Stokes, S. C., Dunning, T., Nazareno, M. and Brusco, V. 2013. *Brokers, Voters, and Clientelism: The Puzzle of Distributive Politics*. New York: Cambridge University Press.

Tanzi, V. 2011. *Government Versus Markets: The Changing Economic Role of the State*. New York: Cambridge University Press.

van Biezen, I. and Kopecký, P. 2007. The state and the parties: Public funding, public regulation and rent-seeking in contemporary democracies. *Party Politics* 13:2, 235–254.

Velasco, A. 2000. Debts and deficits with fragmented fiscal policymaking. *Journal of Public Economics* 76:1, 105–125.

Volkens, A., Lehmann, P., Matthieß, T., Merz, N., Regel, S. and Werner, A. 2015. *The Manifesto Data Collection*. Manifesto Project (MRG/CMP/MARPOR). Version 2015a. Berlin: Wissenschaftszentrum Berlin für Sozialforschung (WZB).

Weingast, B. R., Shepsle, K. A. and Johnsen, C. 1981. The political economy of benefits and costs: a neoclassical approach to distributive politics. *Journal of Political Economy* 89:4, 642–664.

Ylisalo, J. 2015. The fiscal commons: assessing the limits and possibilities of a metaphor. *Homo Œconomicus* 32:3/4, 331–354.

Chapter Eight

Universal Social Policies and Clientelistic Party Strategies in Latin America

Sarah A. Berens and Saskia Ruth-Lovell

INTRODUCTION

Welfare states in developing countries are challenged in many ways: they suffer from resource scarcity, economic volatility, and institutional inefficiencies. But apart from these structural weaknesses, social policies are first of all a product of the political decision-making process that take into account voter interests, party strategies, and the influence of dominant groups such as business elites and labour unions (see Fairfield and Garay 2017; Huber and Stephens 2001; Mares 2003). The type of welfare coalitions that are produced have historical roots in the structure of the class system (Huber and Stephens 2012) and economic policies of the past (see Wibbels and Ahlquist 2011). While many low- and middle-income countries are adopting more progressive welfare policies such as Conditional Cash Transfers (CCTs) and welfare subsidies to encounter severe income inequality and poverty (Brooks 2015; Carnes and Mares 2014; Díaz-Cayeros and Magaloni 2009; Garay 2016), we still find many welfare policies in place that distribute benefits disproportionally to the income structure (see Lindert, Skoufias, and Shapiro 2006). The poor benefited from governments' increasing incentives to invest in human capital to remain competitive at the global market (see Rudra 2008) and also from international efforts to foster basic health care provision in recent decades. But universal social policies – that have been identified as significant for poverty and inequality reduction (Korpi and Palme 1998; Rothstein 2011) – are largely absent in low- and middle-income democracies. In contrast, several states rather appear to have come to a halt in a developmental stalemate, with high-income inequality, weak state capacity and a less cohesive society which Rothstein (2011, 146) identified as 'low-trust-corruption-inequality trap'. Latin America represents the region with the most inegalitarian income distribution. Despite the large share of low-income earners, why are regressive social policies so persistent?

The adoption and reform of social policies is also a function of the diverse relationships between voters and political parties, which essentially determines whose interests are represented. Especially in low- and middle-income countries parties do not always follow policy-based mobilization strategies, but may also buy-off voters to ensure support via clientelistic practices (Kitschelt 2000). In simplified terms, programmatic parties allow interest representation of their entire constituency following the given electoral rule, while clientelistic parties have the opportunity to selectively represent only a certain share of their constituency, buying off the rest (see Gibson 1997; Luna 2014; Magaloni, Diaz-Cayeros, and Estévez 2007). We therefore argue: when individuals do not use their vote to make programmatic choices but cast it based on clientelistic exchanges the resulting electoral outcome should influence the type of social policies that are implemented (e.g., Calvo and Murillo 2004; Remmer 2007; Weitz-Shapiro 2014).

Following the definition put forward in the introduction to this volume, we understand clientelism, in a broad sense, as a mobilization strategy of political parties by exchanging material goods and selective benefits for political support and votes (see Ruth-Lovell, chapter 1, in this volume). From the literature on clientelism we know that low-income earners are among the most favoured targets of political machines as their votes come at lower cost (see Dixit and Londregan 1996; Stokes et al. 2013). Relatedly, it is assumed that clientelistic parties do not have incentives to pursue policies which foster economic growth and decrease income inequalities since a positive economic development ameliorates the income structure; and potential clients come at higher prices (see Kitschelt and Kselman 2013; Kitschelt and Wilkinson 2007). Right-wing parties, which prefer a conservative welfare regime, have a comparative advantage in using a clientelistic linkage strategy compared to left-wing parties, as the strategy of clientelism remains self-enforcing for a right-wing party, while it would be a self-undermining strategy for a left-wing, pro-poor social policy promoting, party. The same holds for a clientelistic party: adopting a conservative welfare agenda is a self-enforcing strategy, whereas a left-wing agenda would erode the clientelistic linkage in the long run. While in recent years researchers focused on disentangling the relationship between clientelism and social policy implementation in small-N studies and sub-national comparisons (e.g., De La O 2013; Magaloni, Diaz-Cayeros, and Estévez 2007; Weitz-Shapiro 2014), until now, this relationship has not been tested in a large-N comparative analysis yet. In this chapter, we aim to reduce this gap by addressing the following two interlinked research questions: does clientelism decrease the likelihood of political parties to pursue a progressive social policy agenda? And if so, do party systems that are more inflicted by clientelism provide more conservative social policies in the end?

Hence, we study the link between clientelism and social policy advocacy, on the one hand, and social policy outcomes, on the other hand. We focus our empirical analysis on the Latin American region (LA hereafter) for two reasons. First, clientelistic practices are prevalent throughout LA but the degree of clientelism varies both between and within countries (Hilgers 2013; Kitschelt and Kselman 2013). Second, the study of social policy and welfare states in LA has advanced considerably during the last two decades with respect to both the categorization of welfare state regimes as well as the analysis of different (de facto) outputs and outcomes of social policies (e.g., Mares and Carnes 2009; Pribble 2013; Rudra 2008).

In the first part of our analysis we focus on the meso-level and on the type of policy platforms clientelistic parties' offer. A central prerequisite for the proposed mechanism to work is that clientelistic parties score high on less redistributive social policies in their party platforms. Therefore, we start out with a cross-sectional analysis on the link between parties efforts on clientelistic practices and their orientation regarding several social policies, making use of expert survey data provided by the Democratic Accountability and Linkages Project (DALP) (Kitschelt 2013). Subsequently, we employ a pooled time-series cross-section regression analysis with panel-corrected standard errors on macro-level data on the degree of clientelistic versus programmatic linkages in the respective party system provided by the Varieties of Democracies Project (VDem) (Coppedge et al. 2016) in the country's party system for a set of eighteen Latin American countries from 1990 to 2012. We study the effect of clientelism on several social policy outcomes (infant mortality rate, secondary female school enrolment, life expectancy, and poverty) to take into account the limited information expenditure data convey (Baum and Lake 2003; Kittel and Winner 2005; Ross 2006).

The first part of our analysis reveals that, on the party level, clientelism indeed goes together with a more conservative policy advocacy on several social policy dimensions, likely contributing to more residual welfare states in the region. Moreover, studying social policy outcomes in the second part of our analysis, we find that an increase in clientelism on the party system-level augments the infant mortality rate and decreases female school enrolment, two indicators for the progressivity of welfare state policies. Also the life expectancy is lower in countries that experience higher levels of clientelism. While the effects on infant mortality and school enrolment suggest that clientelism appears to be linked to less pro-poor oriented welfare state policies, the latter finding also shows that social security, which usually rather profits the already better-off, is equally negatively affected.

THEORETICAL FRAMEWORK

Clientelism and Parties' Social Policy Platforms

Most traditional theories of democratic representation, rest upon the assumption of policy-based behaviour of both political parties and voters (Manin, Przeworski, and Stokes 1999; Powell 2004). Meaning that parties mobilize support by promising voters to implement specific policies if they are elected, and that voters base their party choice in elections on the best fit between their own interests and the policy programs parties offer. However, elected representatives will respond only to the policy preferences of citizens if they are selected and judged by this logic. Thus, institutional mechanisms only structure political parties' scope of action but do not determine the substance on which base they are accountable and responsive to their voters (Kitschelt 2000).

The linkage concept is a useful analytical tool to overcome this implicit assumption and to study the relationship between political parties and the electorate without a predetermined focus on programmatic party competition (e.g., Kitschelt 2000, see Ruth-Lovell, chapter 2, in this volume). Following the linkage concept, political parties may mobilize electoral support following a programmatic linkage strategy and appeal to their voters with policy programs. These programs consist of policy bundles concerning a range of solutions to the problems of a society. In this regard, parties that pursue a programmatic linkage strategy induce voters to signal their policy preferences at election time (Downs 1957; Manin, Przeworski, and Stokes 1999). In contrast, political parties may also rely on a clientelistic linkage strategy, defined here in the broader sense as the distribution of material goods and selective benefits by political parties for political support and votes (e.g., Hopkin 2006; Stokes 2007). Unlike the programmatic linkage, clientelism undermines the chain of democratic representation (Powell 2005). Since 'the use of the vote as a currency to buy material benefits subverts the ostensible purpose of the electoral process in a representative democracy' (Hopkin 2006, 410), a negative effect on parties' responsiveness to the policy preferences of the voters may be expected. This is especially important since clientelism builds on *economic* inequalities and translates them into *political* inequality. Drawing upon Dixit and Londregan's (1996) seminal work on the diminishing utility of income, clientelistic appeals are less conducive the higher an individual's income. Consequently, the poor value clientelistic handouts more. If political parties in government focus their policy programs more on voters that are not inclined to give their vote in exchange for material inducements, clientelism may induce inequality in democratic representation in favour of high-income and high-skilled constituencies (e.g., Luna 2014; Weitz-Shapiro

2014). This may then lead to a regressive social policy outline of clientelistic parties, since rich constituencies are, on average, more likely represented on a programmatic basis. Consequently, when considering political parties' responsiveness to voter demands in less developed democracies, clientelism needs to be factored in.

Recent research highlights that parties which build on clientelistic support favour some policies over others, especially in the area of social policy (Pribble 2013; Ruth and Salazar Elena 2016; Stokes et al. 2013; Tzelgov and Wang 2016). To determine the effect of clientelism on the quality of social policy we need to investigate which specific welfare policy programs clientelistic parties favour. Arguments in the literature highlight that clientelistic parties rather pursue policies that favour the free market instead of the state in ruling the economy, that are rather discretionary than universalistic, and that are more conservative than progressive (e.g., Kitschelt 2000; Kitschelt and Wilkinson 2007; Tzelgov and Wang 2016).

This is especially important if we consider that political parties may use linkage-mixing to win elections (see Magaloni, Diaz-Cayeros, and Estévez 2007). In line with the *portfolio-diversification theory*, linkage-mixing may be the consequence of either risk-aversion of political elites – addressing the same constituency with different linkage strategies to hedge electoral losses – or the parallel appeal to diverse constituencies which are then combined into one electoral coalition (see Gibson 1997; Luna 2014; Magaloni, Diaz-Cayeros, and Estévez 2007). However, the combination of a clientelistic linkage with a specific programmatic outline to maximize a party's utility may come at some cost. Some political parties seem to be able to combine programmatic and clientelistic strategies more effectively than others (Gibson 1997; Hilgers 2009; Luna 2014; Magaloni, Diaz-Cayeros, and Estévez 2007; Singer and Kitschelt 2011). More specifically, portfolio-diversification seems to be more likely on the right side of the political spectrum since leftist policies are usually grounded on universalistic principles, which are less combinable with particularistic exchanges. It is, therefore, plausible that the type of ideologically grounded universalistic principle affects the feasibility of clientelism (Weitz-Shapiro 2012). Especially left-libertarian parties that focus on social inequality issues and redistribution may compromise their credibility when engaging in clientelistic practices (Kitschelt 2000; Weitz-Shapiro 2014). Adopting a left-wing, pro-poor social policy agenda would clearly represent a self-undermining strategy for a clientelistic party, whereas a conservative welfare agenda that redistributes on a contribution-based logic would be self-enforcing regarding returns to clientelism. From a utility-maximizing perspective, clientelistic parties should therefore promote a regressive social policy.

Based on these arguments we can state the following hypothesis:

Hypothesis 1: Ceteris paribus, clientelistic parties are more likely to pursue regressive social policies

Clientelism and Social Policy Outcomes

If the proposed overlap between the clientelistic linkages and a conservative stance on social policy for political parties holds, this could explain part of the variation in welfare state policies that we observe in LA. Social security has the most far-reaching historical roots in the region compared to health care and education policy. Basic social insurance systems emerged in the beginning of the twentieth century (Haggard and Kaufman 2008). Benefits were however only accessible for a small circle of elites, following a Bismarckian style, and the exclusionary nature still marks the design of social security today. Regressive social policy favours high-income earners, as returns do not decrease with increasing income. With respect to the region, it is mostly health care and education expenditures that generate a more progressive outcome (Huber and Stephens 2012), meaning that the resource distribution is proportional to the individual's means and needs and increases with decreasing income. However, the nature of the distributive effect of education and health care policies depends, for instance, on the sector of education (primary or tertiary education) and the type of health care (e.g., basic health care or employment related health insurance) that is supported by the government. Lloyd-Sherlock (2009) emphasizes that improvements in primary education and basic health care are not far-reaching enough to significantly reduce income inequality in LA. Nevertheless, the popularity of social assistance programs such as CCTs in the last two decades (Carnes and Mares 2015) and the continuous increase of these programs prove the endeavour to address severe poverty and income inequality by many LA governments (see Brooks 2015). So far, CCTs reach rather favourable results with regard to their distributive effects (see Fiszbein, Schady, and Ferreira 2009). Lindert, Skoufias, and Shapiro (2006) find a more progressive impact of social assistance programs compared to conventional welfare services, but they also point out that the subsidies are too small to make a significant change to the income structure. It is the 'truncated' nature of the LA welfare states (De Ferranti et al. 2004) which reproduces inequity by favouring formal sector workers and privileged groups such as the military and civil servants (Garay 2016). Hence, persisting regressive and conservative social policy is problematic for the poor not only in terms of short-term effects but also in the long run.

Welfare states in Latin America struggle especially with the negative effects of international market integration and globalization (Kaufman and

Segura-Ubiergo 2001; Rudra 2008).[1] Economic downturn is particularly detrimental for the country's welfare generosity as low- and middle-income countries lack the financial capacities to pursue anti-cyclical spending strategies (Wibbels 2006). In contrast, democratic development facilitates the promotion of more generous welfare systems (Huber, Mustillo, and Stephens 2008; Huber and Stephens 2012). According to Huber, Mustillo, and Stephens (2008), left parties do not necessarily spend more on social policies in absolute terms in Latin America, but they foster progressive social policies so that the type of social policy varies by incumbent party. Drawing upon the classical Meltzer-Richard model (1981), increased income inequality should induce greater spending on welfare because of the changing distance between mean and median voter. But researchers have illustrated that the Meltzer-Richard model mostly fails at the macro-level (see Kenworthy and McCall 2008). Only at the micro-level it finds empirical support (see Finseraas 2009), demand for redistribution rises with increasing income inequality, especially when focusing on higher income earners as recently demonstrated by Rueda and Stegmueller (2016) for the U.S. and the OECD context in general. Similarly, there is empirical evidence which shows that the LA public is sensitive to the fairness or unfairness of income distribution (Cramer and Kaufman 2011), so that one could expect larger support for more progressive social policies. But already Dion and Birchfield (2010) illustrated for a large sample of developing countries that public opinion is much less driven by economic self-interest when it comes to social policy issues in contexts that are less developed. The question is, why we still see rather conservative and regressive social policies in place in the LA context that is so very dominated by high levels of income inequality.

We argue that it is clientelism, which hinders the development of more generous and universal social policies. Clientelism erodes the substantive relationship between voters and parties as it distorts the responsiveness of political parties towards their policy preferences. We expect countries, which foster party competition based on clientelistic electoral mobilization strategies to perform less well on social welfare. In line with the arguments stated in the previous section, it is exactly the propensity of clientelistic parties to target low-income earners and to favour status quo enhancing social policies for the middle- and high-income earners that make the perseverance of conservative welfare states more plausible (Berens and Ruth 2014). In contrast, several empirical studies confirm a strong link between electoral pledges (i.e., policy advocacy) and promise fulfilment in policy-making (e.g., Bischof forthcoming; Mansergh and Thomson 2007; Thomson et al. 2017) for programmatic parties. As emphasized above, clientelistic parties have the opportunity to represent only a certain share of their constituencies on substantive grounds, while the rest is bought

(Magaloni, Diaz-Cayeros, and Estévez 2007). The mechanics of linkage-mixing together with the logic of diminishing marginal utility of income therefore favours the political interests of middle- and high-income earners (Dixit and Londregan 1996; Luna 2014; Magaloni, Diaz-Cayeros, and Estévez 2007), which tend to be more conservative in their social policy preferences in the LA context (see Berens 2015). We therefore expect to find more conservative social policies – visualized through poor performance on social welfare indicators – in countries that are more prone to clientelistic behaviour. As emphasized above, the poor benefit most from social expenditures on health care and primary and secondary education (Baum and Lake 2003; Ross 2006). Hence, when clientelism is strong, investments in health care and primary and secondary education are less likely. We pose the following hypothesis:

Hypothesis 2: Ceteris paribus, social welfare performance – especially with respect to health and education – should be lower in countries with more clientelistic party systems

One might argue that clientelism works as an equivalent to the welfare state since benefits are provided here as well, differing only in the allocation key and the conditionality of the exchange (for a discussion see Kitschelt 2000; Stokes et al. 2013). In this sense, clientelism may be seen as an appropriate electoral strategy – for both parties and voters – in places where political institutions are dysfunctional (Gay 1998; Hilgers 2009, 2011; Kitschelt 2000). Furthermore, from a clients' perspective the exchange of particularistic goods may be perceived as a viable solution to social problems (Auyero 1999; Hilgers 2009). In some situations clientelism may even enhance political participation of poor constituencies. Poor non-voters may be mobilized through clientelistic exchanges ('turnout buying') and such patron-client interaction may provide poor citizens with basic information on democratic participation (Hilgers 2009; Nichter 2008). However, non-programmatic social policy is unable to harmonize the income distribution as clientelistic benefits are exclusive in nature, supporting the persistence of truncated welfare systems (see De Ferranti et al. 2004). Moreover, vote buying may lead to serious consequences not only to those individuals who sell their votes but also to classes of voters and the public in general like inefficient resource allocation, reduced influence over public policy, and diminished political accountability of representatives (Stokes et al. 2013, 245–254). Empirical findings contradict the assumption of a substitution effect (e.g., Hilgers 2009) and the descriptive statistics below also hint towards a negative relationship between clientelism and generous social policy.

EMPIRICAL ANALYSIS

We begin with an analysis at the party level regarding a political party's degree of clientelism and its stance on social policy issues as well as the general left-right ideological scale. After studying the relationship based on expert survey ratings on party positions and linkage strategies, in part I, we move on to investigate the relationship between clientelism and conservative social policies based on welfare state outcomes over time, in part II of the analysis.

Clientelism and Social Policy Positions (Part I)

In order to operationalize the degree of clientelism on the meso-level we build on data provided by the Democratic Accountability and Linkages Project (DALP, Kitschelt 2013). In this survey experts have been asked to rank political parties' efforts with respect to several clientelistic practices.[2] A total of five questions on different practices have been asked, using a categorical scale ranging from 1 to 4 with higher values indicating a more frequent use of the respective practice. Building the mean of the expert responses a quasi-continuous measure of a parties' degree of each practice is derived. Experts are asked to indicate party's efforts to attract voters by providing consumer goods' (B1), 'preferential public benefits' (B2), 'preferential access to employment opportunities' (B3), 'by offering them preferential access to government contracts or procurement opportunities' (B4), and finally, to indicate a 'party's effort to attract voters and the businesses for which they work by influencing regulatory proceedings in their favor' (B5). Following Kitschelt and Kselman (2013), we use these five items to build an overall index of clientelism that ranges from 1 (a negligible effort or none at all) to 4 (a major effort). Moreover, experts were also asked to rank political parties regarding their position on the left-right ideological dimension (D6) as well as the issue dimensions of social spending on the disadvantaged (D1) and public spending (D3) in general, all of which use a 10-point scale (with higher values indicating more conservative positions).

In addition, we include both meso- and macro-level control variables: On the meso-level, we control for a political party's emphasis on a programmatic linkage strategy (item E2). The question is categorical and ranges from 1 to 4, with higher values indicating a more frequent use of this linkage type. The mean expert rating of a party indicates its emphasis on the linkage type. We also control for (logged) party age and party seat share as two additional meso-level factors that might be correlated with our main variables of interest. Data on party age and party seat share is taken from Bolleyer and Ruth

(2018). On the macro-level, we control for two-party system characteristics – polarization and fragmentation – and two systemic context factors – democratic and economic development. For party system polarization we use the Taylor-Herman index (Taylor and Herman 1971) based on political parties, left-right placements and weighted by their seat share in national legislatures. To capture party system fragmentation we calculate the effective number of parliamentary parties (ENPP, Laakso and Taagepera 1979). Additionally, we control for the level of democracy using a country's polity 2 score (provided by Polity IV, Marshall, Jaggers, and Gurr 2016) and economic development using a country's GDP per capita score in the respective year (provided by the WDI, The World Bank Group 2017).

To test the relationship between a party's degree of clientelism and its stance on several political issues, we rely upon a two-level hierarchical linear random-intercept model with the respective policy dimensions as the dependent variables (Hox 2010). The model to test *Hypothesis 1* is specified as follows:

$$Policy\ Dimensions_{jk} = \beta_0 + \beta X_{jk} + \beta Z_k + U_{jk}$$

Subscript j (=1, . . . , J) refers to the units on the party level and the subscript k (=1, . . . , K) refers to the country level. The linear predictor of the dependent variable is modelled by an intercept β_0, a vector of coefficients on the party level (X) and a vector of coefficients on the country level (Z). For the random effect U_{jk} a normal distribution with a zero mean and a variance of σ_ε^2 is assumed.

Table 8.1 reports the results for three models, one for each of the three issue dimensions: social policy (M1), public spending (M2), and the overall left-right dimension (M3). The models in Table 8.1 corroborate our expectations formulated in H1. Across all three policy dimensions, parties are on average farther to the right end of each policy scale the more they expend efforts to mobilize voters using clientelistic practices. Hence, clientelistic parties are less likely to promote extensive pro-poor social spending, and thereby, are in essence against redistributing income. They are also rather against an extensive state role in providing health insurance, pensions, and schooling. Finally, this tendency to more conservative positions is also mirrored in clientelistic parties' location on the left-to-right ideological scale. As can be seen in Table 8.1, an increase in the degree of clientelism by one point, leads to a quite substantive move by more than two points to the right on the 10-point scale. But of course, these observations are correlational in nature so that we illustrate here which choices 'go together' when looking at preferences for a certain linkage strategy and the promotion of more progressive versus conservative social policies. To illustrate this relationship

Table 8.1   Clientelistic Linkage and Social Policy Positions

	M1:	M2:	M3:
	Social Spending Issue-Dimension	Public Spending Issue-Dimension	Left-Right Dimension
Clientelistic Linkage	**1.15**···	**1.16**··	**2.27**···
	(0.30)	**(0.35)**	**(0.50)**
Programmatic Linkage	−0.39	**−0.87**·	**−1.11**⁺
	(0.37)	**(0.43)**	**(0.61)**
Party Age	0.00	0.00	−0.00
	(0.00)	(0.00)	(0.00)
Party Seat Share	−0.02	−0.01	−0.02
	(0.01)	(0.01)	(0.02)
ENPP	0.04	−0.05	−0.01
	(0.07)	(0.09)	(0.12)
Polarization	0.03	0.02	0.02
	(0.05)	(0.06)	(0.08)
Democracy Level	**0.33**··	**0.24**⁺	**0.56**··
	(0.11)	**(0.13)**	**(0.18)**
GDP p.c.	−0.00	0.00	−0.00
	(0.00)	(0.00)	(0.00)
Constant	0.11	2.51	−0.50
	(1.81)	(2.15)	(3.01)
Var(constant)	−1.07	−0.80	−0.56
	(0.85)	(0.58)	(0.60)
Var(residual)	0.05	0.20·	0.56···
	(0.09)	(0.09)	(0.09)
N (parties)	84	84	84
Log-Likelihood	−146.98	−158.68	−184.85
BIC	342.71	366.11	418.44
Chi²	31.14	29.69	48.23

Note: Standard errors in parentheses, ⁺$p < 0.10$, ·$p < 0.05$, ··$p < 0.01$, ···$p < 0.001$.
Sources: DALP data from 2009 Kitschelt (2013) and Bolleyer and Ruth (2018).

graphically, Figure 8.1 shows the predicted probabilities of the degree of clientelism on our three dependent variables (i.e., policy dimensions).

Clientelism and Social Policy Outcomes (Part II)

In order to operationalize the degree of clientelism on the macro-level and over time we use data from the Varieties of Democracies project (VDem, Coppedge et al. 2016), which provides information at the party system level on the degree of clientelistic versus programmatic linkages for a wider time span than the DALP which is a cross-section for 2009.[3] The VDem data is based on expert ratings on the following question: 'Among the major parties,

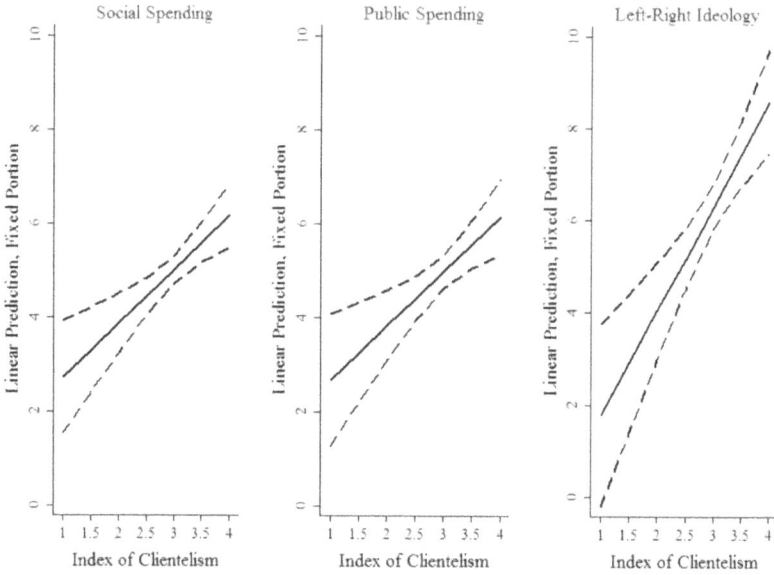

Figure 8.1   Predicted Probabilities of Clientelism on Policy Dimensions
Note: Predicted probabilities of clientelism on social spending, public spending and the overall left-right dimension with confidence intervals at the 95 per cent level.

what is the main or most common form of linkage to their constituents?'[4] The answer categories are: 'clientelistic: constituents are rewarded with goods, cash, and/or jobs', 'mixed clientelistic and local collective', 'local collective: constituents are rewarded with local collective goods, e.g., wells, toilets, markets, roads, bridges, and local development', 'mixed local collective and policy/programmatic', and 'policy/programmatic: constituents respond to a party's positions on national policies, general party programs, and visions for society'. For ease of interpretation we recode lower values reflecting a programmatic linkage and higher values a more clientelistic linkage in the party system. The scale is an ordinal one which is 'converted to interval by the measurement model' (Coppedge et al. 2016, 126), so that it ranges from 1 (programmatic) to 5 (clientelistic).

Concerning the dependent variables in this part of our analysis, instead of looking at expenditures, we focus on social policy outcomes which are more reliable measures for welfare (Baum and Lake 2003; Ross 2006). Ross (2006, 861) promotes the focus on the infant mortality rate (IMR) as it is 'typically concentrated in the lowest income quintile' and it 'is also a sensitive measure of many other conditions – including access to clean water and sanitation, indoor air quality, female education and literacy, prenatal and neonatal health services, caloric intake, disease, and of course, income'. Hence, our first social policy outcome indicator, IMR, is measured by infants dying before the age of one and reflects the progressivity of health care policies. Secondly, we study the effect of clientelism on secondary female education, as outcome of progressive public policy on education. The female gross secondary school enrolment is defined as follows: 'Gross enrollment ratio is the ratio of total enrollment, regardless of age, to the population of the age group that officially corresponds to the level of education shown' (WDI, The World Bank Group 2017). We opt for *female* education since it is a more conservative indicator of education for the poor as even in countries with less developed education systems it is usually men who receive some education. Thus, when females are reached, we take it as an indicator for a more thorough and inclusive education system (see Baum and Lake [2003] for a similar rationale). We use *secondary* rather than primary education as primary school enrolment is usually fostered by CCTs and programs that are not necessarily always at the discretion of governments but also promoted by international actors such as the IMF, the World Bank or donors. Thirdly, we use the life expectancy rate as proxy for the scope of social security in Latin America (see Pribble 2011) as poverty in old age can strongly reduce the rate. Finally, we consider the poverty gap (i.e., the percentage of the population living below the poverty line of a minimum of 1.90$ per day) as a general account of the redistributive and pro-poor nature of the country's welfare system. All indicators are derived from the Worldwide Development Indicators of the World Bank (WDI, The World Bank Group 2017).

To set up the model specification for these welfare indicators as dependent variables we follow the standard approaches from the literature (Baum and Lake 2003; Kaufman and Segura-Ubiergo 2001; Ross 2006) and add the following controls: GDP per capita, trade openness (imports plus exports divided by GDP), the inflation rate and the official exchange rate, size of the population, population above sixty-five years of age, and the unemployment rate (The World Bank Group 2017). We also control for the Gini coefficient (Solt 2009, 2016), the level of democracy (Polity IV, scale from −10, autocracy, to 10, democracy), and include a dummy variable for the ideological slant of the government (left or right, centre is taken as reference category) from Murillo, Oliveros, and Vaishnav (2010).[5] While Huber, Mustillo, and Stephens (2008) promote the expectation that the progressivity of social policies is increased by the left in Latin America, recent findings from Fairfield and Garay (2017) and Brooks (2015) challenge this assumption with new insights. Finally, we hold constant how much the government spends on social policies in general (in per capita USD, ECLAC 2016) to factor in governmental social policy output. We use a one-year lag for social expenditures and GDP per capita to factor in some time for adjustment, as responses are less likely to be immediate. Furthermore we use a lag of five years for the democracy measure since Gerring, Thacker, and Alfaro (2012) found evidence that it is the length of democratic experience that matters for welfare indicators.[6]

For the pooled time-series cross-section analysis we use an OLS regression with panel-corrected standard errors (PCSE) due to our continuous dependent variables. The subscripts k indicates countries and t refers to years. We add country (α) and time (γ, decade dummies) fixed effects as there might be unobserved heterogeneity. X illustrates a set of control variables. The model is specified as follows:

$$Welfare\ Indicators_{kt} = \beta_0 + \beta_1 + \beta^2$$
$$Clientelism_{kt} + \beta X_{kt} + \alpha_k + \gamma_t + \varepsilon_{kt}$$

Holding constant the level of income inequality and economic factors such as trade openness and the level of GDP per capita, our estimates from the pooled time-series cross-section OLS regression – presented in Table 8.2 – show that countries with more clientelistic party systems score lower on

Table 8.2 Pooled Time-Series Cross-Section OLS Regression with Fixed Effects: Clientelistic Linkage and Welfare Indicators for Eighteen Latin American Countries, 1990–2012

	M4	M5	M6	M7
	IMR	Life Expect.	School Enrol.	Poverty
Clientelistic Linkage$_{t-1}$	1.905**	−0.303***	−1.685+	0.651
	(0.667)	(0.092)	(0.992)	(0.441)
Left Presidency$_{t-1}$	0.383	−0.005	−3.995*	0.271
(Ref. Category: Centre)	(0.488)	(0.066)	(1.661)	(0.400)
Right Presidency$_{t-1}$	0.497	0.011	−1.439	0.383
	(0.457)	(0.060)	(2.066)	(0.493)
Social Spending per Capita	0.002	−0.001+	−0.008	0.002
	(0.002)	(0.000)	(0.008)	(0.003)
Unemployment Rate	0.090	−0.014	0.269	0.208**
	(0.064)	(0.014)	(0.251)	(0.077)
Gini Coefficient	0.299*	−0.040+	1.003**	0.498***
	(0.148)	(0.024)	(0.373)	(0.117)
Pop>65	−7.926***	2.211***	17.700***	−2.011*
	(0.927)	(0.134)	(2.805)	(0.999)
Population	−0.000***	0.000*	0.000	0.000
	(0.000)	(0.000)	(0.000)	(0.000)
GDP per Capita	0.002**	−0.000	0.000	−0.001
	(0.001)	(0.000)	(0.002)	(0.001)
Inflation	0.016*	−0.003*	−0.036	0.010
	(0.007)	(0.001)	(0.039)	(0.017)

	M4	M5	M6	M7
	IMR	Life Expect.	School Enrol.	Poverty
Official Exchange Rate	0.000	0.000*	−0.000**	0.000
	(0.000)	(0.000)	(0.000)	(0.000)
Trade Openness	−0.052**	0.009**	0.020	0.007
	(0.017)	(0.003)	(0.057)	(0.020)
Polity IV$_{t-5}$	0.002	0.005	0.110	0.067
	(0.112)	(0.018)	(0.264)	(0.093)
90s	1.027**	−0.181**	−2.543*	−0.059
	(0.338)	(0.057)	(1.102)	(0.543)
Constant	74.773***	54.940***	−126.487***	−6.436
	(13.166)	(1.942)	(31.094)	(11.606)
N	214	214	169	166
N (countries)	18	18	18	17
Wald Chi²	9,268.92	7,376.96	2,938.95	3,277.47
R²	0.966	0.999	0.939	0.745

Note: Standard errors in parentheses. Fixed effects are not displayed. $^+p < 0.10$, $^*p < 0.05$, $^{**}p < 0.01$, $^{***}p < 0.001$. The sample is unbalanced due to missing data in some countries for some of the control variables (e.g. information on the poverty gap is missing for Guatemala).
Sources: VDem (2016), World Bank World Development Indicators (2017), Murillo and Oliveros (2010), Solt (2009), Marshal et al. (2016), and ECLAC (2016).

social indicators. To illustrate the substantive effect of clientelism on our four welfare indicators we plot their predictive marginal effects in Figure 8.2. More clientelistic linkages in a party system go together with a higher infant mortality rate (IMR) as illustrated in Model 4. The effect is significant at the 1 per cent level, and given a mean of IMR of 26.2 (standard deviation = 13.12) an increase of 1.9 is substantial. Also, female education is significantly reduced when clientelism is more pronounced (see Model 6), although the effect is only significant at the 10 per cent level. The mean of female secondary school enrolment in our sample is 74.42 with a standard deviation of 17.74, so that an increase of clientelism by one unit reduces enrolment by 1.7 units on average. Considering the life expectancy ratio (Model 5), we also find a significant negative effect of clientelism. The poverty level increases by more than 1 percentage point when comparing very programmatic to very clientelistic party systems (see panel d in Figure 8.2). The poverty gap has a mean of 4.89 in our sample and a standard deviation of 3.84, so that the increase is not negligible. But the effect on the poverty gap falls short of the 95 per cent confidence level.

Figure 8.2 shows that the pattern of the effect of clientelism holds across all welfare indicators. While our independent variable, the clientelistic linkage indicated by higher values on this scale, is barely or not significant in the last two panels, we see a significant effect in the upper panels regarding the

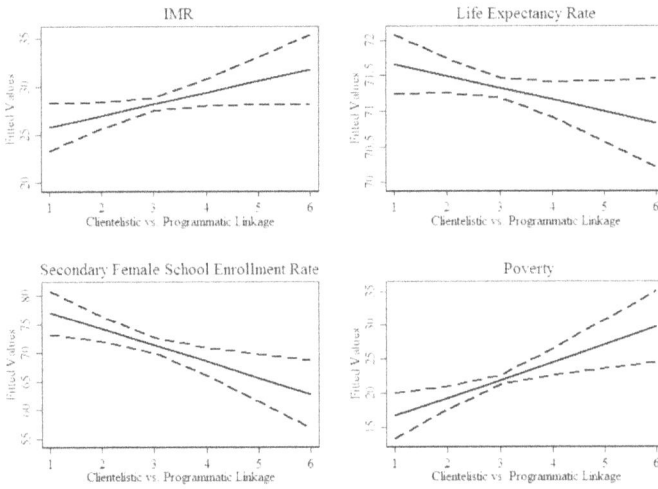

Figure 8.2   Predicted Probabilities with Confidence Intervals at the 95 Per Cent Level
Note: Predicted probabilities of clientelism on four welfare indicators with confidence
intervals at the 95 per cent level.

infant mortality rate (upper left corner) and the life expectancy rate (upper
right corner). The confidence intervals do not overlap at the lowest and highest levels of the linkage scale. Even though the impact on the life expectancy
rate, which stands as a proxy for social security policies, seems to be steep-
est, the magnitude is stronger for IMR and school enrolment. There seems
to be a tendency that progressive social policies are less compatible with
clientelism in the party system compared to more conservative or residual
social policies, but the aggregated nature of our analysis does not allow us to
draw firm conclusions on this claim. Given the well-known shortcomings of
pooled time-series cross-sectional analysis (Kittel and Winner 2005), missing observations for some country-years, and the macro perspective of the
analysis, further research that taps into the causal mechanism is needed. We
can therefore only partially support H2.

DISCUSSION

We now turn to the joint discussion of these results, tying them back to the
arguments stated in the theoretical section of this chapter. As highlighted
early on, the causal chain between clientelism and regressive welfare states
consists of several steps, of which we test two in our analysis. We argue, in
the first part, that the presence of clientelistic linkages between parties and

their voters holds the danger of systematically underrepresenting specific segments in society, especially in the area of social policy. Our results support the assumed connection between the degree of clientelism and a more regressive stance on social policy and economic issues in general, thereby confirming H1. Note that this relationship is robust even when controlling for the degree of programmatic linkages a party deploys. Moreover, the more a political party emphasizes a programmatic linkage strategy the more likely it advocates left leaning policies – at least with respect to public spending and the overall left-right dimension (see Table 9.1). These findings support arguments put forward by Kitschelt (2000) and Weitz-Shapiro (2014) that clientelistic parties face credibility costs with respect to their policy platforms.

We cannot infer from a political party's stance on social policy issues on implemented social policy and its distributive outcomes, as this is a long causal chain that is influenced by further aspects. For established democracies, at least, several studies have found a significant connection between political parties' policy promises and the policies they enact if they are in power (Mansergh and Thomson 2007; Thomson et al. 2017). For the Latin American context, however, it can be questioned that political parties are reliable in their programmatic appeal as Stokes (2001) has illustrated for the 1990s, when left parties suddenly propagated neoliberal policies after they achieved office based on a left campaign. Moreover, all parties are equally constrained by resource scarcity so that the willingness to spend does sometimes just not meet the available means (see Huber, Mustillo, and Stephens 2008). Since we do not test this link in the causal chain, we need to interpret the findings from the first part of our empirical analysis with caution. To investigate the last chain in the causal process linking clientelistic behaviour of political parties to social policy outcomes, we conducted several regression analyses of the influence of clientelism on different welfare indicators. While we find only weak support for an effect of clientelism in a party system on our overall indicator of poverty (Model 7, Table 9.2), we find a significant and negative effect of clientelism on female school enrolment and the life expectancy rate (Models 5 and 6), and a highly significant and positive effect on IMR in Models 4. The analysis on party positions on the public spending issue explicitly refers to pro-poor social policies versus the support of private solutions and voluntary insurance systems. Here, clientelism goes very well together with the latter stance. In terms of welfare state outcomes we do, however, not see such a clear divide between pro-poor and more conservative social policies. Both types seem to be refuted by clientelistic parties. The lack of a clear finding on discrimination between social policy types through clientelism might be due to the crudeness of our welfare outcome measures. There might be much more regional variation in welfare provision that we miss through our national level measures. Furthermore, we still lack means to hold constant the impact of CCTs on welfare state outcomes and the level of discretion that governments have on their performance (see Diaz-Cayeros, Estévez, and Magaloni 2016).

Hence, this study is only a first step into the analysis of welfare state policies and clientelism. While the measure of the degree of programmatic vs clientelistic linkage usage in a country's party system established by VDem (Coppedge et al. 2016) finally allows to study the impact of clientelism over time, it also comes with shortcomings in its conceptual specification. For example, it assumes that party systems can be placed on a dimension that runs from fully clientelistic to fully programmatic, thereby excluding the possibility of different types of linkage-mixing by political parties (e.g., Luna 2014; Magaloni, Diaz-Cayeros, and Estévez 2007)

We need to develop better measures for clientelism over time to trace its impact on social policy in low- and middle-income countries.

CONCLUSION

Classical theories on democratic representation often emphasize the beneficial consequences of parties competing in free and fair elections with each other for the votes of their citizens, leading to famous models of responsible party government or the mandate perspective of government. However, these theories rest on the assumption of a programmatic link between voters and parties, a link that has been challenged by evidence from new democracies, and is lately questioned also in more established democracies (Kitschelt and Kselman 2013). Thus, we make use of the linkage concept and factor in clientelistic practices that may subvert the beneficial consequences of democratic representation by hindering the policy-signalling power of a vote (Hopkin 2006). The contribution of our analysis is twofold: First we show that clientelistic parties are indeed less supportive of pro-poor oriented social policies in their party platforms, indicating that they might be an obstacle to welfare state development in the long term. Second, a party system that is classified as being more clientelistic goes together with lower social welfare, especially for the poor. Clientelism, thus, seems to pose a serious hurdle to political reforms toward more universal social welfare states in Latin America.

In this chapter we placed our emphasis on the nexus between social policy and clientelism. But distributive politics and poverty alleviation does not only work through transfers. Implications of clientelism for fiscal policies is so far a very underdeveloped field of research. Moreover, recent findings from Holland (2015, 2016) on forbearance illustrates, on the one hand, the need to take into account the actual enforcement of written policy decisions and laws, and on the other, the crucial role of labour market policies and labour regulations for poverty and inequality. By raising entry hurdles to the labour market, clientelistic parties might increase obstacles for informal sector workers to have access to employment related social policies such as pensions and thereby provide benefits to public employees – the classical clients. Understanding the clientelistic parties' strategic choices which policies to promote does therefore need a broad approach that encompasses more than just social policies. Next to the adjacent fields of taxation and labour law, infrastructure and environmental politics could be equally affected.

NOTES

1. But as Rudra (2008) emphasizes it is mostly the middle-income group that experiences cutbacks.

2. For detailed question wordings and scales, see the DALP online questionnaire available at https://sites.duke.edu/democracylinkage/, accessed August 2017.

3. Note that we find a positive correlation of $r = 0.429$ (significant at $p < 0.10$) between the country mean of the DALP indicator used in part I of this chapter and the VDem indicator used in part II for the year 2009.

4. The following clarification for the expert is provided: 'A party-constituent linkage refers to the sort of "good" that the party offers in exchange for political support and participation in party activities'.

5. The original scale goes form 1 (left) to 5 (right) presidencies, which we recode to left (1 and 2), centre (3) and right (4 and 5).

6. The estimation results on the clientelistic linkage variables is robust to variation in the lag structure. Results are available on request.

REFERENCES

Auyero, Javier. 1999. 'From the Client's Point(s) of View': How Poor People Perceive and Evaluate Political Clientelism. *Theory and Society* 28: 297–334.

Baum, Matthew A., and David A. Lake. 2003. The Political Economy of Growth: Democracy and Human Capital. *American Journal of Political Science* 47(2): 333–347.

Berens, Sarah. 2015. Preferences on Redistribution in Fragmented Labor Markets in Latin America and the Caribbean. *Journal of Politics in Latin America* 7(3): 117–156.

Berens, Sarah, and Saskia P. Ruth. 2014. Bad Bargains – Does Vote-Buying Hinder Progressive Social Policy in Latin America? Presented at the ECPR Joint Sessions of Workshops, Salamanca, Spain.

Bischof, Daniel. forthcoming. Do Parties Walk Like They Talk? Ideological Congruence Between Party Rhetoric & Policy-Making. *West European Politics*.

Bolleyer, Nicole, and Saskia P. Ruth. 2018. Elite Investments in Party Institutionalization in New Democracies: A Two-Dimensional Approach. *The Journal of Politics* 80(1): 288–302.

Brooks, Sarah M. 2015. Social Protection for the Poorest: The Adoption of Antipoverty Cash Transfer Programs in the Global South. *Politics & Society* 43(4): 551–582.

Calvo, Ernesto, and María Victoria Murillo. 2004. Who Delivers? Partisan Clients in the Argentine Electoral Market. *American Journal of Political Science* 48(4): 742–757.

Carnes, Matthew E., and Isabela Mares. 2014. Coalitional Realignment and the Adoption of Non-Contributory Social Insurance Programmes in Latin America. *Socio-Economic Review* 12(4): 695–722.

———. 2015. Explaining the 'Return of the State' in Middle-Income Countries: Employment Vulnerability, Income, and Preferences for Social Protection in Latin America. *Politics & Society* 43(4): 525–550.

Coppedge, Michael, John Gerring, Staffan I. Lindberg, Svend-Erik Skaaning, Jan Teorell, David Altman, Michael Bernhard, M. Steven Fish, Adam Glynn, Allen Hicken, Carl Henrik Knutsen, Kyle Marquardt, Kelly McMann, Farhad Miri, Pamela Paxton, Daniel Pemstein, Jeffrey Staton, Eitan Tzelgov, Yi-Ting Wang, and Brigitte Zimmerman. 2016a. V-Dem [Country-Year/Country-Date] Dataset v6.2. In, ed. Varieties of Democracy (V-Dem) Project.

———. 2016b. V-Dem Codebook v6. In, ed. Varieties of Democracy (V-Dem) Project.

Cramer, Brian D., and Robert R. Kaufman. 2011. Views of Economic Inequality in Latin America. *Comparative Political Studies* 44(9): 1206–1237.

De Ferranti, D., G. E. Perry, F. H. H. Ferreira, and M. Walton. 2004. *Inequality in Latin America and the Caribbean: Breaking with History?* Washington, DC: The World Bank.

De La O, Ana. 2013. Do Conditional Cash Transfers Affect Electoral Behavior? Evidence from a Randomized Experiment in Mexico. *American Journal of Political Science* 57(1): 1–14.

Díaz-Cayeros, Alberto, and Beatriz Magaloni. 2009. Poverty, Inequality, and Democracy. Aiding Latin America's Poor. *Journal of Democracy* 20(4): 36–49.

Diaz-Cayeros, Alberto, Federico Estévez, and Beatriz Magaloni. 2016. *The Political Logic of Poverty Relief: Electoral Strategies and Social Policy in Mexico.* Cambridge: Cambridge University Press.

Dion, Michelle L., and Vicki Birchfield. 2010. Economic Development, Income Inequality, and Preferences for Redistribution. *International Studies Quarterly* 54 (2): 315–334.

Dixit, Avinash, and John Londregan. 1996. The Determinants of Success of Special Interests in Redistributive Politics. *Journal of Politics* 58(4): 1132–1155.

Downs, Anthony. 1957. *An Economic Theory of Democracy.* New York: Harper & Row Publishers.

ECLAC. 2016. CEPALSTAT. Databases and Statistical Publications. In, ed. Economic Commission for Latin America and the Caribbean.

Fairfield, Tasha, and Candelaria Garay. 2017. Redistribution Under the Right in Latin America: Electoral Competition and Organized Actors in Policymaking. *Comparative Political Studies* 50(14): 1871–1906.

Finseraas, Henning. 2009. Income Inequality and Demand for Redistribution: A Multilevel Analysis of European Public Opinion. *Scandinavian Political Studies* 32(1): 94–119.

Fiszbein, A., N. R. Schady, and F. H. H. Ferreira. 2009. *Conditional Cash Transfers: Educing Present and Future Poverty*. Washington, DC: World Bank Publications.

Garay, Candelaria. 2016. *Social Policy Expansion in Latin America*. New York: Cambridge University Press.

Gay, Robert. 1998. Rethinking Clientelism: Demands, Discourses and Practices in Contemporary Brazil. *European Journal of Latin American and Caribbean Studies* 65: 7–24.

Gerring, John, Strom C. Thacker, and Rodrigo Alfaro. 2012. Democracy and Human Development. *The Journal of Politics* 74(1): 1–17.

Gibson, Edward L. 1997. The Populist Road to Market Reform. Policy and Electoral Coalitions in Mexico and Argentina. *World Politics* 49(3): 339–370.

Haggard, Stephan, and Robert R. Kaufman. 2008. *Development, Democracy, and Welfare States: Latin America, East Asia, and Eastern Europe*. Princeton, NJ: Princeton University Press.

Hilgers, Tina. 2009. 'Who Is Using Whom?' Clientelism from the Client's Perspective. *Journal of Iberian and Latin American Research* 15(1): 51–75.

———. 2011. Clientelism and Conceptual Stretching: Differentiating Among Concepts and Among Analytical Levels. *Theory and Society* 40(5): 567–588.

———, ed. 2013. *Clientelism in Everyday Latin American Politics*. Basingstoke: Palgrave Macmillan.

Holland, Alisha C. 2015. The Distributive Politics of Enforcement. *American Journal of Political Science* 59(2): 357–371.

———. 2016. Insurgent Successor Parties: Scaling Down to Build a Party After War. In *Challenges of Party-Building in Latin America*, eds. Steven Levitsky, James Loxton, Brandon Van Dyck, and Jorge I. Domínguez. Cambridge: Cambridge University Press. 273–304.

Hopkin, Jonathan. 2006. Clientelism and Party Politics. In *Handbook of Party Politics*, eds. Richard S. Katz and Bill Crotty. London: Sage. 406–421.

Hox, Joop J. 2010. *Multilevel Analysis. Techniques and Applications*. Second Edition. New York: Routledge.

Huber, Evelyne, and John D. Stephens. 2001. *Development and Crisis of the Welfare State: Parties and Policies in Global Markets*. Chicago: University of Chicago Press.

———. 2012. *Democracy and the Left: Social Policy and Inequality in Latin America*. Chicago: University of Chicago Press.

Huber, Evelyne, Thomas Mustillo, and John D. Stephens. 2008. Politics and Social Spending in Latin America. *The Journal of Politics* 70(02): 420–436.

Kaufman, Robert R., and Alex Segura-Ubiergo. 2001. Globalization, Domestic Politics, and Social Spending in Latin America: A Time-Series Cross-Section Analysis, 1973–97. *World Politics* 53(4): 553–587.

Kenworthy, Lane, and Leslie McCall. 2008. Inequality, Public Opinion and Redistribution. *Socio-Economic Review* 6(1): 35–68.

Kitschelt, Herbert. 2000. Linkages Between Citizens and Politicians in Democratic Polities. *Comparative Political Studies* 33(6/7): 845–879.

———. 2013. *Democratic Accountability and Linkages Project*. Durham, NC: Duke University Press.

Kitschelt, Herbert, and Daniel M. Kselman. 2013. Economic Development, Democratic Experience, and Political Parties' Linkage Strategies. *Comparative Political Studies* 46(11), 1453–1484.

Kitschelt, Herbert, and Steven I. Wilkinson. 2007. Citizen-Politician Linkages: An Introduction. In *Patrons, Clients, and Policies. Patterns of Democratic Accountability and Political Competition*, eds. Herbert Kitschelt and Steven I. Wilkinson. Cambridge: Cambridge University Press. 1–49.

Kittel, Bernhard, and H. Winner. 2005. How Reliable Is Pooled Analysis in Political Economy? The Globalization-Welfare Nexus Revisited. *European Journal of Political Research* 44: 269–293.

Korpi, Walter, and Joakim Palme. 1998. The Paradox of Redistribution and Strategies of Equality: Welfare State Institutions, Inequality, and Poverty in the Western Countries. *American Sociological Review* 63(5): 661–687.

Laakso, Markku, and Rein Taagepera. 1979. 'Effective' Number of Parties. A Measure with Application to West Europe. *Comparative Political Studies* 12(1): 3–27.

Lindert, Kathy, Emmanuel Skoufias, and Joseph Shapiro. 2006. Redistributing Income to the Poor and the Rich: Public Transfers in Latin America and the Caribbean. Social Safety Nets Primer Series #0605, The World Bank.

Lloyd-Sherlock, Peter. 2009. Social Policy and Inequality in Latin America: A Review of Recent Trends. *Social Policy & Administration* 43(4): 347–363.

Luna, Juan Pablo. 2014. *Segmented Representation: Political Party Strategies in Unequal Democracies*. Oxford: Oxford University Press.

Magaloni, Beatriz, Alberto Diaz-Cayeros, and Federico Estévez. 2007. Clientelism and Portfolio Diversification: A Model of Electoral Investment with Applications to Mexico. In *Patrons, Clients, and Policies. Patterns of Democratic Accountability and Political Competition*, eds. Herbert Kitschelt and Steven I. Wilkinson. Cambridge: Cambridge University Press. 182–205.

Manin, Bernard, Adam Przeworski, and Susan C. Stokes. 1999. Elections and Representation. In *Democracy, Accountability, and Representation*, eds. Adam Przeworski, Susan C. Stokes, and Bernard Manin. Cambridge: Cambridge University Press. 29–54.

Mansergh, Lucy, and Robert Thomson. 2007. Election Pledges, Party Competition, and Policymaking. *Comparative Politics* 39(3): 311–329.

Mares, Isabela. 2003. *The Politics of Social Risk: Business and Welfare State Development*. Cambridge: Cambridge University Press.

Mares, Isabela, and Matthew E. Carnes. 2009. Social Policy in Developing Countries. *Annual Review of Political Science* 12(1): 93–113.

Marshall, Monty, Keith Jaggers, and Ted Robert Gurr. 2016. Polity IV Project. Political Regime Characteristics and Transitions, 1800–2015. In *Dataset Users' Manual*. Vienna, VA: Center for Systemic Peace.

Meltzer, Allan H., and Scott F. Richard. 1981. A Rational Theory of the Size of Government. *Journal of Political Economy* 89(5): 914–927.

Murillo, María Victoria, Virginia Oliveros, and Milan Vaishnav. 2010. *Dataset on Political Ideology of Presidents and Parties in Latin America.* New York: Colombia University. Available at https://virginiaoliveros.com/data/ accessed August 2017

Nichter, Simeon. 2008. Vote Buying or Turnout Buying? Machine Politics and the Secret Ballot. *American Political Science Review* 102(1): 19–31.

Powell, G. Bingham. 2004. Political Representation in Comparative Politics. *Annual Review of Political Science* 7(1): 273–296.

———. 2005. The Chain of Responsiveness. In *Assessing the Quality of Democracy*, eds. Larry Diamond and Leonardo Morlino. Baltimore, MD: Johns Hopkins University Press. 62–76.

Pribble, Jennifer. 2011. Worlds Apart: Social Policy Regimes in Latin America. *Studies in Comparative International Development* 46(2): 191–216.

———. 2013. *Welfare and Party Politics in Latin America.* Cambridge: Cambridge University Press.

Remmer, Karen L. 2007. The Political Economy of Patronage: Expenditure Patterns in the Argentine Provinces, 1983–2003. *The Journal of Politics* 69(2): 363–377.

Ross, Michael. 2006. Is Democracy Good for the Poor? *American Journal of Political Science* 50(4): 860–874.

Rothstein, Bo. 2011. *The Quality of Government: Corruption, Social Trust, and Inequality in International Perspective.* Chicago: University of Chicago Press.

Rudra, Nita. 2008. *Globalization and the Race to the Bottom in Developing Countries. Who Really Gets Hurt?* Cambridge: Cambridge University Press.

Rueda, David, and Daniel Stegmueller. 2016. The Externalities of Inequality: Fear of Crime and Preferences for Redistribution in Western Europe. *American Journal of Political Science* 60(2): 472–489.

Ruth, Saskia P., and Rodrigo Salazar Elena. 2016. Designing Loopholes: Clientelism and Social Policy Design in Mexico. Presented at the 'New' Policy Design Research: When and How Does Policy Design Matter? Zurich.

Singer, Matthew, and Herbert Kitschelt. 2011. 'Do Everything' (DoE) Parties: When Can Politicians Combine Clientelistic and Programmatic Appeals. Presented at the Workshop on Democratic Accountability Strategies, Durham, May.

Solt, Frederick. 2009. Standardizing the World Income Inequality Database*. *Social Science Quarterly* 90(2): 231–242.

———. 2016. Standardizing the World Income Inequality Database*. *Social Science Quarterly* 97(5): 1267–1281.

Stokes, Susan C. 2001. *Mandates and Democracy. Neoliberalism by Surprise in Latin America.* Cambridge: Cambridge University Press.

———. 2007. Political Clientelism. In *The Oxford Handbook of Comparative Politics*, eds. Carles Boix and Susan C. Stokes. Oxford: Oxford University Press. 604–627.

Stokes, Susan C., Thad Dunning, Marcelo Nazareno, and Valeria Brusco, eds. 2013. *Brokers, Voters, and Clientelism. The Puzzle of Distributive Politics.* Cambridge: Cambridge University Press.

Taylor, Michael, and V. M. Herman. 1971. Party Systems and Governmental Stability. *American Political Science Review* 65: 28–37.

The World Bank Group. 2017. *World Development Indicators (WDI).* http://datatopics.
    worldbank.org/world-development-indicators/ accessed July 2017.

Thomson, Robert, Terry Royed, Elin Naurin, Joaquín Artés, Rory Costello, Laurenz
    Ennser-Jedenastik, Mark Ferguson, Petia Kostadinova, Catherine Moury, François
    Pétry, and Katrin Praprotnik. 2017. The Fulfillment of Parties' Election Pledges:
    A Comparative Study on the Impact of Power Sharing. *American Journal of Politi-
    cal Science* 61(3): 527–542.

Tzelgov, Eitan, and Yi-Ting Wang. 2016. Party Ideology and Clientelistic Linkage.
    Electoral Studies 44: 374–387.

Weitz-Shapiro, Rebecca. 2012. What Wins Votes: Why Some Politicians Opt Out of
    Clientelism. *American Journal of Political Science* 56(3): 568–583.

———. 2014. *Curbing Clientelism in Argentina. Politics, Poverty, and Social Policy.*
    Cambridge: Cambridge University Press.

Wibbels, Erik. 2006. Dependency Revisited: International Markets, Business Cycles,
    and Social Spending in the Developing World. *International Organization* 60(2):
    433–468.

Wibbels, Erik, and John S. Ahlquist. 2011. Development, Trade, and Social Insur-
    ance. *International Studies Quarterly* 55(1): 125–149.

Chapter Nine

Clientelism and Political Budget Cycles

Evidence from Health Policy in Italy

Francesco Stolfi

INTRODUCTION

In the past twenty years there has been sustained scholarly attention to the contextual factors affecting the size of Political Budget Cycles (PBCs), that is electorally motivated cycles in fiscal variables. More specifically, PBCs are 'regular, periodic fluctuation[s] in a government's fiscal policies induced by the cycle of elections' (Alt and Rose 2007, 845). The underlying assumption in the literature is that changes in the institutions or resources that make up the context in which actors make fiscal policy will modify their decisions (Drazen 2001; Franzese 2002a). In other words, PBCs are produced by manipulable variables, and they can be modified. In this chapter I am particularly interested in the effect of clientelism on electoral cycles in distributive spending. As argued in the introduction of this volume, clientelistic practices may distort governance as access to public resources and services is granted to individuals in exchange for their political support rather than based on formal rules of public policies (De La O 2013; Stokes et al. 2013, chapter 1). However, until now the actual impact of clientelism on public spending has seldom been tested empirically.

Therefore, this chapter aims to systematically analyse the relationship between the extent of clientelism and the distortion in public policy in regional jurisdictions. Specifically, it assesses how different indicators of clientelism affect the Political Budget Cycles (PBCs) of personnel spending in the health sector of the Italian regions. I focus on personnel spending as this type of spending is especially prone to be manipulated in a particularistic manner for short-term electoral purposes (Ames et al. 2005). Consequently, the chapter focuses on one subtype of clientelistic practices, namely patronage, which is defined as electorally motivated favouritism in the distribution of government jobs (Afonso et al. 2015, 908; Hicken 2011; Kitschelt 2000; Piattoni 2001; Stokes 2007).

Italy is a most likely case to analyse this question since it has one of the highest levels of patronage spending in Europe at the national level (Kopecký and Spirova 2011, 908) as well as significant variation across regions (see table A1 in the Appendix). Moreover, focusing on the sub-national level in one single country allows me to control for other institutional features that can have an impact on the size of PBCs, such as electoral rules (Chang 2008; Lizzeri and Persico 2001; Milesi-Ferretti et al. 2002; Persson and Tabellini 2003), transparency of the budget process (Alt and Lassen 2006b; Saporiti and Streb 2008), quality of the media (Akhmedov and Zhuravskaya 2004), and the experience with democracy (Akhmedov and Zhuravskaya 2004; Brender and Drazen 2005). Finally, I focus specifically on the health sector since this is by far the largest policy competence of the Italian regions, with health care spending representing more than 70 per cent of regional expenditure (ISAE 2004, 39).

The chapter has both theoretical and policy implications well beyond the Italian case. The connection between the two heretofore separates literatures on clientelism, and PBCs points to difficulties in managing fiscal policy, and specifically reducing PBCs, across contexts that cannot be easily modified through a common institutional framework. Hence, this issue is important both in countries with regional differences, like Italy, and for supranational regimes aiming to harmonize fiscal policies across different national contexts. A case in point is the European Union (EU). Evidence of PBCs has been found in a number of EU Member States (Buti and van den Noord 2004; Efthyvoulou 2012; Mink and de Haan 2006; von Hagen 2006); at the same time, the EU has been engaged in a process of institutional development precisely with the goal of limiting fiscal cycles that are not guided by macro-economic factors (Debrun et al. 2008), a process that the current debt crisis has accelerated.

The chapter is structured as follows: In the first section I briefly place the chapter in the context of the clientelism and PBCs literature. In the second section II introduce the Italian case in the context of health policy and regional politics. The third section describes the operationalization of the main concepts, presents the empirical analysis, and discusses the findings. The final section concludes.

POLITICAL BUDGET CYCLES AND CLIENTELISM

In theory, incumbents have an incentive to engineer Political Budget Cycles (PBCs) parallel to electoral cycles because they gain from being in government. Rational voters, however, should not be fooled by electoral manipulations that simply distort the temporal distribution of spending and taxes. They should not be swayed or should even penalize the electoral manipulation of public spending (Alesina 1988; Peltzman 1992). Faced with the evidence that PBCs do exist, at least in some countries and in some periods, this poses an important empirical puzzle. Until now, the literature has explained differences in the size and nature of PBCs based on the structure of incentives faced by incumbents and by the ability of voters to detect electoral manipulations. Hence, the explanatory focus has been on electoral rules shaping the incentives of policy-makers (Ames 2001; Chang 2008; Lizzeri and Persico 2001; Milesi-Ferretti et al. 2002; Persson and Tabellini 2003), on the transparency of fiscal choices (Alt and Lassen 2006a), on benefits accruing to incumbents from corruption (Shi and Svensson 2006) and on factors affecting voters ability to assess the choices of the incumbents, such as the presence of independent media (Akhmedov and Zhuravskaya 2004) and the length of experience with democracy (Brender and Drazen 2005).

What the literature on PBCs has not yet explored is the potential effect of deeper, structural differences across jurisdictions, namely of behavioural variables that persist over time and operate independently of the institutional framework and of the resources available to actors. In this chapter, I aim to complement the PBC literature by focusing on such differences across fiscal jurisdictions that may cause actors to respond differently even within a broader national context. Specifically, I show that differences in the degree of clientelism across jurisdictions (Italian regions) that otherwise share a similar context explain differences in the size of PBCs across them.

I define clientelism here in the narrow sense of patronage – that is the distribution of public employment for political gain (Hicken 2011; Kitschelt 2000; Piattoni 2001; Stokes 2007). Patronage spending aims to create goodwill among voters through the distorted use of public resources. Consequently, the practice of patronage may have severe consequences on both the timing of public spending and the rules that make up public policy (Remmer 2007).

Moreover, I focus on clientelism as a collective behavioural attribute of a community. Specifically, clientelism is based on a generalized reciprocity (Auyero et al. 2009; Finan and Schechter 2012), namely on people providing resources to others with an immediate return on their cooperative behaviour. Thus I consider clientelism to consist of both a supply and a demand aspect (Piattoni 2001; Shefter 1994): the supply of clientelistic practices on the part of elites, and the demand for, or at least acceptance of, them on the part of voters. Patronage spending is particularistic and entails the subversion of the letter or the spirit of existing rules, and thus the size of distributive PBCs will vary according to the degree of patronage within jurisdictions. The degree to which members of a polity respect the formal rules and consider the interests of the community in their decision-making is a key factor in this argument.

Consequently, I assess the strength of the impact of clientelism on public spending, or at least of the association between the degree of clientelism and the electorally motivated distortion of PBCs in health care spending if one wishes to remain agnostic on causality. I do so by using five indicators of clientelism that are measured independently of the dependent variable, namely the surge in personnel spending close to elections.

My expectation is that more (less) clientelistic communities will have larger (smaller) PBCs. This expectation applies specifically to a particular type of public spending, namely public spending that benefits specific constituencies in order to win their electoral goodwill and that is decided without public debate, that is in a non-transparent manner, and/or by subverting the official criteria that are supposed to regulate decision-making. This definition distinguishes particularistic, electorally targeted from programmatic, need-based, and democratically legitimate government spending (De La O 2013; Stokes et al. 2013).

On the supply side, in more clientelistic regions the average incumbent will be more willing to break the rules because he or she has a lower level of attachment to public spending norms (Ichino and Maggi 2000; Ostrom 2000). On the demand side, voters will be more inclined to electorally reward personal benefits that they receive from this rule-breaking rather than penalize it (Auyero et al. 2009; Finan and Schechter 2012).

Furthermore, beside these direct effects, patronage may affect PBCs indirectly as well. For example, clientelism goes along with increased corruption (Keefer 2007; Keefer and Vlaicu 2008; Sööt and Rootalu 2012), and this in turn increases the benefits of incumbency and thus the incumbents' incentives to manipulate spending close to elections (Shi and Svensson 2006); it increases the degree of tax evasion (Hug and Spörri 2011; Marien and Hooghe 2011), which reduces the actual cost of public spending for voters in clientelistic communities (Katsimi and Moutos 2010), thus increasing the net benefits of electoral rewards to voters; as it slows down economic development (Bjornskov 2012; Knack and Keefer 1997; Putnam 1993) it creates the conditions for distributive PBCs since poorer voters are more susceptible to electoral manipulation of public spending (Auyero 2000; Brusco et al. 2004; Calvo and Murillo 2004; Stokes 2005).

THE ITALIAN HEALTH SERVICE AND
REGIONAL POLITICS

At the sub-national level Italy is divided into twenty regions. Valle d'Aosta, Friuli-Venezia Giulia, Sicily, Sardinia, and Trentino-Alto Adige, this last region being split into the two autonomous provinces of Bolzano and Trento, were created between 1948 and 1963 and given a special, 'autonomous' status reflecting their specific conditions as border, multi-ethnic areas, or islands. The other fifteen 'ordinary' regions were set up in 1970. The national government sets the overall spending and service provision goals of the National Health Service (NHS), but the services are provided and funded either partially or entirely (in the case of some autonomous regions) by the regions. Health spending represents approximately 70 per cent of the regions' budgets (ISAE 2004).

The NHS was created in 1978 to provide equal health services across the national territory. Originally the central government set the guidelines and provided the funding through general taxation, with funds overwhelmingly allocated as conditional grants, while regions and municipalities were tasked with the day-to-day administration. In the early 1990s, in parallel to the reforms increasing the autonomy of regional politics from national politics, a process began that concentrated the administrative responsibilities for the health services in the regions and gradually changed the sources of funding. A major break in terms of funding occurred in 1997, when ordinary regions were given control of a regional tax on business activities (IRAP), with a rate that can vary between 3.5 and 5.5 per cent and is applied to the valued added produced in the region. In the same year regions were also given the power to impose an additional rate of between 0.5 and 1 per cent on national income tax.[1]

Since the creation of the NHS, the national government routinely underfunded the regional provision of health services, transferring funds to the regions that were lower than the expenses in the previous years, thus leading to the creation of deficits that would be covered by the central government in later years (Bordignon and Turati 2009). In order to supersede this informal arrangement, in 2005 an agreement was reached between central and regional governments whereby regions with high deficits would commit to deficit reduction plans which mandate regional tax increases and spending cuts in exchange for new funds from the central government.[2]

Until the early 1990s regional politics, in both autonomous and ordinary regions, was largely an offshoot of national politics, and drew little attention from voters. A series of laws changed from the mid-1990s on strengthened the connection between voters and regional governments. Law 43/1995 mandated the creation of pre-electoral coalitions, where parties indicate their candidate for president of the region, and introduced a seat premium for the winning coalition. Constitutional law 1/1999 mandated that the presidents of the regions be directly elected.

While these reforms have greatly increased the visibility and electoral weight of the regional presidents (Musella 2009), national issues have continued to dominate regional electoral campaigns. Regional votes are cast according to national party affiliations and based on national party systems, and regional parties do not try to distinguish themselves from the positions of the national parties so that the regional political context in the 2000s remained bound to the national one (Loughlin and Bolgherini 2006). Moreover, the influence of the central party organizations on their peripheral structures, a long-standing feature of the relationship between centre and regions (Tarrow 1977), has been reinforced by the electoral systems used in national elections from 1994 on, which have centralized the selection of candidates (Bardi 2007; Giannetti and Laver 2001; Hopkin 2009).

However, regional issues have become more important, and this is especially the case for the health issue (Loughlin and Bolgherini 2006, 149–150). Moreover, a strong link between illicit activities and politics has developed in the health sector: local and regional politicians can appoint health administrators who can then steer public procurement to preferred entrepreneurs, who in turn provide kickbacks to the politicians (Maino 2009).[3]

Incumbents who want to continue to benefit from this state of affairs and thus be re-elected can resort to a typical strategy to gain electoral consensus in Italy: government hiring circumventing the meritocratic criteria that are supposed to regulate hiring in the public sector (Alesina et al. 1999; Hopkin and Mastropaolo 2001). This strategy is especially available in the health sector, which due to its size provides a key opportunity for distributive spending (Hopkin 2009, 94), and indeed regional and local politicians often start their political careers from a background in the health sector (Tronconi and Rioux 2009, 162). Having carried out an analysis of six newspapers for the 1998–2010 period,[4] I have found ten reported cases of electoral manipulations of health spending in apparent violation of existing rules. These manipulations are principally in the area of personnel, in the form of hiring or of the release of salary arrears close to elections.[5]

In sum, the public health sector in Italy provides an ideal testing ground for the argument that clientelism, both on the supply and the demand side, has a significant impact on electoral spending cycles quite aside from the institutional factors that have so far been emphasized in the literature. The following section provides an empirical test of how clientelism (measured with several different indicators) affects the electoral manipulation of personnel spending in the public health sector

EMPIRICAL ANALYSIS

The dependent variable is per capita personnel spending in the public health sector in the Italian regions. The dataset covers all Italian regions for the 1998–2010 period. For most variables I have data separately for each of the two autonomous provinces that make up Trentino-Alto Adige. I therefore have twenty-one sub-national units over a period of thirteen years.

The aim is to assess the extent to which clientelism affects the size of pre-electoral increases in personnel spending in the health sector of the Italian regions. As an electoral mobilization strategy based on the distribution of selective benefits for voters, clientelism presents a supply and a demand aspect (Piattoni 2001; Shefter 1994): the supply of clientelistic practices on the part of the elites, and the demand for, or at least acceptance of, them on the part of voters. The five indicators are derived so as to be conceptually connected to both the supply and the demand side of clientelism.

As an indicator of clientelistic behaviour by the elites (the supply side) I take corruption. Clientelism implies the distortion of the formal rules that regulate government spending in a contingent exchange of benefits for voter support (Kitschelt 2000; Stokes et al. 2013). Just like clientelism, corruption is a reciprocal exchange based on the subversion of rules, and it has therefore been associated with, and used as proxy for, clientelism in the literature (Keefer 2007; Kitschelt 2000; Kopecký and Spirova 2011).

I use the index of the relative corruption of the Italian regions developed by Golden and Picci (2005): the ratio between the value of government spending in infrastructure and the value of the infrastructure actually built in a region. Using standard procedures for assessing the value of infrastructure and the price paid by the government for that infrastructure, controlling for region-specific costs, and based on time series between 1954 and 1998, Golden and Picci create a normalized index (hereafter GP index) with a value of 1 for a region where the ratio of public capital stock to public outlays is equal to the national average (hence, for a region with 'average efficiency and corruption'). The index measures the ability of regional governments to turn their fiscal resources into physical capital and thus public goods for their citizens.[6] Note that in the original index higher values indicate a higher value of the infrastructure stock, and hence lower corruption; in the analysis carried out in this chapter the scale has been inverted for ease of interpretation, so that higher values of the index indicate higher corruption.

The demand side of clientelism can be seen as either the voters' response to the incentives offered by their environment (Kitschelt and Wilkinson 2007; Piattoni 2001) or as an essentially cultural phenomenon that reflects the attitudes of voters (Carlin and Moseley 2015; Weitz-Shapiro 2012). As an indicator for the incentive-based view of the demand side of clientelism I take income inequality, to reflect the established expectation in the literature of an association between inequality and clientelism, as voters at the lower rungs of the income distribution are relatively more dependent on the benefits they receive through personalistic spending (Luna 2014; Stokes 2007; You 2015). For the attitude-based view of the demand for clientelism I use three indicators: two refer to cooperative behaviour (tax evasion and blood donations) and the third to the electoral turnout for referenda. Electoral participation in referenda is untainted by the distortive use of public resources by politicians who want to be elected, and cooperative behaviour is the exact opposite of the contingent exchange that defines clientelism.

For income inequality I use the 2009 regional Gini index; as a measure of tax evasion I use the ratio between undeclared taxable income and reported taxable income for IRAP (the regional tax on economic activities), based on official data of the Italian tax agency (the data are averages for the 1998–2002 period). A value of, for example 90 per cent, means that, for 100 euros reported to tax authorities, an economic actor does not declare (and thus avoids paying taxes on) 90 euros; finally, following Guiso et al. (2004), as measures of cooperative behaviour I employ regional data on average per capita blood donations (as number of standard-weight blood bags) between 2004 and 2007 and the average turnout for referenda held between 1993 and 2009, the latter being an indication of political participation that, unlike votes in national or regional elections, is untainted by potential vote buying or patronage since no elected positions are at stake.[7]

The following table (Table 9.1) reports the correlations among these five indicators of clientelism:

Table 9.1   Correlations among the Clientelism Indicators

	Blood Donations	Referendum Turnout	GP Index	Tax Evasion	Gini Index
Blood Donations	1.0000				
Referendum Turnout	0.4836*	1.0000			
GP Index	0.6156*	0.8256*	1.0000		
Tax Evasion	−0.5172*	−0.7402*	−0.6541*	1.0000	
Gini Index	−0.2118*	−0.5303*	−0.5568*	0.4987*	1.0000

* The coefficient is statistically different from 0 at the 5 per cent level.

I consider the year before the elections as pre-electoral.[8] The election indicator refers to both regional and national elections, and, following Franzese (2000), I measure the electoral cycle by distributing the time of elections between the election year and the pre-election year. The election indicator takes a value equal to the number of the full months before the election month plus the election day divided by the number of days in the election month, all divided by 12; the year before the election takes the complement to 1 of the value for the election year.

A significant issue in the study of electoral cycles is the potential endogeneity of elections, as in parliamentary systems governments might call elections when positive shocks to the economy favour their electoral prospects (Ito and Park 1998; Kayser 2005). For this reason I only focus on scheduled elections, namely the elections that can be taken to be exogenous because they occur at their constitutionally mandated time, considering as constitutionally mandated those elections that take place within one year of the mandated end of the relevant (national or regional) legislature (Brender and Drazen

2005; Shi and Svensson 2006). Over the 1998–2010 period there were three national elections and, for most regions, three regional elections. One of the three national elections (in 2008) and one regional election in three regions (Abruzzo 2008; Molise 2001; Sicily 2008) took place prematurely. Hence, out of a total of 129 national and regional election occurrences, I consider 105 scheduled elections.

I control both for factors that can be expected to specifically impact health spending and for political, institutional, and economic variables that can affect sub-national spending as a whole. Specific controls for health spending are: the size of a region's population, as economies of scale in the prevision of health care may reduce their unitary cost (Costa-Font and Moscone 2008); the regional age structure, here operationalized as the share of the population over sixty-five years of age, as age has a powerful influence on health care costs (Baltagi and Moscone 2010; Cantatero Prieto and Lago-Peñas 2012; Lopez-Casanovas and Saez 2007; Reich et al. 2012; Sanz and Vasquez 2007); and finally, per capita income, as a common finding is that higher incomes are associated with greater expenditure on health (see Cantatero Prieto and Lago-Peñas 2012 and literature cited therein).

As political controls I include, first, the political orientation of regional and national governments. A common expectation in the literature is that the left increases government size and in particular spending on welfare and social policies like health (see the review in Franzese 2002a, and recent research by Katzimi and Sarantides 2012). For the partisan orientation of the national and regional governments I use a dummy taking a value of one if the government is centre-left and of zero if it is centre-right.

A second political control is the competitiveness of elections. The closeness of the electoral competition may affect the incentives of incumbents: incumbents who are certain to win or lose the next elections will be less prone to electoral fiscal expansions than incumbents that face a tighter race (Aidt et al. 2011; Efthyvoulou 2012; Schultz 1995). Measuring the impact of electoral competitiveness on the electoral choices of incumbents is notoriously difficult given the issues of endogeneity that are raised: the vote differences between winners and losers in a district, which are supposed to affect the electioneering choices of incumbents, are also influenced by these choices. We take advantage of the fact that after World War II the political orientation of voters was very stable geographically (Agnew 2007), until populist movements burst onto the scene and upturned the established left-right axis of political conflict in 2013 (Corbetta and Vignati 2014). Therefore, as a measure of competitiveness I use a dummy variable for the electoral contestability of regions, distinguishing between those that are electorally contestable and those that have, throughout the post–World War II period, maintained a consistent left- or right-wing orientation.[9]

Further, I control for the institutional context. First, I control for the regions that, starting in 2007, have been put under oversight of the central government due to their inability to rein in their deficits in previous years.[10] Second, I include the regions' financial autonomy. This refers to the ratio of a region's 'own taxes', namely taxes on which the sub-national government has some control (in terms of setting the tax rate), to its total revenues. The greater the share of own taxes in the total revenues, namely the greater the share of resources for which they are responsible to their voters, the more fiscally conservative sub-national politicians will be, as they will not consider the fiscal resources of their region as part of a national common pool (Jones et al. 2000; Rodden 2002, 2006; Rodden and Wibbels 2002). Moreover, the lower their financial autonomy, the more sub-national governments can expect to be bailed out if they run excessive deficits (Rodden 2002), especially when without a bailout the regional government would fail to provide essential services such as health care (Rodden 2006, 8–9). As a measure of financial autonomy, I use the ratio between the regional taxes earmarked for the health services (IRAP and the additional rate applied to the national income tax) and the total revenues of the regional health systems.

Finally, as economic control I include the regional unemployment rate, to account for the possibility that health policy may be used counter-cyclically (Clark and Milcent 2011). The following table (Table A9.1 in the appendix) summarizes the variables, reports their sources and their expected signs:

As regards the estimation strategy, like much recent PBCs literature (e.g. Alt and Rose 2007; Block 2002; Drazen and Eslava 2010; Shi and Svensson 2006; Vergne 2009), I rely on the Generalized Method of Moments (GMM) (Arellano and Bond 1991), which expunges the impact of fixed effects (Roodman 2006), and use the Windmeijer correction for finite samples (Windmeijer 2005).[11] At least one panel does not present unit roots.[12]

In order to assess the impact of clientelism, namely how it modifies the size of PBCs, I specify the following model, which includes an interaction term between the election indicator and each of the five indicators of clientelism:

$$\text{Spending}_{i,t} = \alpha + \beta \left(\text{Elections}_{i,t} \right) + \sigma \left(\text{Clientelism Indicator}_i \right) +$$
$$\iota \left(\text{Elections}_{i,t} \right) X \left(\text{Clientelism Indicator}_i \right) + \delta \left(\text{Political controls}_{i,t} \right) +$$
$$\gamma \left(\text{Institutional controls}_{i,t} \right) + \rho \left(\text{Unemployment}_{i,t} \right) + \theta_i + \varepsilon_{i,t}$$

where θ_i is the unobserved region effect and $\varepsilon_{i,t}$ is the error term.

Table 9.2 reports the results of the regressions:[13]

Table 9.2 Clientelism and Electoral Cycles

	(1)	(2)	(3)	(4)	(5)
	GP	Gini	Tax Evasion	Blood Don.	Ref. Turnout
Lagged Spending	0.990***	0.961***	0.950***	0.962***	0.923***
	(0.0480)	(0.0349)	(0.0430)	(0.0350)	(0.0467)
Elections	16.77	−74.99	18.05	37.34***	41.56**
	(13.79)	(54.47)	(11.79)	(10.61)	(16.18)
GP	1.464				
	(10.67)				
GP XElections	11.27				
	(7.852)				
Gini		−44.35			
		(141.7)			
Gini XElections		323.8*			
		(185.0)			
Tax Evasion			14.79		
			(28.16)		
(Tax Evasion) XElections			7.096		
			(17.10)		
Blood Donations				−66.84	
				(45.10)	
Blood Don. XElections				−113.5*	
				(61.90)	
Referendum Turnout					−216.2*
					(109.9)
(Ref. Turnout) XElections					−46.10
					(29.72)
Population (Logged)	6.517	3.062	2.552	0.549	6.031**
	(4.011)	(2.731)	(3.144)	(2.615)	(2.788)
Over 65	−0.738	−0.514	−0.634	−0.993	2.169
	(0.707)	(0.612)	(0.589)	(0.766)	(1.340)
Income (p.c.)	0.00277***	0.00316**	0.00357***	0.00355***	0.00447***
	(0.00119)	(0.00125)	(0.00117)	(0.00124)	(0.00148)
Left (Regional)	0.124	0.387	-0.242	0.284	6.104
	(5.338)	(4.520)	(4.422)	(4.525)	(4.756)
Left (National)	−0.0370	−1.227	−1.303	−1.445	−2.127**
	(1.396)	(0.883)	(0.910)	(0.952)	(0.860)
Electoral Contestability	4.983	5.818	5.183	−2.381	−1.724
	(7.609)	(6.652)	(6.460)	(6.787)	(6.081)
Oversight	−5.127	−6.243	−6.230	−7.103	−10.62
	(6.974)	(6.074)	(6.670)	(6.607)	(7.657)
Financial Autonomy	−128.2**	−117.5**	−112.1**	−120.1**	−105.2**
	(43.63)	(44.43)	(48.14)	(43.05)	(49.95)
Unemployment Rate	−0.079	−16.99	−13.80	−35.29	41.18
	(0.794)	(70.08)	(58.77)	(66.56)	(75.80)
Constant	−75.63	−37.79	−51.04	1.138	−53.53

(Continued)

Table 9.2   (Continued)

	(1)	(2)	(3)	(4)	(5)
	GP	Gini	Tax Evasion	Blood Don.	Ref. Turnout
	(63.65)	(66.05)	(54.37)	(54.95)	(47.35)
N	248	248	248	248	248
First-Order Serial Correlation	z = −2.96	z = −2.98	z = −2.97	z = −2.98	z = −3.05
	Pr > z = 0.003	Pr > z = 0.003	Pr > z = 0.003	Pr > z = 0.00	Pr > z = 0.002
Second-Order Serial Correlation	z = 1.31	z = 1.28	z = 1.28	z = 1.28	z = 1.26
	Pr > z = 0.189	Pr > z = 0.201	Pr > z = 0.202	Pr > z = 0.201	Pr > z = 0.207
Sargan Test	chi2(106) = 68.01	chi2(106) = 71.33	chi2(106) = 75.76	chi2(106) = 71.33	chi2(106) = 69.00
	Prob > chi2 = 0.998	Prob > chi2 = 0.996	Prob > chi2 = 0.988	Prob > chi2 = 0.996	Prob > chi2 = 0.998

As the regression coefficients do not give a full picture of the statistical significance of the interaction effects, because the standard errors only refer to a specific value of the conditioning variable (Brambor et al. 2006), one needs to turn to graphical analysis in order to assess the impact of our clientelism indicators on the size of PBCs (Figure 9.1).

Conventionally, the impact of the conditional variable is statistically significant when the upper and lower borders of the 95 per cent confidence intervals are both above (below) the zero line. Figure 9.1 shows that the clientelism indicators have the expected impact on the size of spending cycle: the higher blood donations and referendum turnout, the lower the increase of health personnel spending in the run-up to elections; the higher corruption, tax evasion, and inequality, the higher the increase of health personnel spending in the run-up to elections. For all indicators, the relationship is statistically significant for most of the range of values across the regions.

In order to quantify the difference that clientelism makes to the size of PBCs, we can turn to the regression results in Table 9.2. As an example, let us consider for instance the results for the GP corruption index (indicator for the supply of clientelistic practices). The range of the index for which the impact of clientelism is statistically significant is from 0.688 to its max (1.618), equivalent to the range from the Marche and Campania regions. A linear combination of the coefficients for elections and for the interaction term indicates that the health personnel spending in a full election year increases by approximately 24 euros per capita in Marche, and by 35 euros per capita in

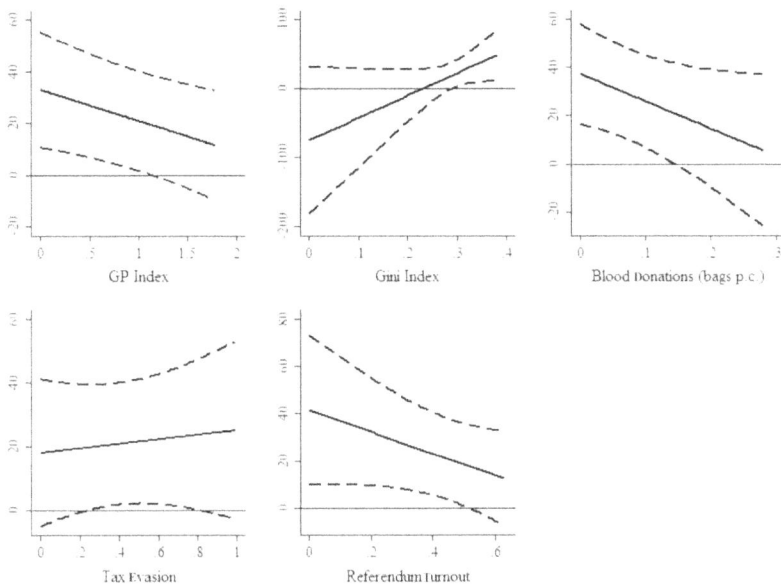

Figure 9.1   Clientelism and Electoral Cycles (a–e)
Note: Panels a–e highlight the increase in health care personnel spending in election year (*y*-axis) with 95 per cent confidence intervals.

Campania. The difference, 11 euros per capita, means that Campania spends approximately 64 million euros more on health personnel spending in an election year than it would if it had the same level of clientelism as Marche.

With regard to the control variables, only per capita income and financial autonomy are consistently significant and have the expected sign across all specifications. A noteworthy finding is that in one specification the political orientation of national (albeit not regional) governments affects personnel spending, with the left spending *less* than the right.

CONCLUSION

This chapter has shown that the degree of clientelism of the Italian regions affects the extent to which regional governments manipulate the fiscal levers at their disposal for electoral reasons. Specifically, I have shown that PBCs in health personnel spending are larger in the more clientelistic regions. This result connects the two distinct literatures on clientelism and contextual political budget cycles and shows that contextual features such as clientelism may affect the size of these cycles. This conclusion adds a new factor to the literature that studies the differences in PBCs across countries (e.g., Alt and Lassen 2006a; Brender and Drazen 2005; Shi and Svensson 2006), and calls for further research at the cross-national level.

Moreover, the finding that contextual features matter has significant policy implications. A vast literature has studied how fiscal rules can be set up to reduce the incentives of policy-makers to produce unsustainable budget outcomes (e.g., Hallerberg 2004; Hallerberg et al. 2009; von Hagen and Harden 1995). This chapter has shown that how well these rules work also depends on relatively long-term features of national or even sub-national jurisdictions.

Finally, the results also have more immediate implications in the European context. The unfolding European debt crisis has stimulated the introduction of new fiscal rules for the members of the Economic and Monetary Union. If, however, these rules are less effective in some member states because of some structural factors, the fiscal tensions that they were supposed to ameliorate may well persist, unless some countries are subject to more stringent rules and controls. However, as the case of Greece shows, this solution raises considerable issues of political acceptability and democratic legitimacy.

APPENDIX

Table 9.3   Distribution, Expected Signs, and Sources of Variables

Name	Min.	Max.	Mean	Std. Dev.	Expected Sign
Clientelism Indicators[†]					
Controls					
Health Personnel Spending [^]	349.82	1083.52	569.94	123.91	
Elections[*]	0	1.31	0.369	0.367	+
Supply Side					
GP Index	0.217	1.638	1	0.416	-
Demand Side					
Gini Index	0.263	0.335	0.296	0.20	+
Tax Evasion	0.13	0.94	0.13	0.07	+
Blood Donations	0.020	0.27	0.13	0.067	-
Referen. Turnout	0.35	0.59	0.46	0.07	-
Log of Population	11.68	16.10	14.36	1.10	-
Age (Share of Pop. over 65)	13.31	26.8	19.79	2.83	+
Income[^]	11,592.9	36,212.8	23,230.98	6,173.46	+
Left (Regional Gov'ts)	0	1	0.62	0.49	+
Left (National Gov'ts)	0	1	0.480	0.96	+
Electoral Contestability	0	1	0.71	0.45	+

Name	Min.	Max.	Mean	Std. Dev.	Expected Sign
Clientelism Indicators[†]					
Controls					
Regions under Oversight	0	1	0.11	0.31	-
Financial Autonomy	0.065	0.70	0.35	0.15	-
Unemployment Rate	0.018	0.28	0.087	0.059	+

^ Per capita euros.

* The maximum value for elections exceeds 1. This is because there are cases of region years with both national and regional elections.

† For the clientelism indicators the expected sign refers to the interaction term.

Sources: Relazione sulla gestione finanziaria delle regioni, various years, Rome: Corte dei Conti; Ministero dell'Interno http://www.interno.gov.it/mininterno/export/sites/default/it/temi/elezioni/; Golden and Picci (2005); ISTAT, *Distribuzione del reddito e condizioni di vita e in Italia – Anni 2008 e 2009, Statistiche in breve*, 29 dicembre 2010; Pisani and Polito (2006); Associazione Volontari Italiani Sangue (AVIS) http://www.avis.it/Statistiche/7/; ISTAT (2011) *Health for All*. Rome: ISTAT; ISTAT. Various years. *Conti economici regionali*. ISTAT: Rome; ISAE. Various years. *Rapporto ISAE*. Rome: ISAE; Calculated by the authors based on data from Caroppo M. S., Turati G. (2007) *I sistemi sanitari regionali in italia riflessioni in una prospettiva di lungo periodo* Milano: Vita d Pensiero; and Ministero dell'Economia e delle Finanze. Various Years. *Relazione generale sulla situazione economica del paese* Rome: MEF.

NOTES

1. In the 1998–2010 period these taxes represented almost 40 per cent of the regional health service revenues, although with significant variation across regions, with the richer regions covering more than 50 per cent and the poorer regions covering less than 20 per cent of their health spending through their own resources. The own resource system created in 1997, which also includes a regional share of the tax on gasoline, is complemented by funds transferred from the centre (these transfers are properly the regional shares of an equalization fund alimented by revenues from VAT) and for the autonomous regions, from the national tax revenues generated in the region.

2. This was part of a series of agreements between the national government and the regions that, starting in 2001, have gradually shifted a number of decisions regarding the health system to the central level.

3. A similar mechanism, connecting distributive policies and favours to politically connected entrepreneurs has been documented in Brazil (Samuel 2003).

4. The newspapers (available through the Lexis-Nexis database) are: Corriere della Sera, Italia Oggi, La Nazione, La Stampa, Il Resto del Carlino, Milano Finanza.

5. The disbursement of late salaries close to elections is a practice that has also been documented in Russia (Akhmedov and Zhuravskaya 2004).

6. In fact, this index is more accurately a measure of corruption-cum-efficiency. As however there is no evidence that there are systematic differences between the regional distribution of corruption and efficiency, the index can be used as a consistent indicator of corruption across regions (Golden and Picci 2005). Moreover,

differences in efficiency can be attributed to non-meritocratic practices in public sector hiring and public procurement.

7. Over this period forty-four referendum questions were voted on, with votes held on eight separate occasions. Questions covered widely disparate issues, including whether judges could work as private consultants, whether to reduce the constraints on workers' dismissals, and whether to severely restrict in-vitro fertilization.

8. In principle, if politicians need to honour their campaign promises in order to retain credibility, then spending should peak *after* rather than *before* the elections (Franzese 2002b). However, if the purpose of spending is simply to generate goodwill for the incumbents (Stokes 2009), then spending should peak before the elections. Alternatively, a pattern of pre-electoral cycles is consistent with voters not trusting politicians to deliver on their electoral promises in the first place, in which case politicians will concentrate spending in the period running up to the elections (Wantchekon 2003).

9. These are Lombardy, Veneto, and Emilia-Romagna in the North, the first two being consistently centre-right and the latter consistently producing Communist (until 1992) or centre-left majorities; Tuscany and Umbria in the Center (left wing) and Sicily in the South (right wing).

10. The regions are Abruzzo (2007–2010), Calabria (2009–2010), Campania (2007–2010), Latium (2007–2010), Liguria (2007–2009), Molise (2007–2010), Piemonte (2010), Puglia (2010), Sardinia (2007–2009), Sicily (2007–2010).

11. I also include year effects: On the one hand, one may expect an increase in health spending over time, due to technological progress (Newhouse 1977), which is consistent with broad international trends (Baltagi and Moscone 2010). On the other hand, starting in 2001, successive agreements between the regions and the central government, which were motivated by the deepening financial problems of the regional health systems, have gradually shifted a number of decisions regarding the health system to the central level, and might have had the effect of reducing spending.

12. Given the likely geographical concentration of health risks (Baltagi and Moscone 2010), I use the IPS test for unit roots (Im et al. 2003), which does not assume a common autoregressive parameter.

13. Note that the use of lagged variables in the GMM specification implies a reduction in the number of cases from the potential total of 273.

REFERENCES

Afonso, Alexandre, Sotirios Zartaloudis, and Yannis Papadopoulos. 2015. "How Party Linkages Shape Austerity Politics." *Journal of European Public Policy* 22 (3): 315–334.

Agnew, John. 2007. "Remaking Italy? Place Configurations and Italian Electoral Politics under the 'Second Republic'." *Modern Italy* 12 (1): 17–38.

Aidt, Toke, Francisco José Veiga, and Linda Gonçalves Veiga. 2011. "Election Results and Opportunistic Policies." *Public Choice* 148 (1–2): 21–44.

Akhmedov, Akhmed, and Ekaterina Zhuravskaya. 2004. "Opportunistic Political Cycles." *The Quarterly Journal of Economics* 119 (4): 1301–1338.

Alesina, Alberto. 1988. "Macroeconomics and Politics." In *NBER Macroeconomics Annual 1988*, Volume 3, edited by Stanley Fischer, 13–62. Boston, MA: MIT Press.

Alesina, Alberto, Stephan Danninger, and Massino Rostagno. 1999. "Redistribution Through Public Employment: The Case of Italy." NBER Working Paper 7387, October.

Alt, James, and David Lassen. 2006a. "Fiscal Transparency, Political Parties, and Debt in OECD Countries." *European Economic Review* 50 (6): 1403–1439.

Alt, James, and David Lassen. 2006b. "Transparency, Political Polarization, and Political Budget Cycles in OECD Countries." *American Journal of Political Science* 50 (3): 530–550.

Alt, James, and Shanna Rose. 2007. "Context-Conditional Political Budget Cycles." In *The Oxford Handbook of Comparative Politics*, edited by Carles Boix and Susan Stokes, 845–867. Oxford: Oxford University Press.

Ames, Barry. 2001. *The Deadlock of Democracy in Brazil*. Ann Arbor, MI: University of Michigan Press.

Ames, Barry, Taeko Hiroi, and Lucio Renno. 2005. "The Political Economy of Personnel Expenditures." *Revista de Economia Politica* 25 (January): 50–69.

Arellano, Manuel, and Stephen Bond. 1991. "Some Tests of Specification for Panel Data." *Review of Economic Studies* 58 (2): 277–297.

Auyero, Javier. 2000. "The Logic of Clientelism in Argentina." *Latin American Research Review* 35 (3): 55–81.

Auyero, Javier, Pablo Lapegna, and Fernanda Poma. 2009. "Patronage Politics and Contentious Collective Action." *Latin American Politics and Society* 51 (3): 1–31.

Baltagi, Badi, and Francesco Moscone. 2010. "Health Care Expenditure and Income in the OECD Reconsidered." *Economic Modelling* 27 (4): 804–811.

Bardi, Luciano. 2007. "Electoral Change and Its Impact on the Party System in Italy." *West European Politics* 30 (4): 711–732.

Bjornskov, Christian. 2012. "How Does Social Trust Affect Economic Growth?" *Southern Economic Journal* 78 (4): 1346–1368.

Block, Steven. 2002. "Political Business Cycles, Democratization and Economic Reform." *Journal of Development Economics* 67: 205–228.

Bordignon, Massimo, and Gilberto Turati. 2009. "Bailing Out Expectations and Public Health Expenditure." *Journal of Health Economics* 28: 305–321.

Brambor, Thomas, William Roberts Clark, and Matt Golder. 2006. "Understanding Interaction Models." *Political Analysis* 14: 63–82.

Brender, Adi, and Allen Drazen. 2005. "Political Budget Cycles in New Versus Established Democracies." *Journal of Monetary Economics* 52 (7): 1271–1295.

Brusco, Valeria, Marcelo Nazareno, and Susan C. Stoke. 2004. "Vote Buying in Argentina." *Latin American Research Review* 39 (2): 66–88.

Buti, Marco, and Paul van den Noord. 2004. "Fiscal Discretion and Elections in the Early Years of EMU." *Journal of Common Market Studies* 42 (4): 737–756.

Calvo, Ernesto, and Maria Victoria Murillo. 2004. "Who Delivers? Partisan Clients in the Argentine Electoral Market." *American Journal of Political Science* 48 (4): 742–757.

Cantatero Prieto, David, and Santiago Lago-Peñas. 2012. "Decomposing the Determinants of Health Care Expenditure." *European Journal of Health Economics* 13 (1): 19–27.

Carlin, Ryan, and Mason Moseley. 2015. "Good Democrats, Bad Targets." *Journal of Politics* 77 (1): 14–26.

Chang, Eric. 2008. "Electoral Incentives and Budgetary Spending." *Journal of Politics* 70 (4): 1086–1097.

Clark, Andrew, and Carine Milcent. 2011. "Public Employment and Political Pressure." *Journal of Health Economics* 30: 1103–1112.

Corbetta, Piergiorgio, and Rinaldo Vignati. 2014. "Direct Democracy and Scapegoats: The Five Star Movement and Europe." *The International Spectator* 49 (1): 53–64.

Costa-Font, Joan, and Francesco Moscone. 2008. "The Impact of Decentralization and Inter-Territorial Interactions on Spanish Health Expenditure." *Empirical Economics* 34 (1): 167–184.

De La O, Ana. 2013. "Do Conditional Cash Transfers Affect Electoral Behavior?" *American Journal of Political Science* 57 (1): 1–14.

Debrun, Xavier, Laurent Moulin, Alessandro Turrini, Joaquim Ayuso-i-Casals, and Manmohan Kumar. 2008. "Tied to the Mast? National Fiscal Rules in the European Union." *Economic Policy* 23: 297–362.

Drazen, Allen. 2001. "The Political Business Cycle After 25 Years." In *NBER Macroeconomics Annual 2000*, edited by Ben Bernanke and Kenneth Rogoff, 75–138. Boston, MA: MIT Press.

Drazen, Allen, and Marcela Eslava. 2010. "Electoral Manipulation via Voter-Friendly Spending." *Journal of Development Economics* 92 (1): 39–52.

Efthyvoulou, Georgios. 2012. "Political Budget Cycles in the European Union and the Impact of Political Pressures." *Public Choice* 153 (3–4): 295–327.

Finan, Frederico, and Laura Schechter. 2012. "Vote-Buying and Reciprocity." *Econometrica* 80 (2): 863–881.

Franzese, Robert. 2000. "Electoral and Partisan Manipulation of Public Debt in Developed Democracies, 1956–1990." In *Institutions, Politics and Fiscal Policy*, edited by Rolf Strauch and Juergen Von Hagen, 61–83. Boston, MA: Kluwer Academic Press.

Franzese, Robert. 2002a. "Electoral and Partisan Cycles in Economic Policies and Outcomes." *Annual Review of Political Science* 5: 369–421.

Franzese, Robert. 2002b. *Macroeconomic Policies of Developed Democracies*. Cambridge: Cambridge University Press.

Giannetti, Daniela, and Michael Laver. 2001. "Party System Dynamics and the Making and Breaking of Italian Governments." *Electoral Studies* 20 (4): 529–553.

Golden, Miriam, and Lucio Picci. 2005. "Proposal for a New Measure of Corruption, Illustrated with Italian Data." *Economics and Politics* 17 (1): 37–75.

Guiso, Luigi, Paola Sapienza, and Luigi Zingales. 2004. "The Role of Social Capital in Financial Development." *American Economic Review* 94: 526–56

Hallerberg, Mark. 2004. *Domestic Budgets in a United Europe*. Ithaca, NY: Cornell University Press.

Hallerberg, Mark, Rolf Strauch, and Jürgen von Hagen. 2009. *Forms of Fiscal Governance: Evidence from Europe*. Cambridge: Cambridge University Press.

Hicken, Allen. 2011. "Clientelism." *Annual Review of Political Science* 14 (June): 289–310.

Hopkin, Jonathan. 2009. "Decentralization and Party Organizational Change." In *Territorial Party Politics in Western Europe*, edited by Wilfried Swenden and Bart Maddens, 86–101. London: Palgrave.

Hopkin, Jonathan, and Alfio Mastropaolo. 2001. "From Patronage to Clientelism." In *Clientelism, Interests, and Democratic Representation*, edited by Simona Piattoni, 152–171. Cambridge: Cambridge University Press.

Hug, Simon, and Franziska Spörri. 2011. "Referendums, Trust, and Tax Evasion." *European Journal of Political Economy* 27: 120–131.

Ichino, Andrea, and Giovanni Maggi. 2000. "Work Environment and Individual Background." *The Quarterly Journal of Economics* 115 (3): 1057–1090.

Im, Kyung So, M. Hashem Pesaran, and Yongcheol Shin. 2003. "Testing for Unit Roots in Heterogeneous Panels." *Journal of Econometrics* 115 (1): 53–74.

ISAE. 2004. *Rapporto Annuale sull'Attuazione del Federalismo*. Rome: ISAE (Istituto di Studi e Analisi Economica).

Ito, Takatoshi, and Jin Hyuk Park. 1998. "Political Business Cycles in the Parliamentary System." *Economics Letters* 27: 233–238.

Jones, Mark, Pablo Sanguinetti, and Mariano Tommasi. 2000. "Politics, Institutions, and Fiscal Performance in a Federal System: An Analysis of the Argentine Provinces." *Journal of Development Economics* 61 (2): 305–333.

Katsimi, Margarita, and Thomas Moutos. 2010. "EMU and the Greek Crisis." *European Journal of Political Economy* 26: 568–576.

Katzimi, Margarita, and Vassili Sarantides. 2012. "Do Elections Affect the Composition of Fiscal Policy in Developed, Established Democracies?" *Public Choice* 151 (1–2): 325–362.

Kayser, Mark. 2005. "Who Surfs, Who Manipulates?" *American Political Science Review* 99 (1): 17–27.

Keefer, Philip. 2007. "Clientelism, Credibility, and the Policy Choices of Young Democracies." *American Journal of Political Science* 51 (4): 804–821.

Keefer, Philip, and Razvan Vlaicu. 2008. "Democracy, Credibility, and Clientelism." *The Journal of Law, Economics, & Organization* 24 (2): 371–406.

Kitschelt, Herbert. 2000. "Linkages Between Citizens and Politicians in Democratic Polities." *Comparative Political Studies* 33 (6/7): 845–879.

Kitschelt, Herbert, and Stephen Wilkinson. 2007. "Citizen-Politician Linkages." In *Patrons, Clients and Policies*, edited by Herbert Kitschelt and Stephen Wilkinson, 1–49. Cambridge: Cambridge University Press.

Knack, Stephen, and Philip Keefer. 1997. "Does Social Capital Have an Economic Payoff?" *The Quarterly Journal of Economics* 112 (4): 1251–1288.

Kopecký, Petr, and Maria Spirova. 2011. "'Jobs for the Boys?'" *West European Politics* 34 (5): 897–921.

Lizzeri, Alessandro, and Nicola Persico. 2001. "The Provision of Public Goods Under Alternative Electoral Incentives." *American Economic Review* 91 (1): 225–239.

Lopez-Casanovas, Guillem, and Marc Saez. 2007. "A Multilevel Analysis of the Determinants of Regional Health Care Expenditure." *European Journal of Health Economics* 8 (1): 59–65.

Loughlin, John, and Silvia Bolgherini. 2006. "Regional Elections in Italy." In *Devolution and Electoral Politics*, edited by Daniel Hough and Charlie Jeffery, 140–156. Manchester: Manchester University Press.

Luna, Juan Pablo. 2014. *Segmented Representation*. Oxford: Oxford University Press.

Maino, Franca. 2009. "Il sistema sanitario italiano tra contenimento della spesa, malasanità e politicizzazione." In *Politica in Italia*, edited by Gianfranco Baldini and Anna Cento Bull, 67–86. Bologna: Il Mulino.

Marien, Sofie, and Marc Hooghe. 2011. "Does Political Trust Matter?" *European Journal of Political Research* 50: 267–291.

Milesi-Ferretti, Gian Maria, Roberto Perotti, and Massimo Rostagno. 2002. "Electoral Systems and Public Spending." *Quarterly Journal of Economics* 117: 609–657.

Mink, Mark, and Jakob de Haan. 2006. "Are There Political Budget Cycles in the Euro Area?" *European Union Politics* 7 (2): 191–211.

Musella, Fortunato. 2009. *Governi monocratici*. Bologna: Il Mulino.

Newhouse, Joseph. 1977. "Medical Care Expenditure." *Journal of Human Resources* 12 (1): 115–125.

Ostrom, Elinor. 2000. "Collective Action and the Evolution of Social Norms." *The Journal of Economic Perspectives* 14 (3): 137–158.

Peltzman, Sam. 1992. "Voters as Fiscal Conservatives." *Quarterly Journal of Economics* 107 (2): 327–361.

Persson, Torsten, and Guido Tabellini. 2003. *The Economic Effects of Constitutions*. Cambridge, MA: MIT Press.

Piattoni, Simona. 2001. "Clientelism in Historical and Comparative Perspective." In *Clientelism, Interests and Democratic Representation*, edited by Simona Piattoni, 1–30. Cambridge: Cambridge University Press.

Pisani, Stefano, and Polito. Cristiano. 2006. "Analisi Dell'evasione Fondata Sui Dati Irap." *Documenti di lavoro dell'ufficio studi, Ministero dell'Economia e delle Finanze*. Rome: Ministero dell'Economia e delle Finanze.

Putnam, Robert. 1993. *Making Democracy Work*. Princeton, NJ: Princeton University Press.

Reich, Oliver, Cornelia Weins, Claudia Schusterschitz, and Magdalena Thöni. 2012. "Exploring the Disparities of Health Care Expenditure in Switzerland." *European Journal of Health Economics* 13 (2): 193–202.

Remmer, Karen. 2007. "The Political Economy of Patronage." *Journal of Politics* 69 (2): 363–377.

Rodden, Jonathan. 2002. "The Dilemma of Fiscal Federalism." *American Journal of Political Science* 46 (3): 670–697.

Rodden, Jonathan. 2006. *Hamilton's Paradox*. New York: Cambridge University Press.

Rodden, Jonathan, and Erik Wibbels. 2002. "Beyond the Fiction of Federalism." *World Politics* 54 (July): 494–531.

Roodman, David. 2006. "How to Do xtabond2." Center for Global Development, Working Paper Number 103.

Samuel, David. 2003. *Ambition, Federalism, and Legislative Politics in Brazil.* Cambridge: Cambridge University Press.

Sanz, Ismael, and Francisco Vasquez. 2007. "The Role of Ageing in the Growth of Government and Social Welfare Spending in the OECD." *European Journal of Political Economy* 23 (4): 917–931.

Saporiti, Alejandro, and Jorge Streb. 2008. "Separation of Powers and Political Budget Cycles." *Public Choice* 137: 329–345.

Schultz, Kenneth. 1995. "The Politics of the Political Business Cycle." *British Journal of Political Science* 25 (1): 79–99.

Shefter, Martin. 1994. *Political Parties and the State.* Princeton, NJ: Princeton University Press.

Shi, Min, and Jakob Svensson. 2006. "Political Budget Cycles." *Journal of Public Economics* 90 (8–9): 1367–1389.

Sööt, Mari-Liis, and Kadri Rootalu. 2012. "Institutional Trust and Opinions of Corruption." *Public Administration and Development* 32: 82–95.

Stokes, Susan. 2005. "Perverse Accountability: A Formal Model of Machine Politics with Evidence from Argentina." *American Political Science Review* 99 (3): 315–325.

Stokes, Susan. 2007. "Political Clientelism." In *The Handbook of Comparative Politics,* edited by Carles Boix and Susan Stoke, 604–627. Oxford: Oxford University Press.

Stokes, Susan. 2009. Pork, by Any Other Name . . . Building a Conceptual Scheme of Distributive Politics. *2009 Conference of the American Political Science Association,* Toronto.

Stokes, Susan, Thad Dunning, Marcelo Nazareno, and Valeria Brusco. 2013. *Brokers, Voters, and Clientelism.* Cambridge: Cambridge University Press.

Tarrow, Sidney. 1977. *Between Center and Periphery: Grassroots Politicians in Italy and France.* New Haven, CT: Yale University Press.

Tronconi, Filippo, and Christophe Rioux. 2009. "The Political Systems of Italian Regions Between State-Wide Logics and Increasing Differentiation." *Modern Italy* 14 (2): 151–166.

Vergne, Clemence. 2009. "Democracy, Elections and the Allocation of Public Expenditures in Developing Countries." *European Journal of Political Economy* 25: 63–77.

von Hagen, Jürgen. 2006. "Political Economy of Fiscal Institutions." In *The Oxford Handbook of Political Economy,* edited by Barry R. Weingast and Donald A. Wittman, 464–478. Oxford: Oxford University Press.

von Hagen, Jürgen, and Ian Harden. 1995. "Budget Processes and Commitment to Fiscal Discipline." *European Economic Review* 39: 771–779.

Wantchekon, Leonard. 2003. "Clientelism and Voting Behavior." *World Politics* 55 (3): 399–422.

Weitz-Shapiro, Rebecca. 2012. "What Wins Votes: Why Some Politicians Opt Out of Clientelism." *American Journal of Political Science* 56 (3): 568–583.

Windmeijer, Frank. 2005. "A Finite Sample Correction for the Variance of Linear Efficient Two-Step GMM Estimators." *Journal of Econometrics* 126 (1): 25–51.

You, Jong-sung. 2015. *Democracy, Inequality and Corruption.* Cambridge: Cambridge University Press.

Chapter Ten

Misusing the Reform

New Public Governance in the Service of Clientelism

Anka Kekez[1]

INTRODUCTION

The study of public management and policy reforms is often divided between literature that traces different reform practices in developed, Western democracies, and that which addresses reforms in other contexts, including new democracies and countries in transition and post-conflict societies. Of course, any attempt to break down this distinction has to take into account the fact that different societies have different prevailing conditions and mechanisms. This signifies that a mere transfer of reforms implemented in one setting to another one is not possible, but that specific governance legacies and political agency are inevitable so as to render the effects of those reforms in an altered manner. At the same time, models developed in one context do have an impact – albeit not always the desired one – when implemented elsewhere. In the end, understandings of real reform efforts can refine and elaborate models of the reform process and stand relevant in a broader range of societies.

This chapter aims to address what occurs in a young democracy such as Croatia in which the scope conditions of reform processes were to a large extent shaped by one political party that governed Croatia for twenty-one out of the twenty-nine years since the country's independence. Acting as the incumbent in the context of state-building, war, and post-war transition, the HDZ (Croatian Democratic Union) developed into a party with a wide and strong organization maintained through party penetration into state institutions and the public sector during the 1990s. The centralized nature and the size of the network of territorial organizations covering every municipality created a sort of a vicious cycle for the HDZ. In this vicious cycle the state was used to strengthen party organization by means of employment of party activists in the public sector, and the party organization in turn was used to support the electoral base and deliver electoral support (Henjak, Zakošek, and Čular 2013). Other parties in power could not use this mechanism to the same degree.

As the patronage-driven strategy guided many executive decisions regarding the organization of various public services, this chapter asks what happens to policy implementation and service delivery when public management reforms 'meet' a politicized policy-making context. The chapter is therefore structured as follows: firstly, it provides a brief overview of reform doctrines that affected the study and practice of policy implementation in the last thirty years. After elaborating the implications that different types of citizen-politician linkages can have on executive decisions on the adoption and execution of the management reform, it discusses the effect of the patronage-driven strategy of a ruling party on the reform outcome. To examine this, the chapter focuses extensively on one domain of social policy in a case study design, analysing the results of the elderly care reform in Croatia. The last section discusses the implications of the findings and provides readers with some concluding thoughts.

MODELS OF PUBLIC MANAGEMENT REFORM AND PUBLIC SERVICE DELIVERY

The crisis of modern democracies has over the past few decades led to an intensified scientific and practical quest for the solution of the long-conceptualized tension between the democratic idea of citizen participation in the governing process and the liberal idea of enlightened leadership by the political elite and the more recently favoured technocratic one. In the 1980s, in the public management and public policy domain this quest was complemented by the widely acknowledged necessity to reform the rigidity of the traditional bureaucratic government (D. Osborne and Gaebler 1992). The initial reform propositions did lean more towards the elitist idea of the New Public Management (NPM) thinking which proposed the replacement of hierarchy with markets and contracts while importing of business-like concepts, values, and tools into the functioning of public bureaucracy (Pollitt and Bouckaert 2011). By empowering public managers and making them responsible for operationalizing government priorities and contracting service delivery to private actors, NPM stimulated the efficiency and flexibility of the public service, but neglected its democratic quality (Pierre 2012).

As a reaction to the latter effect of NPM and as an answer to citizen alienation from institutions of political representation, the 1990s yielded New Public Governance (NPG) as a quite different reform path, which searched for solutions to policy problems based on the inclusion of a wider spectrum of actors in the policy processes, thus endorsing more collaborative forms of service delivery. In order to foster effectiveness and democratic quality of public service, New Public Governance (NPG) proposed replacement of hierarchies and markets as central steering mechanisms with a network of actors stemming from the government, market and civil society (S. P. Osborne 2010; Pollitt and Bouckaert 2011). This reliance on networks in NPG is accompanied by the idea of working in partnerships toward producing joint results and with stress on citizens' engagement in the design and delivery of public services (Pestoff, Brandsen, and Verschuere 2013).

NPM and NPG, with an abundance of variations in the existing labels for the former, are often presented as key competing reformist strategies in scholarly discussions. Hoverer, reforms in many Northern and Western European countries involved not just visions of managerialist or participatory modernization of state apparatus, but also devotion to preservation of Weberian foundations of public services such as 'assumptions of a positive state, a distinctive public service and particular legal order' (Pollitt and Bouckaert 2011, 120). Recently labelled as Neo-Weberian State (NWS), this reform model combines efforts toward reaffirmation of the role of the state as a driving force in facing challenges of modern society, with the shift from rule-following toward the holistic focus on meeting citizens' needs. NWS-inspired solutions to citizens' needs may occasionally rely on the employment of market-based tools, but their core strength is in the professionalism and in the quality of state-based services (Pollitt 2008; Pollitt and Bouckaert 2011).

As a consequence of diverse reform strategies, contemporary public management is marked by a wide range of practices with the existence of multiple dominant modes rather than a single one (Pollitt and Bouckaert 2011). The plurality of management practices is especially evident in the delivery of public services. As Table 10.1 demonstrates, this nowadays varies not just in relation to the types of actors that can be in charge for the production of public services, but also in relation to managerial tasks involved in the realization of different service-delivery arrangements (Alford and O'Flynn 2012; Hill and Hupe 2014).

In the in-house provision of public services as the service-delivery arrangement most congruent with the NWS model, government agencies maintain monopoly over the production of public services. With managerial reliance on inputs, management of the overall service-delivery process is focused on the assignment of explicit mandates to public sector organizations. At the scale of organizations, these mandates are further clarified and substantiated via sufficient resources. With hierarchical vertical connections and rules as a central management mechanism, management of street-level work is focused on internalization of regulations and standard operating procedures. Compliance with the rules is ensured through provision of leadership and on-the-job

Table 10.1   Service Delivery Arrangements: Background Reform Models and Core Management Tasks

	Public Service-Delivery Arrangements		
	Provision by Public Sector Organizations	*Outsourcing and Contracting*	*Partnerships and Collaboration*
Background Reform Model	Neo-Weberian State	New Public Management	New Public Governance
Management of Delivery Process	Assigning public sector organizations with explicit mandates	Creating a framework for competitive procurement	Enabling a meaningful participation of societal actors
Management of Inter-Organizational Relations	Stipulating mandates and substantiating them with resources	Defining performance targets and ensuring contract compliance	Building and nurturing trust, shared values, and partnering relations
Management of Street-Level Work	Combining orientation toward rule-following with focus on results and citizens' needs	Combining results-based personnel management with service orientation	Professionals engaging with citizens in the creation of service quality

Sources: Author's own elaboration, based on Alford and O'Flynn (2012), Hill and Hupe (2014), and Pollitt and Bouckaert (2011).

training (Hill and Hupe 2014). Nevertheless, in the NWS-inspired modernization of resources management within the government sector, strict reliance on rule-following in this service-delivery mode is accompanied by orientation toward achievement of results and toward addressing citizens' needs and wishes (Pollitt 2008; Pollitt and Bouckaert 2011).

In NPM-inspired service-delivery arrangements, such as the contracting-out, output-based performance management becomes central. For the management at the system scale, this implies the emphasis on the creation of a framework for competitive procurement of public services production (Alford and O'Flynn 2012; Hill and Hupe 2014). While the given framework enables arrangements with various private, public, or non-profit contractors, relations with the selected ones are defined though contracts specifying not only costs but also performance targets and output standards (English and Guthrie 2003; Pollitt 2003). Within this setting, the management of inter-organizational relations is oriented towards ensuring contract compliance. Along the same line, the management of individual interactions implies the reliance on result-oriented personnel management and the creation of incentives for the prevalence of service orientation (Hill and Hupe 2014; Pollitt and Bouckaert 2011; Thomann, Hupe, and Sager 2017).

Lastly, the collaborative arrangements induced by NPG reform strategy imply managerial activities through which a government enables a meaningful participation of societal actors in the service-delivery process (Hill and Hupe 2014). Those activities include invitation and selection of participants and creation and maintenance of network of organizations that will act as service providers, and development of ways to manage strategic and operational complexity that comes with collaborative arrangements (Agranoff and McGuire 2004). To ensure intrinsic cooperation and participation, instead of adoption of rules or specification of outputs, the management of inter-organizational relations is focused on the building and nurturing of trust, reciprocity, and social capital (Alford and O'Flynn 2012; Hill and Hupe 2014; Klijn 2010). For the management of street-level work, this implies engagement of employees of organizations mandated with the collaborative service provision in the creation of knowledge and quality together with citizens, networks, and communities (Brandsen and Honingh 2016).

FORCES BEHIND REFORMS: FOCUS ON POLITICAL FACTORS

Goals and management tools introduced by means of one or by a fusion of more reform models undoubtedly have significant impact on the service-delivery arrangements that the management reform can result in. Nevertheless, the choice of a particular model and its materialization into service-delivery practice are also determined by numerous forces that can be at work in driving, guiding and restraining management change (Christensen and Lægreid 2012). After analysing public management reforms in twelve Western democracies, Pollitt and Bouckaert (2011) offered the conceptualization of public management reform in which they apply a top-down approach to the reform process, and they attribute executive politicians and/or senior civil servants a key role in conceiving and executing the change of public management. Although it is central for the adoption of a specific reform package, elite decision-making on management change is shaped through the interplay of three large groups of factors, namely background socio-economic influences, political pressures, and features of administrative system.

The first group of factors includes the effects of global economic forces and national socio-demographic aspects that provide incentives for politicians and civil servants to look for ways of easing the strain on the system. The second cluster of factors concerns structural and dynamic elements of the political system. While the former refers to general features of a system, such as the type of executive government, the latter encompasses the influx of management reform ideas combined with the pressure from citizens and party-political ideas. In taking a broader view, Pollitt and Bouckaert (2011) attribute the upsurge of reforms over the last thirty years to socio-economic factors and to the supply of management reform ideas. On the other hand, political system actors – particularly groups with a vested interest in the *status quo* – not only can act as sources of incentives but may also demonstrate a lack of interest for management reform or even recalcitrance to change. Resistance to change can also originate from the third group of factors which entails cultural, structural, and institutional characteristic of the administrative system, often proven difficult to transform in more than merely incremental ways.

General conceptualization of the public management reform process developed by Pollitt and Bouckaert (2011) presents an open schematic and heuristic tool that can accommodate specific empirical contexts and a variety of more specific explanations for different outcomes of management reforms. What is more, if looking more closely into those dynamic elements of a political system, party-political ideas and their influence on management reform can thus be conceived through the lens of strategic forms of the linkage that politicians and parties develop with citizens in general or with subsets of citizens as those target populations of specific public policies. In competitive democracies, these strategies can take the form of programmatic competition or the form of clientelistic exchange, both of which tend to have significant, although divergent, influence on the public management reform (see Table 10.2).

When appealing to the general electorate, politicians tend to mobilize voters by promising them a successful delivery of goods favoured by and accessible to the whole polity. In this mode of strategic linkages, which Kitschelt and Wilkinson (2007) refer to as the programmatic valence policy competition, politicians compete not by promising different packages of preferred public goods, but by demonstrating own abilities to successfully provide them. Such electoral mobilization strategy is mainly focused on the salient issues such are the employment, national security, monetary stability, or national health care (Kitschelt and Wilkinson 2007). Nevertheless, the incidence of scandals or the widespread dissatisfaction with the standards of public services might trigger public outcry for public management reform. Such pressure, in turn, may induce politicians to appeal to citizens by demonstrating commitment to a more accountable, effective, or hospitable public sector (Pollitt and Bouckaert 2011).

When the mobilization strategy is focused on target populations of specific policies, on the other hand, the goods being offered to voters have the nature

Table 10.2 Types of Citizen-Politician Linkages and Their Implications for Management Reform

	Strategic Citizen – Politician Linkages			
	Programmatic Valence Policy Competition	*Programmatic Policy Competition*	*Clientelistic Policy Competition*	*Clientelistic Patronage*
Focus of Electoral Mobilization Strategy	General electorate	Target populations of specific policies	Target populations of specific policies	Individual citizens
Features of Party Competition	Politicians compete by demonstrating own abilities to successfully provide salient goods	Spatial or directional competition based on indirect unconditional exchange	Competition based on conditional and direct exchange	Allocation of valuable goods as the reward or payments for political support
Nature of Goods Offered to Voters	Goods that are favoured by and accessible to the whole polity	Club goods that are typical part of (re) distributive policies	Club goods mainly in a form of highly selective benefits	Private goods, primarily appointments and jobs in the public sector
Position of Political Leaders toward Public Management Reform	Inclination to demonstrate commitment to the reform, if public management gains saliency	Supporting or promoting reforms, especially in policies highlighted by their program	Reluctance toward reform, due to interest in preservation of high political discretion	Resistance or even inclination toward the politicized re-engineering of reform ideas

Sources: Author's own elaboration based on Kitschelt and Wilkinson (2007), Cruz and Keefer (2015), Pollitt and Bouckaert (2011), Kopecký et al. (2016), Chandra (2007), Grindle (2012), Peters (2010).

of club goods which include, but are not limited to, differential access to social insurance benefits, tax schemas, and other, categorical social benefits. Club goods are typically part of redistributive policies providing benefits to one and imposing burdens to other categories of citizens. When developing voter mobilization strategy focused on such goods, politicians can choose between a programmatic or a clientelistic linkage with targeted constituencies. The choice of the former, which Kitschelt and Wilkinson (2007) refer to as the programmatic policy competition, implies spatial or directional competition with other parties based on the offer of distributive policies targeting voters with different policy preferences. The choice of the clientelistic strategy, on the other hand, implies party competition based on conditional exchange. Politicians thus offer the provision of highly selective benefits to targeted groups of citizens and expect political support in the form of votes or various contributions to political party in return (Kitschelt and Wilkinson 2007).

When becoming office incumbents, parties that have opted for the programmatic path will frame the design and implementation of policies to achieve indirect exchange with their constituencies while hoping that policy outcomes will ensure sufficient support for the re-election of their party. In the application of rules guiding the distribution of benefits and costs, party preferences of policy implementers and beneficiaries will not affect their status. Clientelistic office holders, on the other hand, will engage in the formulation and implementation of policies mainly to ensure the conditions for direct and contingent exchange with their clients. By favouring ambiguous rules to allow them significant discretion over the implementation process, they try to maintain the large leeway for politicized tailoring of benefits to the needs of targeted citizens whose voting behaviour can be predicted and monitored (Kitschelt and Wilkinson 2007; Piattoni 2001).

The choice between these two strategies can significantly affect the fate of the public management reform. As evidence from studies encompassing both large and smaller samples of countries suggests, political systems in which public sector reforms were evaluated as more or less successful are characterized by the prevalence of programmatic parties (Cruz and Keefer 2015; Geddes 1996). In countries ruled by parties that tend to opt for the clientelistic mode of electoral mobilization, on the other hand, reformist initiatives are often countervailed by the reluctance of politicians and groups with a vested interest in the preservation of high political discretion (Cruz and Keefer 2015; Pollitt and Bouckaert 2011). By analysing evaluations of World Bank public sector reform loans in over 100 countries, Cruz and Keefer (2015) even evidenced the smallest chances of success for those reform meant to increase the transparency of public sector financial management.

Additionally, public management reform efforts can be significantly undermined by a particular kind of clientelistic practices referred to as party patronage, in which allocation of valuable, rare and private goods occurs in retail transactions to individual citizens who receive those goods as a reward for loyalty or payments for past support (Chandra 2007; Kitschelt and Wilkinson 2007). Even though the wide list of goods that can be exchanged through this type of citizens-politicians linkage encompasses public service projects and contracts, personal rewards and gifts, as well as privileged access to medical care, land, or housing, a more precise definition limits the concept to its most widespread form which refers to the politicized allocation of appointments and jobs in the public and semi-public sector (Kopecký and Spirova 2011;

Kopecký et al. 2016). In its latter meaning, party patronage is linked closely with the phenomenon labelled by public administration literature as the politicization of civil service. In its most dominant interpretation, this refers to the replacement of merit-based criteria with political ones in the recruitment and management of public servants (Dahlström 2012; Peters and Pierre 2004; Rouban 2012)

When strictly bound to politicization of civil servants' careers and activities, however, patronage neither has to be clientelistic, nor does it directly lead to illegal or corruptive practices. Public jobs allocated through patronage may undoubtedly be used as a resource for vote-buying and building the network of loyal party supporters. On the other hand, it can also function as a management tool used by political leaders to gain or maintain control over the state apparatus and public policies. Political appointees can therefore be placed or employed in core civil service, state-owned companies, agencies, or even organizations contracted by the government not just to receive a reward for their political support, but also to guarantee the design and implementation of public policies that will correspond with politicians' aims (Kopecký and Spirova 2011; Kopecký et al. 2016; Rouban 2012).

These two motivations can function both separately and combined, and, as recent research on patronage conducted in twenty-two countries demonstrated, the pattern of patronage tends to be linked to its scope (Kopecký et al. 2016). In political systems in which politicization is limited to senior positions in civil service, patronage is mainly motivated by the desire to control the bureaucracy so that political appointees act as high-ranked intermediaries between politicians and the state apparatus. On the other hand, in polities characterized by substantial politicization which spreads wide across and deep into state institutions, patronage tends to simultaneously function as a control and electoral resource. Political appointees in such systems mainly act as parts of a network of political activists and supporters which penetrate the state apparatus, while enabling the party not only to pursue its policy goals but also to capture state resources for clientelistic purposes (Kopecký et al. 2016).

Clientelistic deals through which jobs are given to political allies are widespread in countries with high levels of economic inequality and job instability, with the latter exhibiting the tendency to amplify the value of public employment. The inclination to engage in patronage practices of this type can nevertheless be found among political actors in most advanced democracies, at the local level, in particular, and it can lead to ethically problematic or even illegal practices (Keefer 2007; Kitschelt and Wilkinson 2007; Rouban 2012). Patronage-driven elected officials have been argued to need opportunities for retail transactions and are consequently incentivized to engage in the distortion of policy design and implementation (chapter 1 in this volume;

Chandra 2007). Proven to be a highly adaptive strategy of electoral mobilization, patronage may not only generate resistance to management reform but
even incentivize politicians to engage in the re-engineering of reform ideas
and tools so as to fit in their rent-seeking needs (Grindle 2012; Peters 2010).

The latter implication is of particular interest for this chapter, as reformist
ideas introduced to improve policy implementation and service delivery can
be misused by rent-seeking elected officials for exploitation of public jobs in
patronage purposes (Kekez 2018a). By seeking to identify which reform ideas
and tools are prone to patronage-driven misuse and to describe what kind of
service-delivery practices may be induced with such rent-seeking enterprise,
what follows below examines the origins and fate of a reformist initiative deal-
ing with provision of non-institutional care of older persons in Croatia.

RESEARCH DESIGN

The research employed a case-oriented research strategy while focusing
extensively on the home care of older persons, identified by a recent comparative study as a case in which the aspiration of the ruling party to preserve
or spread patronage practices within the public sector shaped the course and
the outcomes of service management reform (Kekez 2018a). The study analysed the reform of Croatian social services induced in 2000s with the inad-
equacy of the system of facilities for residential care, the ageing of the total
population and change in the family structure, all of this creating the need for
novel solutions in the provision of social services. In older persons' policy,
this purpose was served the best, as declared by the government that led the
reform process, with home care services designed to support older citizens in
their homes and assist them in everyday activities such as personal hygiene,
shopping, and cooking.

The home care service existed with the same content since the communist
era policies, but it had a rather insignificant role in the general system of
elderly care and was not made available in many rural and less developed
urban communities. In seeking ways to counteract both groups of problems,
the national government decided to launch the reformist *Program of Intergenerational Solidarity* in 2004. The programme functioned in parallel with the
existing home care services and was promoted as an innovative community-
based solution for the prevention of institutionalization of older persons. The
novelty of this reform was also related to the fact that its main promoters
were core executive politicians who, especially in welfare policies, often
demonstrated a lack of interest in service management reforms. In this case,
however, politicians took a very proactive role and provided reformist efforts
with leadership, as well as with access to significant budgetary funds. Strong

political engagement in the re-organization of service provision induced rapid growth of home care, but the patronage-driven strategy of the ruling party affected many executive decisions regarding actual adoption of reformist goals and principles (Kekez 2018a).

In order to identify which management ideas and tools were used or mis-used in this reform and to describe what kind of service-delivery practices the reform yielded, the collection and analysis of data was focused on the provision of home care service a decade after the reformist program was launched. As to the methods and sources of data collection, interviews as the main sources of evidence were combined with policy documents and official statistical data related to the reform and the provision of the chosen social service. The interviews were conducted with thirty participants ranging from care givers to beneficiaries, from national government officials and public managers to civil society groups, as well as from local officials and public managers, to coordinators of non-profit, private, and public organizations providing the service. Interviews were conducted in different country regions by the author of the chapter, in the period between July 2013 and March 2014. All of the interviews were recorded and transcribed.

Qualitative data collected was processed by means of within-case analyses (Miles and Huberman 1994) that mounted to provide in-depth insight into service-delivery practice of selected service. Data was initially coded with the use of a provisional scheme of pattern codes based on the conceptualization of service-delivery arrangements presented in the first part of the chapter (see Table 10.1). As this part of the analysis was also used to identify and fill the gaps in the existing conceptualization of service-delivery practices, provisional pattern codes were used in an open manner. The coding units adding some new insights were therefore extracted and further coded with the use of more inductive types of descriptive and interpretative codes. The repeated regularities arising from inductive codes were formalized in the last coding cycle to create new pattern codes assigned to the existing ones. An important result of such a coding process was the identification of a new service-delivery arrangement distorted with patronage practices.

FINDINGS

Home care of older persons, as indicated in the analysis of documents and interviews at hand, has represented one of the most developing but also the most heavily fragmented social service over the past decade. Not only was this service locally supported and organized by a countless variety of actors at the time when research data was collected, but it was also nationally coordinated through two completely disconnected programs. While the service was provided within the traditional state social care system in the first program, in the second one the provision relied on the 'system of intergenerational solidarity' in which home care was nationally coordinated, but managed by county and local governments.

During 2013 and 2014, when the data for the study was collected, both programs were coordinated by the Ministry of Social Policy and Youth, but until 2012 the second program was run separately by the Ministry for Family, Veterans, and Intergenerational Solidarity. The latter ministry existed from 2003 to 2011, during the two terms of the Croatian Democratic Union (HDZ) government. After the change of government in late 2011, the second program was placed under the authority of the new Ministry of Social Policy and Youth. Even though this institution also coordinated the home care within the social care system, the integration and restructuring of the arrangements for the provision of services for senior citizens was postponed until the full enforcement of a new Act on Social Care adopted at the beginning of 2014.

As the analysis of documents and interviews has indicated, both programs preserved their structure in the meantime, as well as the activities and techniques developed by the previous government. The evidenced features of the home care management are summarized in Table 10.3 and further elaborated in text that follows it.

In the first, traditional, home care program, the state maintained monopoly over assignment of the right to home care service and mandated it to the de-concentrated network of public bodies – to the Centres for Social Work (CSWs). Since the beginning of 2000s the bureaucratized arrangements for service provision, nevertheless, were complemented with New Public Management-inspired contracts which CWSs were signing with Centres for Nursing and Care or Social Welfare Homes for the older persons. Even though the framework for subcontracting was allowing both private and non-profit actors to act as providers, contracting choices reflected the Ministry's inclination toward public institutions. In the year 2012, for 73 per cent of the beneficiaries encompassed by this program, home care was outsourced to thirty-three Social Welfare Homes, all founded by county governments and subsidized by the central state. For the remaining 23 per cent of beneficiaries, care was provided by twenty nine Nursing Centres, institutions specialized for elderly care and founded either by municipal governments or non-profit organizations such as the Caritas and the Red Cross (Ministry of Social Policy and Youth 2013a).

In relation with the CSWs, the central government preserved the director role and was providing them with resources and assignments defined by strict rules and protocols outlined in the thick social care regulation. With contracted providers, the state took up the role of a regulator and an inspector, while shifting its focus toward ensuring contract compliance. Contracts signed between CSWs and Welfare Homes or Nursing Centres were hence not so much about the stipulation of rules of conduct as they were about the

Table 10.3　Reformed Management of the Home Care Provision: Key Features

	Parallel Arrangements for Service Provision with the 'New' Home Care Program Overshadowing the 'Old' One-	
	'Old' Home Care Program: Combination of In-House with Contracting Provision	*'New' Home Care Program: Politicized Partnerships and Collaboration*
Background Reform Model	New Public Management ideas added on pre-existing bureaucratic service management	New Public Governance ideas used for the creation of a new arrangement, but merged with patronage practices
Management of Delivery Process	Ensuring explicit mandates and creating a framework for contracting	Fostering local ownership, but keeping informal political control
Management of Inter-Organizational Relations	Providing subordinate bodies with resources and assignments while ensuring contract compliance of service providers	Local political executives left with the possibility to pursue their own interests and to use their own capacity in arranging care provision
Management of Street-Level Work	Flexible, but standardized service that was granted under very strict rules	Local politicians authorizing home care teams or politicizing micro-management Care giver designs service with users

specification of expected performance and outputs of service provision. Even though the CSWs had no mandate to interfere in the operative decisions made by contracted providers, the control over service delivery was ensured with the codification of quality standards and related overseeing authority of the state inspection.

The contractual provision of home care was marked by flexible, but at the same time standardized organization of service provision. On the other hand, the assignment of the right to the service to individual beneficiaries proved to be not as flexible. Acting as case managers, the CSWs were applying strict means which were testing the approval of the right to home care. As emphasized by a professional providing home care, the combination of strictness in the approval and flexibility in service provision resulted in a nicely designed service that was rather resistant to any kind of manipulation, but was rarely used:

Home care is nicely designed and providers follow standards, but the fact is that this service is relatively rarely assigned based on the approval of the CSWs. The census prescribed by the Social Care Act is really low and not many citizens can pass the means test. Senior citizens which could even be eligible, are either not aware of its existence or do not know how to get it. (Manager in Centre for Social Welfare)

Official data confirms this statement and, as Figure 10.1 shows, in the year 2013, home care within this program was provided only to 7 per cent of the total number of beneficiaries encompassed by two national home care programs.

More flexibility in service arrangement and a much wider outreach was accomplished with arrangements developed in the course of the reform by the Ministry of the Family, Veterans' Affairs and Intergenerational Solidarity (MFVAIS) which in 2004 established a pilot of home care services and expanded it to a nation-wide *Program of Intergenerational Solidarity* in the year 2007. As Figure 10.1 shows, by the year 2013, this program completely overshadowed the traditional home care and with more than 15,500 users and a 93 per cent share in number of overall national home care beneficiaries, became the most comprehensive, most expensive and, accordingly, the most politically attractive program among all home care services.

Inspirations for the design of new home care program were the principles, goals, and instruments of New Public Governance thinking. The reform of

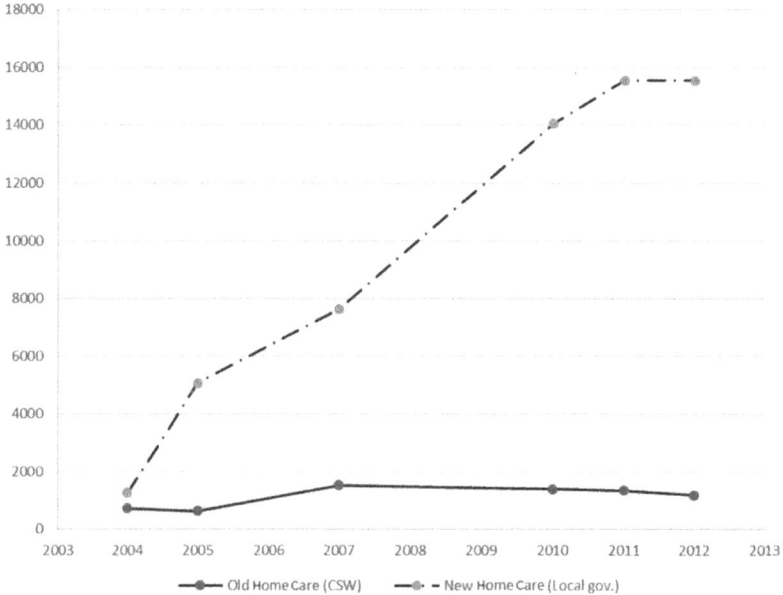

Figure 10.1   Users of 'Old' and 'New' Home Care Programs: Trends over the Past Ten Years
Sources: Reports published by MFVAIS and Ministry of Social Policy and Youth

the arrangement for care provision envisioned the empowerment of beneficiaries and their engagement in service delivery. That was to be achieved not
through network of bureaucratized social care institutions or in NPM-fashion
but via collaboration between state and local, typically non-profit community
actors. The development of home care provision was organized by means of
partnership agreements – with the national government signing an agreement
on co-funding and cooperation with the regional/local governments, which
then in turn organized the provision themselves or together with non-profit
organizations and homes for the older persons.

Agreements were signed for two versions of partnership arrangements:
solo home care and home care that was complemented with the state's support to local units that wanted to open a day care centre in their community.
While the program was managed by the MFVAIS, decisions on the funding of
home care service were done through an open call and the process of competition among counties and municipalities which expressed interest for service
provision. For the combined care, funding was not decided based on open
calls, but agreements were signed with those municipalities that demonstrated
devotion and results in providing home care.

While mobilizing local political leaders and community stakeholders
towards a joint care for older citizens, the MFVAIS acted as the enabler. The
analysis of qualitative and quantitative data referring to the implementation
of the program revealed that this role, however, was combined with the role
of a clientelistic capo in practice, while the realization of a collaboration was
followed by the distortion of home care provision with patronage practices of
the ruling party. The choices on the state funding, as the political official in
the Ministry of Social Policy and Youth highlighted, reflected the real needs,
but political links were employed as well:

> *The financing of home care within the Program of intergenerational solidar-*
> *ity is mainly centralized – counties and municipalities are participating in the*
> *costs with approx. 23%. As to, well, how to say, the management of the Program*
> *during the previous government – cooperation agreements with counties and*
> *municipalities were not only reflecting the need to expand the service in certain*
> *communities, but were also a matter of discretional decisions made by politi-*
> *cians. (Assistant Minister)*

The perception of additional political criteria employed in the decision-
making process was also present among counties and municipalities that
competed for financial support:

> *We couldn't get the funds because, to be quite honest, politics played a role*
> *here – we just have a different party in power. We contacted the Ministry of*
> *Intergenerational Solidarity and the Minister. Even more than that, the former*

county mayor and I went to Zagreb and reached an agreement with program
coordinators . . . but we just could not reach the point of signing the contract.
Unlike us, one municipality in our county area was able to get the signature,
but the fact is that the local government there was at that time formed by HDZ.
(Senior civil servant in regional/local government)

Here it is important to qualify that the affiliation of the mayor or the political profile of county/city/commune council most plausibly acted just as an
additional, but not the only decision-making criterion. As emphasized by the
interviewed actors, for counties and municipalities that had a different political profile than the national executive it was still possible to receive funding:

We contacted the Ministry in 2006 and offered cooperation. The Ministry soon
invited our representatives to a meeting and a few months later we signed the
contract. In the beginning we thought that the funding decision is exclusively
political – but as our county government was formed by a different political
option, the Ministry demonstrated to us that we were wrong. (Senior civil ser-
vant in regional/ local government 2)

Nevertheless, the fact that municipalities not fitting the political criteria
were still able to receive funding does not dismiss the account of many interviewed actors on the biased selection of actors participating in the service-
delivery network. This account was also supported by the statistical analysis
on the structure of fund recipients. By the end of 2011, which was the year
in which HDZ lost the national election, the number of signed agreements
for home care services encompassed fifty nine counties and municipalities,
out of which 89 per cent had a mayor who was a member of political parties
in government – HDZ and its coalition partners – even though HDZ and its
partners were in power in only 66 per cent out of 576 Croatian counties, cities
and communes (see Figure 10.2).

In comparison, combined home and day care agreements were signed with
thirty municipalities, 70 per cent of which were ruled by HDZ and partners.
Combined care in which funding was primarily a matter of a discretional
decision made by higher civil servants, not politicians, reflects a wider perspective of party power share much more than the solo home care funding.
After the program was placed under the new Ministry for Social Policy and
Youth, there were no more open calls for solo home care. However, as the
result of a strong opposition of supported localities to the restructuring of the
program, partnership agreements from the end of 2011 were just re-signed at
the beginning of 2012 and 2013.

In the second half of 2013, when data on home care management was
collected, local actors included in the service-delivery network were still
strongly opposing any changes in organization of service provision. In their

■ Only Home Care   ▨ Home Care + Day Care

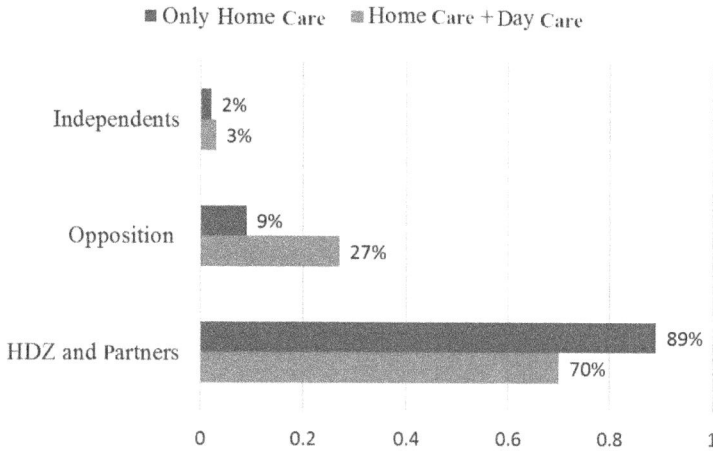

Figure 10.2 'New' Home Care: Structure of Fund Recipients in the Period, 2010–2013
Source: Ministry of Social Policy and Youth (2013b)

interviews, they emphasized the fear of losing national funding and their devotion to keeping their authority over the actual service management as the main reasons behind this opposition. Even though MFVAIS and its elected officials kept tight control over the selection process, the mandate for service management was devolved to local governments. Moreover, once the partnership agreements were signed, the central government would actually leave the local political executive with the possibility to pursue their own interests and to use their own capacity for making autonomous operative decisions. National civil servants acting as program coordinators were given the task of nurturing the realization of the established implementation partnerships accordingly.

Collaboration and local ownership instead of subordination and reliance on the national initiative were to be steered though managerial reliance on trust as well as by the 'golden thread' that implied steering through controlling the budget and personnel. Partnership agreements would specify some outputs on the expenses, personnel for care provision and the number of beneficiaries per employee, but civil servants that were managing the program had no way to check their implementation. So although reports sent to the Ministry by counties and municipalities were pointing that standards outlined in partnership agreement were met by all municipalities, interviews with actors indicated that practice varied significantly in reality:

> *In our home-care program, the city government provides co-funding and doesn't interfere in service provision. It is my responsibility, as a team leader,*

> *to coordinate and monitor the work of geronto-hostesses. . . . I am also writing reports to the Ministry. But I know about more than one case in which home care team-leaders are not the ones creating the narrative and financial reports. Municipality mayors are not letting them do so. . . . They just say: 'What do you care, just sign the financial report' . . . and those team leaders sometimes may not even know what is written in that report. (Home care team coordinator in a non-profit organization)*

Due to the lack of nationally applied oversight mechanisms and loose vertical couplings between civil servants in the Ministry and the funded units of regional/local government, the actual application of collaboration was dependent on the leadership style of local and national political executives. As a result, while in some counties and municipalities politicians left the micro-management to home care team leaders or community organizations, in others local governments decided to manage the care provision directly and politicize it. The latter choice in most cases implied that the decisions on recruitment of home care staff were made not only based on a candidate's competences but also in accordance with her or his party affiliation.

In this way, trust as a management mechanism was often replaced by party patronage. As one local public manager described, in the localities in which this scenario took place, the recruitment of party supporters as service providers became the biggest concern for the local political executive and, when election time comes, so did the monitoring of their compliance with the clientelistic bargain:

> *In our county area, it was often the case that the biggest fuss was about the recruitment of direct service providers. The most important question was who will get the job, and in answering that question, party affiliation or connection with the party was crucial. Then, before the local election, the party would watch closely who was actively lobbying for whom. (Senior civil servant in regional/local government 3)*

As often indicated by the interviewed actors, politicized hiring of home care staff was more present in communities in which home care was designed as the municipal program with care givers as municipal employees. Despite the fact that national program coordinators were frequently reminding counties and municipalities that the practice corresponding with the program's premises would be to give up the recruitment and management of home care teams, out of a total of 1,045 caregivers that in 2012 acted as service providers, 39 per cent of them were still directly employed and coordinated by local governments (Ministry of Social Policy and Youth 2013b).

In the communities included in the service-delivery network, the inclusion of beneficiaries in service provision was not associated with means' testing, but was guided by general indicators such as age, health, the existence of a family support, and left to the discretion of home care teams. As the program guidelines were just framing the basic elements of service, such as cleaning the house or making lunch, direct service providers were the ones designing the specific combination of these elements and adjusting it to the needs of each beneficiary. Although the interviewed actors were often criticizing such a high level of discretion, they have nevertheless emphasised that the flexible implementation setting enabled the creation of relevant, accessible and user-centred service for the older persons.

> *This program reached beneficiaries who might have had an income slightly above the income census but did not have appropriate support and were thus in need. What is more, as users of home care are passive by default and often not able to pursue their rights, the fact that the service was coming to them gave solutions for obstacles which the social care system fights with because of its immobility. (Researcher/consultant)*

However, in communities branded by patronage practices, as vividly illustrated by a former program coordinator, staff recruitment choices were sometimes made in direct opposition to user needs or wishes:

> *We received complaints from the field that mayors were misusing their pow-ers. For example, after the recent local election, the party that was running the government changed in City X. As soon as he/she gained power as the new mayor, he/she changed the whole home care team. Although we act as program coordinators, we had no mandate to give them orders. All we could do was to ask the mayor not to do that, but that had no effect. Unfortunately, after the old team was fired, beneficiaries were really sad and deprived because they grew attached to their former geronto-hostesses. But with politics there is no mercy. (Managerial civil servant in Ministry of Social Policy and Youth)*

In the localities in which service delivery was distorted by patronage prac-tices, local politicians also demonstrated a tendency to reinforce user depen-dence instead of empowerment by presenting home care services as direct material incentives for electoral behaviour. In that way, the NPG-inspired reform of home care became a route for accommodation of political and spoil-seeking interests of the ruling party.

CONCLUSION

Theorizing and studying different public management reform models, particularly New Public Management and New Public Governance, has often proven to be laden with normative propositions about the design of management practices in the delivery of public services. This normative focus guided research of New Public Management and New Public Governance towards the mapping of managerial practices designed to improve efficiency of service delivery, rather than towards identifying the effects of each model on the service-delivery process, the effectiveness of accountability mechanisms, representation of citizens' policy preferences, and consequently on democracy itself (Eikenberry 2007).

Although research focused on New Public Management is also heavily tilted towards normative prescriptions, frequent and wide practical application of the New Public Management strategy has nevertheless uncovered that the approach exhibits significant negative side effects on coherence and coordination in implementation of public policy (Pierre 2012). On the other hand, in normative discussions the effects of New Public Governance are still most commonly identified as the strength of the NPG model in acting as an amplifier of interactions between actors, facilitator of knowledge-sharing in the policy process, as well as enabler of more legitimacy for governmental actions in the eyes of citizens (Buuren, Klijn, and Edelenbos 2012).

This chapter illustrates the usefulness of a joint use of public policy, public management, and political governance perspectives in describing and analysing the public management reform process and the effects it produces. The presented case study has shown the ways in which NPM and NPG ideas did set quite diverse contexts for the two home care reform initiatives detailed here. Although NPM-inspired reform of 'old' home care brought about new focus of service managers on performance measurement-based control in services delivery and on holistic focus on meeting citizens' needs, it did not replace traditional focus on regulatory and oversight functions and reliance on central steering by state agencies, that is ministries. While succeeding in limiting the ability of political parties to integrate political patronage in the service management, this mixture of hierarchical and market-driven accountability failed to bring about mobilization of under-utilized resources within local communities, including civil society networks, in the organization of service provision.

By contrast, an influx of New Public Governance reform ideas guiding the creation of a 'new' home care, did bring changes directed toward more interactive horizontal management with the use of extremely soft steering mechanisms. However, the change that took place in this home care program has also brought to light New Public Governance blind spots. Among others, these include NPG's side effects such as the potential to blur out accountability or enable the misuse of engagement procedures by an unrepresentative local elite (Bell and Hindmoor 2009; Pollitt and Bouckaert 2011). Managerial reliance on trust instead on contracts or rules, as the analyses of 'new' home care program showed, might place rent-seeking politicians in the position of control of the service-delivery process and enable them to use the NPG-inspired reform to insert political interests into the selection of actors that will act as service providers or users. In other words, it can enable politicians to create opportunities and resources for advancing rent-seeking objectives, and even to use these opportunities on the expenses on objectives set by public policy (Kekez and Henjak 2019).

However, it also has to be noted that the analysis also showed that the politicization of the reform process and of soft steering tools might have positive effects. These include wider encompassment of citizens in targeted communities or the recruitment of organizationally underdeveloped, but politically important local units into a network of service providers. On the other hand, as public resources are often very limited, politicization might result in an unequal availability of the service, as well as in the perception that a transfer of funds to selected providers and the delivery of service to individual users are being used as direct material incentives directed at shaping electoral behaviour. This perception need not apply to all providers and beneficiaries of the service, but it can nevertheless seriously damage its sustainability prospects when the clientelistic party loses power and new political actors take over. If provision of services is heavily politicized, change of governing party can result in a deliberate gutting of a policy or service provision directed at limiting resources available to actors affiliated with the previous governing party, or, in order to free resources for party patronage available to a new governing party.

Due to that, after the 2011 national elections in which HDZ lost power, the home care program immediately ended up on the new government's list for complete restructuring. After the several failed attempts, in the New Public Management–inspired integration of the 'old' and 'new' home care that took place in April 2014, local units were removed from the implementation loop and Centres for Social Welfare became focal points in communities. To ensure better control over the implementation, partnership agreements were replaced by licensing and contracting, mean's test was re-introduced and service content prearranged for each category of users. Such restructuring fostered development of the perception that values of accountability, equal treatment and efficiency have been protected, but at the same time it reversed the course of service development by causing significant reduction in the number of service users and the inability of direct service providers to accommodate user's full needs.

NOTE

1. This chapter is based on the author's doctoral dissertation completed at the Faculty of Political Science, University of Zagreb (Kekez 2018b).

REFERENCES

Agranoff, Robert, and Michael McGuire. 2004. *Collaborative Public Management: New Strategies for Local Governments*. Washington, DC: Georgetown University Press.

Alford, John, and Janine O'Flynn. 2012. *Rethinking Public Service Delivery: Managing with External Providers*. Basingstoke: Palgrave.

Bell, Stephen, and Andrew Hindmoor. 2009. *Rethinking Governance: The Centrality of the State in Modern Society*. Cambridge: Cambridge University Press.

Brandsen, Taco, and Marlies Honingh. 2016. "Distinguishing Different Types of Coproduction: A Conceptual Analysis Based on the Classical Definitions." *Public Administration Review* 76 (3): 427–35. https://doi.org/10.1111/puar.12465.

Buuren, Arwin van, Erik-Hans Klijn, and Jurian Edelenbos. 2012. "Democratic Legitimacy of New Forms of Water Management in the Netherlands." *International Journal of Water Resources Development* 28 (4): 629–45. https://doi.org/10.1080/07900627.2011.627756.

Chandra, Kanchan. 2007. "Counting Heads: A Theory of Voter and Elite Behavior in Patronage Democracies." In *Patrons, Clients, and Policies: Patterns of Democratic Accountability and Political Competition*, 84–109. Cambridge: Cambridge University Press.

Christensen, Tom, and Per Lægreid. 2012. "Administrative Reforms in Western Democracies." In *The SAGE Handbook of Public Administration*, 577–89. London: SAGE Publications Ltd. https://doi.org/10.4135/9781446200506.

Cruz, Cesi, and Philip Keefer. 2015. "Political Parties, Clientelism, and Bureaucratic Reform." *Comparative Political Studies* 48 (14): 1942–73. https://doi.org/10.1177/0010414015594627.

Dahlström, Carl. 2012. "Introduction to Part Seven: Politics and Administration." In *The SAGE Handbook of Public Administration*, edited by B. Guy Peters and Jon Pierre, 361–69. London: SAGE Publications Ltd.

Eikenberry, Angela M. 2007. "Symposium – Theorizing Governance Beyond the State: Introduction." *Administrative Theory & Praxis* 29 (2): 193–97. https://doi.org/10.1080/10841806.2007.11029585.

English, Linda M., and James Guthrie. 2003. "Driving Privately Financed Projects in Australia: What Makes Them Tick?" *Accounting, Auditing & Accountability Journal* 16 (3): 493–511. https://doi.org/10.1108/09513570310482354.

Geddes, Barbara. 1996. *Politician's Dilemma: Building State Capacity in Latin America*. Berkeley: University of California Press.

Grindle, Merilee Serrill. 2012. *Jobs for the Boys*. Cambridge, MA: Harvard University Press.

Henjak, Andrija, Nenad Zakošek, and Goran Čular. 2013. "Croatia." In *Handbook of Political Change in Eastern Europe*, edited by Sten Berglund, Joakim Erman, Deegan Krause, and Terje Knutsen, 443–80. Cheltenham: Edward Elgar Publishing.

Hill, Michael, and Peter Hupe. 2014. *Implementing Public Policy: An Introduction to the Study of Operational Governance*. 3rd ed. London: Sage.

Keefer, Philip. 2007. "Clientelism, Credibility, and the Policy Choices of Young Democracies." *American Journal of Political Science* 51 (4): 804–21.

Kekez, Anka. 2018a. "Public Service Reforms and Clientelism: Explaining Variation of Service Delivery Modes in Croatian Social Policy." *Policy and Society*, 1–19. https://doi.org/10.1080/14494035.2018.1436505.

Kekez, Anka. 2018b. *Influence of Institutions and Actors on the Reform of Implementation Management: A Comparative Analysis of Social Services in Croatia.* University of Zagreb, Zagreb.

Kekez, Anka, and Andrija Henjak. 2019. 'Problems of Captured Collaboration: From Political to Politicized Metagovernance'. In Collaboration in Public Service Delivery: Promise and Pitfalls, edited by Anka Kekez, Michael Howlett and M Ramesh, 203–22. Cheltenham: Edward Elgar Publishing.

Kitschelt, Herbert, and Steven Wilkinson. 2007. "Citizen-Politician Linkages: An Introduction." In *Patrons, Clients, and Policies: Patterns of Democratic Accountability and Political Competition*, edited by Herbert Kitschelt and Steven Wilkinson, 1–49. Cambridge: Cambridge University Press.

Klijn, Erik-Hans. 2010. "Trust in Governance Networks: Looking for Conditions for Innovative Solutions and Outcomes." In *The New Public Governance? Emerging Perspectives on the Theory and Practice of Public Governance*, edited by Stephen P. Osborne, 351–65. London: Routledge.

Kopecký, Petr, Jan-Hinrik Meyer Sahling, Francisco Panizza, Gerardo Scherlis, Christian Schuster, and Maria Spirova. 2016. "Party Patronage in Contemporary Democracies: Results from an Expert Survey in 22 Countries from Five Regions." *European Journal of Political Research* 55 (2): 416–31. https://doi.org/10.1111/1475-6765.12135.

Kopecký, Petr, and Maria Spirova. 2011. "'Jobs for the Boys'? Patterns of Party Patronage in Post-Communist Europe." *West European Politics* 34 (5): 897–921.

Miles, Matthew B., and A. M. Huberman. 1994. *Qualitative Data Analysis: An Expanded Sourcebook*. Thousand Oaks, CA: Sage Publications.

Ministry of Social Policy and Youth. 2013a. *Katalog prava i usluga za odrasle osobe (Catalog of Rights and Services for Adult Persons)*. Zagreb Author.

———. 2013b. *Popis područja i provoditelja programa pomoć u kući i dnevni boravak s pomoći u kući u razdoblju 2010–2013. (List of Localities and Contracted Actors for the Implementation of Home Care and Day Care Programs in 2010–2013)*. Zagreb Author.

Osborne, David, and Ted Gaebler. 1992. *Reinventing Government: How the Entrepreneurial Spirit Is Transforming the Public Sector*. Boston: Addision-Wesley Publishing Company.

Osborne, Stephen P., ed. 2010. *The New Public Governance? Emerging Perspectives on the Theory and Practice of Public Governance*. London: Routledge.

Pestoff, Victor, Taco Brandsen, and Bram Verschuere. 2013. *New Public Governance, the Third Sector, and Co-Production*. New York: Routledge.

Peters, B. Guy. 2010. *The Politics of Bureaucracy: An Introduction to Comparative Public Administration*. London: Routledge.

Peters, B. Guy, and Jon Pierre. 2004. *The Politicization of the Civil Service in Comparative Perspective: A Quest for Control*. London: Routledge.

Piattoni, Simona. 2001. *Clientelism, Interests, and Democratic Representation: The European Experience in Historical and Comparative Perspective*. Cambridge: Cambridge University Press.

Pierre, Jon. 2012. "Governance and Institutional Flexibility." In *The Oxford Handbook of Governance*, edited by David Levi-Faur, 187–201. Oxford: Oxford University Press.

Pollitt, Christopher. 2003. *The Essential Public Manager*. Maidenhead: Open University Press.

———. 2008. "An Overview of the Papers and Propositions of the First Trans-European Dialogue (TED1)." *The NISPAcee Journal of Public Administration and Policy Special Issue: A Distinctive European Model? The Neo-Weberian State* 1 (2): 9–16.

Pollitt, Christopher, and Geert Bouckaert. 2011. *Public Management Reform: A Comparative Analysis-New Public Management, Governance, and the Neo-Weberian State*. 3rd ed. Oxford: Oxford University Press.

Rouban, Luc. 2012. "Politicization of the Civil Service." In *The SAGE Handbook of Public Administration*, 380–92. London: SAGE Publications Ltd.

Thomann, Eva, Peter Hupe, and Fritz Sager. 2017. "Serving Many Masters: Public Accountability in Private Policy Implementation." *Governance*, 1–21. https://doi.org/10.1111/gove.12297.

Chapter Eleven

The Bureaucracy as an Opportunity Structure for Neopatrimonialism

Trends and Determinants in Argentina and Brazil (1990–2010)

Luciana Cingolani

INTRODUCTION

The concept of state capacity acquired great centrality in discussions around what should be expected from bureaucracies in developing countries and young democracies. But while state capacity became increasingly important to account for a multiplicity of phenomena in the development discourse, it has been equally stretched in its interpretation (Hendrix 2010; Hanson & Sigman 2011; Cingolani 2013; Cingolani, Thomsson, & de Crombrugghe 2015).

Depending on their disciplinary lenses, scholars place a greater weight to either pro-adaptability or pro-predictability administrative structures and rules to build capacity. Pro-adaptability structures would enable politics to shape civil service behaviour in order to better respond to changing democratic preferences. Pro-predictability structures, on the other hand, would exacerbate the divide between politics and the bureaucracy in order to guarantee credible commitment in the hands of semi-autonomous bureaucratic organizations.

In their quest for capacity building, developmental bureaucracies are indeed faced with this double challenge. In order to show they walk towards democracy and rule of law, they must build strong constraints to executive powers, while in order to signal steering capacity they require sufficiently strong executives, able to implement changing democratic preferences.

Yet we know very little about the historical paths developing countries take to resolve this tension, or the determinants of different resulting balances. Empirically this is a daunting task, inasmuch as it requires a detailed account of how 'complex configurations of organizations' (Zuvanic, Iacoviello, & Rodriguez Gustá 2010) operate and change over time. In fact, the empirical knowledge about state bureaucracies is still in its infancy (Brans 2003; Lapuente 2007; Dahlström, Lapuente, & Teorell 2010; Fukuyama 2012). The absence of readily available measures of civil service characteristics has prompted an all-encompassing understanding of the state and little differentiation of its many elements in cross-country empirical comparisons.

I argue, however, that understanding the resulting balance between pro-adaptability and pro-predictability bureaucratic structures has crucial implications for the political system, and in particular for the organizational structures that give rise and sustain clientelistic practices. I contend that strong imbalances between pro-adaptability and pro-predictability dynamics create structures of opportunity that increase the feasibility of political patronage.

Very simply, when bureaucratic practices favour a tight coupling of politics and the bureaucracy, the resulting balance facilitates adaptability to new contexts, in detriment of stability. But although adaptability may introduce better governance in fast-changing polities, the institutional configurations leading to it can also trigger excellent opportunities for the personalistic or partisan allocation of state resources. This imbalance will be reflected in the organizational configurations of the state, and lead to extended powers to maximize the extraction of rent and the chances of survival in office of the political ruling coalition.

Following the book's central argument, the appropriation by the ruling coalition of otherwise neutral bureaucratic resources has a direct impact on the output side of democratic legitimacy, as it distorts policy design in favour of those more willing to engage in clientelistic practices.

The present chapter aims to enrich discussions about neopatrimonialism, clientelism and administrative capacity in at least two directions: first, by presenting a solid empirical strategy to measure patterns of interactions between the political and bureaucratic realms, and second, by exploring the political economy dimensions that exist behind more (or less) tightly coupled realms. In order to achieve these objectives, the chapter exploits an originally compiled database on bureaucratic structures, civil service appointments, career paths and agencification trends in Argentina and Brazil between 1990 and 2010.

The findings suggest that Brazil displays a more pronounced separation between the politics and bureaucratic realms, with civil service structures that are more robust to changing political cycles. Although Brazil is known for high levels of legislative corruption, these findings would suggest a more reduced structure of opportunity for neopatrimonial practices than in its neighbouring country over this twenty-year period. Consistent with classic veto player theories, the comparative analysis shows that political economy determinants leading to a fragmented polity have resulted in a more predictable environment in Brazil (and hence less coupled realms), while a more compact and centralized institutional setting in Argentina has led to a bureaucracy more likely to be captured politically.

The next section briefly explains the research setup and methodology used. The third section presents the two cases and an examination of how each country behaves regarding the political economy dimensions that I consider important for the degree of (de-)coupling of the political and administrative realms. Section four presents the original database, the empirical strategy for the measurement of (de-)coupling of realms, and the main results. Section five provides a brief conclusion and some lessons learned.

RESEARCH OBJECTIVES AND DESIGN

As previously mentioned, two main research objectives guide my analysis. The first is the development of an empirical strategy that is able to capture the degree of inter-dependence in the dynamics of the politics-administration realms. This can be understood as to which extent the permanent bureaucratic structures are affected by changing political cycles, very much in the vain of Woodrow Wilson's original ideas on the separation between politics and the bureaucracy (1887). I argue that having clarity on the empirical patterns of these dynamics can be highly informative of the vulnerabilities to neopatrimonial practices.

Neopatrimonialism is here defined as a hybrid regime where patrimonial personalistic dominance coexists with rational-legal authority, following Erdmann and Engel (2007). This hybrid nature makes it especially suitable for young democracies like Brazil and Argentina. These scholars argue that neopatrimonialism is '*characterized by insecurity about the behavior and role of state institutions (and agents)*' (p. 105). In my framework, this insecurity translates into lack of predictability, which is accentuated by a stronger dominance of the politics realm over the bureaucratic. Following this logic, and given that for comparative purposes it is important to capture *degrees* of neopatrimonialism, I contend that a stronger dominance of personalistic and unpredictable rule in the mix represents a higher degree of neopatrimonialism.

The second objective is to undertake a broad and multi-dimensional analysis of the political economy reasons behind the patterns found in the two countries. For this, I explore a series of institutional, economic and historical determinants that may have contributed to the clearer separation of the two realms in Brazil, in contrast to Argentina's tight coupling of politics and administration.

For both research goals, the methodology chosen consists of a comparative historical analysis of the two countries between 1990 and 2010. For the first goal, I use originally compiled empirical data that is objective and equivalent in the two cases. From this data, specific statistical measures are extracted in order to capture the desired patterns. For the second goal, I resort to scholarly literature and secondary sources that have traced the behaviour of each country in each dimension over time.

INSTITUTIONS IN ARGENTINA AND BRAZIL

In this section I first provide an overview of the institutional characteristics of the two countries, and why they are generally comparable for my study. In the second part, however, I delineate some important institutional differences that I expect to have an impact in my outcome variable, that is, the nature of the interactions between politics and the bureaucracy.

Overview

Argentina and Brazil enjoy a substantial degree of similarity in their constitutions and recent institutional history. As many other Latin American countries, both underwent re-democratization in the early eighties, after several consecutive cycles of democratic and authoritarian rule during the twentieth century. Both are presidential systems with bicameral legislatures and a federal territorial organization, where governors and municipal leaders are elected by the people. This federal structure was particularly strengthened through a wave of 'functional decentralization' reforms during the 1990s that involved greater fiscal responsibilities as well as increased decision-making capacity over sensitive areas such as health or education to the sub-national level (Montero 2001). Both countries have acquired proportional electoral systems for their lower chambers, although that of Brazil is more proportional, which has induced a fragmented Congress and a coalition style of governance. In both cases, however, the president enjoys very strong constitutional powers and can issue decrees and veto legislation. In both cases the constitution allows up to two consecutive four-year terms in office since 1994, while immediate re-election was previously banned. In both countries sub-national politics play a key role at the national level.

Regarding their bureaucracies, some institutional differences arise. Although both civil services are highly positioned in terms of quality within the Latin American universe, Brazil ranks first in a meritocracy index developed by Longo (2004), with 87 out of 100 points (highly meritocratic), while Argentina ranks fourth with 52 points (mixed meritocratic/patronage). Regarding career management systems or functional capacity, Brazil also ranks first (61 points), with important competitiveness schemes introduced, internal equity and clear wage management systems, while Argentina (46 points) is among the mid-range countries where competitiveness is rather low and inequality high, in spite of some measures introduced. The latter country also suffers from high-forced rotation of high-performers (Zuvanic et al. (2010).

Their economic governance and structures also vary greatly. Brazil's economy is five times bigger than that of Argentina, and counts on a highly diversified industry and services sectors. Argentina's economy is centred around agricultural commodity exports and some industrial by-products. More details about the economic contrast between the countries are provided in section 4.

Adaptability and Predictability: Political Economy Determinants

In this sub-section, I argue that although both countries are generally comparable in terms of their institutions, they differ on a number of dimensions that matter for the degree of coupling between the political and administrative realms. These involve a combination of historical, legal, political and economic factors, and include both political economy incentives for key relevant players, as well as historically rooted traditions and customs that go well beyond the period of the study. These dimensions are:

- **The influence of Congress and its oversight capacity.** It is expected that a stronger congressional influence will encourage a clearer separation between politics and the bureaucracy, as bureaucrats will need to respond to two different principals.
- **The party system and the formation of government.** It is expected that single-party governments represent a higher threat to bureaucratic autonomy, as there are no cross-party examinations in the daily management of the bureaucracy.
- **The management of the civil service and the administrative traditions in place.** This is of course a central aspect of the coupling of the political and administrative realms. It is expected that a civil service that has undergone more reforms towards autonomy has a more independent behaviour from the changing political coalitions over time.
- **The depth of structural reforms that took place in the 1990s.** It is expected that deeper liberal-oriented reforms fostering more meritocratic and cost-efficient public services are conducive to more autonomous bureaucracies.
- **The economic structure.** It is hypothesized that a less concentrated economic structure with multiple powerful actors will also foster more

autonomous bureaucracies, since they will have more incentives to apply impersonal managerial principles.

In what follows, I describe how each dimension behaves in Argentina and Brazil.

Congressional influence and oversight. Over the last decades, Argentina has undergone a series of institutional changes affecting the level of political influence over both the centralized and semi-autonomous administration. During the first post-democratic governments of Alfonsin (1983–1989) and Menem (1989–1999) all reforms to the organizational chart of the administration were exclusively passed through congressional legislation. With the aim of favouring rapid state restructuring, the De la Rúa administration (2000–2001) succeeded in having Congress delegate these powers to the executive in March 2001,[1] in the context of what was conceived as a third-generation administrative reform after the two waves of 1991/1992 and 1995/1996.

Although this reform failed to take off following a major governance crisis, and delegation was originally intended to last one year only, administrative reform by decree was never reversed, not even well after the economic recovery of 2003–2004. These powers were largely used by the subsequent administrations, both for rearranging cabinet charts, as well as deciding upon the structure of independent agencies.

The picture for Brazil is more mixed. The Brazilian Constitution of 1988 clearly defined the presidential and congressional powers regarding public administration reform. In its Article 61 section II it grants the president the exclusive power to initiate legislation creating or terminating public offices, functions and positions in both the centralized and semi-autonomous administration, as well as salary increases for public officials. These changes needed to be subsequently approved by both chambers of Congress with ordinary majorities. In 2001 an amendment was introduced,[2] allowing the president to reform federal structures by decree, as long as they do not involve an increase in expenses or the creation or termination of offices. Offices can be terminated by decree only in the cases where these are left vacant. Article 37 section XIX, on the other hand, stipulates that only by means of a special law shall an autonomous agency be created, which limits presidential unilateral powers in this respect.

Coalition government versus single-party systems. Party system configurations as well as electoral laws are critical aspects when explaining the higher propensity of Brazil towards more predictable policy-making in comparison to Argentina. Brazil is famous for its so-called coalition presidentialism (Abranches 1988), largely determined by a proportional open-list electoral system. This characteristic of the electoral system has led to all post-democratic administrations to govern by wide-coalition agreements, which often do not even reach the needed majorities to pass legislation in Congress.

Collor de Mello governed through a conservative coalition of between two and five parties, that together totalled up to 44 per cent of the seats in the lower house, while his party alone (PRN) only accounted for 5–8 per cent of the seats. This weak position was partially responsible for his ousting from power in 1992. Franco, a centrist technocrat led the government with a five-party coalition for most of his mandate, with between 55 and 60 per cent of the seats. Cardoso took over from Franco with a coalition of a similar leaning of between three and five parties, with 45 to 77 per cent of the seats in the lower house. Lula da Silva led a leftist coalition of as much as nine parties with majorities varying between 40 and 70 per cent of the seats (Cheibub Figueiredo 2011; Praca, Freitas, & Hoepers 2011). Thus, in spite of the fact that Brazilian presidents enjoy strong constitutional powers, when it comes to legislation they are obliged to strike deals with many different sectors.

Argentina, on the other hand, has had a bipartisan system with majoritarian single-party governments alternating in power for most of its recent history, with a relative predominance of the Peronist party. This system was partially disrupted towards the late nineties, when a two-party coalition took power for the first time, to only last twenty-four months in office. After this, the party system resembled more the dominant type, with the Kirchnerist neo-peronist party enjoying a hegemonic position, while the opposition remained highly fragmented. This aspect of Argentine politics has largely turned the Congress into a 'rubber stamp' institution at certain points, and made it highly dependent on party discipline. One consequence of all this has been a frequent reversal of structural laws and a generalized trend towards high intertemporal variation in policy-making.

Civil service systems and traditions. In spite of several attempts to centralize and professionalize public servants' careers, Argentina maintains a weak and fragmented system of human resources management in the public sector, largely determined by partisan concerns. Until the 1940s, Argentina had no rules for civil service recruitment. After the Perón administrations (1945–1955) a few educational conditions were imposed, although the dominance of the Peronist party since then set the civil service on a path of wide-scale partisan appointments as a double strategy to control policy-making and secure loyalties (Scherlis 2013; Sikkink 1993). In turn, at least three different administrative career systems have co-existed throughout the post-democratic years: (a) meritocratically elected elite corps; (b) a wider institutionalized categorization system; and (c) mostly internationally funded short-term consultants (e.g., Oszlak 1997).

Regarding the first, former Argentine president Raúl Alfonsín founded in 1985 a public school that competitively recruited highly skilled candidates to work for the public service. After graduation, these were meant to occupy key positions within the permanent bureaucracy and serve as coordination agents between ministries, while the executive could freely appoint and rotate them. These elite corps, named Governmental Agents Corps or AGs were recruited irregularly until 1993, when president Menem discontinued the program, in spite of which the already formed AGs continued to perform important roles across all different ministries. A wider and more inclusive approach to bureaucratic careers was undertaken through the National System for the Administrative Profession – SINAPA, introduced in 1992, which created an exhaustive salary scale and classifications for different functions and experience levels. SINAPA created incentives for professionalization but did not represent a unified system of cadre formation nor fostered any *esprit de corps*. Also, recurrent recruitment freezes meant that the access to SINAPA was unequal. Finally, Argentina has had to resort to short-term contracting, a legal alternative introduced in 1995 by decree. In this scheme, the funding comes from external donor institutions, and contracts can be unilaterally terminated. This system reinforced the existing fragmentation, giving rise to a so-called *parallel bureaucracy* (Zuvanic & Iacoviello 2005; Zuvanic et al. 2010).

The fragmentation can also be observed in the role and strength of cadre formation schools. In 1973 Argentina founded the Institute for Public Administration – INAP, designed as the main training school for public servants. Over time, however, it lost its autonomy and relevance, until it became a marginal and low-budgeted unit, used mostly at the convenience of the party in power. A similar attempt was made through the Institute of Government Economists, which opened in 1994 but dissolved in the year 2000.

Brazil, on the other hand, has the oldest formal civil service in Latin America (Grindle 2012). Judged to have the most consolidated Weberian administration and greatest level of continuity in the region, it was one of the first to establish a civil service career. The first recruitment exams took place in 1937, when President Getúlio Vargas created the Department for Administrative Services or DASP, an undersecretary designed to monitor and unify the standards of the federal civil service. In addition, meritocratic systems of recruitment were foreseen by all constitutional texts since Vargas. Throughout the following decades, these efforts were implemented only in small areas of the state that came to be known as pockets of efficiency such as the Central Bank, the National Economic Development Bank (BNDE), or public companies like Petrobras or CVRD for mining (Evans 1989; Geddes 1986). By the time Brazil re-entered democratic life in 1985, it combined meritocratic recruitment in pockets of efficiency with personalistic recruitment in other areas (Gaetani and Heredia 2002). Over the last decades, nevertheless, Brazil's bureaucracy has opened-up to New Public Management results-based principles, as well as representative bureaucracy principles, introducing quotas for women and underprivileged groups (Villoria Mendieta 2007).

Schools of public administration in Brazil have in turn acquired greater relevance than those in Argentina. Specialized sectors such as the military and the diplomatic corps count on specific training centres existing since the 1940s, such as the Air Force Academy (1941) for the former and Rio Branco Institute (1945) for the latter. Similar organizations were born during the 1970s, such as the Higher School of Financial Administration – ESAF (1973) and the Foundation for Administrative Development – FUNDAP (1974) (Pacheco 2000).

In 1952 the Brazilian School for Public Administration and Enterprise – EBAPE was founded by the Getúlio Vargas Foundation. In spite of being private, it acquired a key role in training both public officers and businessmen, and built partnerships with a number of important international organizations. Apart from training, it produced relevant research and publications on public policies. A second important school is the National School of Public Administration – ENAP, born in 1986, and its predecessor the FUNCEP NGO, born in 1980. The ENAP was modelled after the French National School of Administration – ENA, to become an elite cadre formation that would fill the ranks of the career permanent bureaucracy, against the backdrop of Brazil's new democratic life. Although institutionalized entry competitions were partially interrupted in the early 90s, the ENAP never stopped training the staff of the most insulated areas within the Brazilian state, such as the Treasury or the Central Bank. The ENAP re-gained momentum during the regulatory reforms of the mid-1990s.

Regulatory reforms of the 1990s. Several Latin American countries undertook state reform initiatives during the early 1990s. A common feature of these reforms was the establishment of independent regulatory agencies in the wake of liberal reforms, emulating similar transformations in Europe and the U.S. one decade earlier. Both Argentina and Brazil faced strong incentives to privatize public sector companies as a way to improve fiscal outcomes and attract foreign investors.

The hyperinflation crisis of 1989, however, prompted Argentina to initiate reforms urgently, with the premise of dramatically downsizing the state instead of foreseeing a more comprehensive and strategically planned public management approach. A second wave of reforms took place in the mid-1990s, also fostered by an economic crisis, the *tequila crisis* of 1995. These reforms included further lowering of public spending, along with increases in taxes meant to balance fiscal accounts. The organizational chart of the cabinet was dramatically altered and simplified, but once again financial results remained at the centre, while managerial aspects were marginally considered. Yet, the second reform lacked generalized support from different players, and run short in its scope, unable to meet its targets like the first one. Other reform attempts took place during the De la Rúa government in 2000 that were unsuccessful and interrupted by the economic turmoil of 2001/2002. Although the initiatives introduced represented progressive improvements, the Argentine public administration remains largely neo-patrimonial – in particular at the provincial and municipal levels – and barely prevents that party members and followers get privileged access to it (Scherlis 2013).

In Brazil, a profound reform started during the first Cardoso government with the aim of replicating the model of independent regulatory agencies following OECD guidelines in order to consolidate the permanent bureaucracy's career system. These reforms happened through a series of laws, but were also safeguarded as constitutional amendments, meaning that changes to the public service management need to reach constitutional status.

Parallel to the consolidation of the permanent career system, the reforms also aimed at introducing New Public Management guidelines, such as results-based management, flexibility in contract termination for public servants, more autonomy for agencies and more accountable officials.

Regarding independent agencies in Brazil, these reforms stipulated that governor selection would happen through executive appointment based on expertise and subject to senatorial approval. Governors would also enjoy fixed mandates, and normally be accompanied by a board of directors or assisted by advisory councils. The autonomy granted to agencies meant that they would enjoy vast decision-making powers and manage their own budgets. In order to enforce accountability, however, a widespread system of public consultations, public hearings and complaint mechanisms would fall on the agency (Mattos 2007). Cardoso's reforms also granted new momentum to public administration schools, such as in the case of the ENAP. A new wave of widespread training programs was implemented for all sectors of the civil service, as well as applied research increased (Pacheco 2000).

Other isolated measures enhanced the career system in Brazil. In the federal bureaucracy, 4 per cent of public servants hold so-called DAS positions (Direcao e Assessoramento Superior), which make up the top-level bureaucracy. A few particular measures protect these positions: they are appointed by the President under recommendation of the Planning Ministry; they enjoy big salary incentives; and since 2005 it was established that 75 per cent of lower level DAS and 50 per cent of higher level DAS should be filled with career bureaucrats (Praca, Freitas, & Hoepers 2011).

The reforms had profound and comprehensive results, and strengthened the bureaucratic career system (Gaetani & Heredia 2002). Although meritocratic recruitment was judged successful and is implemented on a wide scale (Longo 2005), on Lula's arrival, clashes occurred between ministers and independent agencies (Mattos 2007). In 2004 a bill was passed[3] devolving procurement legislation and other regulatory aspects to ministers, signalling some degree of reversal of Cardoso's meritocratic reforms.

Economic structure. Argentina and Brazil enjoy overall similarities regarding their economic profiles, but also important differences. They both belong to the upper middle-income group of countries, with a GDP per capita of 18,400 U.S. dollars (PPP) for Argentina, versus 12,100 for Brazil (est. 2012). Yet, Brazil's economy is five times bigger in total GDP size, and its sectoral composition more diversified and developed.

In Argentina, basic agricultural products represent 10.6 per cent of GDP; the industry accounts for 30.8 per cent, and the service sector for another 58.5 per cent. Manufactured goods make up about one-third of all exports, half of which are agricultural by-products such as food processing, oils, and biodiesel. Argentina's exports represent 21.8 per cent of GDP (World Bank 2011a).

In Brazil, the agricultural sector represents 5.5 per cent of the economy, industry another 27.5 per cent, and services 67 per cent, with manufactured goods making up 56 per cent of all exports (World Bank 2011b). Brazil is the seventh economy worldwide and has the second-biggest industrial sector in the Americas, after the United States. Its industries range from automobiles, autoparts, steel, and petrochemicals to computers, aircraft, and consumer durables. Its service sector is also highly diversified. In total, Brazil attracts six times higher inflows of foreign direct investment than Argentina. The domestic economy has enormous relevance and exports only represent 11.9 per cent of GDP.

A combination of active developmental plans in Brazil, along with a greater weight of industrial interests fostered a continuous feedback mechanism that shaped state structures in favour of these sectors. Sikkink (1993) provides a detailed description of the interplay between bureaucracy and domestic economic interests in comparative perspective. While both countries had developmental plans during the 1960s, President Kubitschek in Brazil relied on the more neutral administrative 'pockets of efficiency' established earlier on, while Frondizi in Argentina attempted to build a parallel bureaucracy for this purpose only.

Frondizi, of the Intransigent Radical Union Party – UCRI needed to struggle with a permanent bureaucracy consisting mostly of Peronist loyalists who consolidated their positions during previous decades of Peronist dominance. When Frondizi called upon a number of committees to decide the strategic planning of foreign investment, the move was largely seen as a '*parallel government*' and failed to endure. Frondizi was ousted by a coup in 1962, four years after taking office. Some differences can be observed, for example in the comparison of public entities in charge of coordinating and allocating resources for the productive sector, such as the BNDE in Brazil and the Banco Industrial – BI in Argentina. The BNDE enjoyed overall autonomy and had a long-term perspective, with several international experts providing advice such as the World Bank. The Argentine BI was less autonomous, and ended up favouring short-term credits and benefiting certain industries over others. Beneficiaries became dependent on these short-term credits and opposed reforms to the bank. The turnover of directors was markedly high (Sikkink 1993).

In other words, the interactions between politicians, bureaucrats and industrialists was more virtuous and intertemporally balanced in Brazil, which led to overall higher levels of regulatory predictability in this country.

EMPIRICAL STRATEGY AND RESULTS

The Database

For each country, I compiled a database gathering information on several aspects of the national public administration over a twenty-year period. First, I recorded the existing organizational chart for each year under study, meaning an exhaustive listing of all the organizational units within the executive power in the form of ministries and all their depending secretaries and under-secretaries. Over the twenty-year period, these total 1,061 for Argentina and 1,569 for Brazil.[4] Second,

I collected the names of semi-autonomous agencies existing between 1990 and 2010 along with their dates of creation, their location in the organizational chart, as well as some additional information about their legal form. These agencies amount to seventy-four in Argentina and forty-six for Brazil. Third, I collected data on the names and dates of appointment and removal of the head officials in each of these organizational units throughout the period, both in agencies and all cabinet units, a total of 1,419 for Argentina and 1,643 for Brazil. Finally, combining the former three items, I built a database for each country with the career paths of the officials entering the sample.[5] Although the database is highly exhaustive, around 20 per cent of the data points are random missings.

Measurement and Results

The information in the database allows me to conduct a comparative analysis of the inter-dependence between permanent administrative structures and changing political cycles. As mentioned before, administrative adaptability potential is understood as a country's capability of introducing changes in the central administrative apparatus in correspondence with changes in democratic preferences. Predictability, on the other hand, is the capacity to maintain long or medium-term policy commitments.

The adaptability to democratic preferences is here captured through the analysis of different patterns within the central administration (ministries and sub-units), while predictability is analysed through semi-autonomous administrative bodies such as independent agencies.

Adaptability. I compare Argentina and Brazil on two adaptability dimensions. Higher marks on these dimensions would be signalling more tightly coupled political and administrative realms. First, I compute a simple formula to measure inter-annual variations in the organizational charts (OCV) for each country, as follows:

$$OCV_j = \frac{\sum_{i=1}^{8}\left(U_{ij}^{n} - U_{ij-}^{n}\right)^2}{\sum_{i=1}^{8} MAX\left[U_{ij}^{n}; U_{ij-1}^{n}\right]}$$

Where j are the years between 1991 and 2010 (since data starts in 1990), i are the individual organizational units, where units (U) can be of a nature m (Ministry), s (Secretary) or u (Undersecretary). U_{ij}^{m}, U_{ij}^{s}, and U_{ij}^{u} equal 1 if they exist and 0 otherwise, so that, for example $U_{2,1999}^{m} = 1$ is the existence of ministry 2 in 1999, and the same for secretaries and undersecretaries. The index ranges between 0 (no change at all) and 1 (complete change). Changes happen when either a new unit is created or terminated or its denomination is changed. If, for example all ministries would change from one year to the next the index would take on a value of 1, as each ministry will automatically drag changes in their depending units (each sub-unit is considered different if they are under a different ministry even when its particular denomination does not change). If only one undersecretary would be eliminated or changed from one year to the next, then the index would take on a value close to 0, which will depend on the total number of units. The higher the total number of units, the less weight each one will have in the index, naturally weighting its individual importance for overall bureaucratic change.

Because data exists for both countries at all three administrative levels in all sectors the index is promising in terms of its comparative capacity. The existence of organizational units is computed on the 1st of July each year to avoid transitional periods, which usually take place at the beginning of the year in both cases.

The levels of change over time provide a first comparison of the degree of political control over the bureaucratic structure, interpreted as higher adaptability to democratic preferences but at the same time greater opportunities for personalistic use of state structures by political parties and elected officials.

The graph shows several interesting findings. First, Argentina has on average 0.15 more points of organizational chart variation than Brazil, which

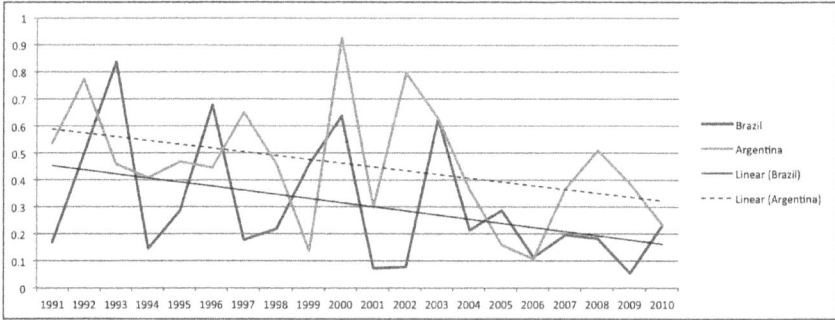

Figure 11.1   Organizational Chart Changes in Argentina and Brazil, 1990–2010
Source: Author's compilation

represents around 30 per cent more changes on an annual basis. Also, in both countries variations are largely dependent on changes in presidential mandates and/or economic transformation episodes. Argentina experiences peaks during the massive privatization and state reform initiatives of the early nineties (1992), second generation state reforms (1996), changes in the governing party (2000 and 2002), the severe economic crisis of the early 2000s (2002), and to a lesser extent the arrival to power of Mr Kirchner (2003) and Mrs Kirchner (2008). In Brazil the first peak corresponds to the aftermath of the impeachment of Collor de Mello and arrival of Franco (1993); the second to the arrival of Cardoso (1996); the third most likely to the aftermath of the devaluation and economic crisis of 1999 (1999/2000), and the last one to the arrival of Lula da Silva (2003). A third finding suggests that a clear downward trend can be registered in both cases. Interpreting this is not straightforward, but one possibility is that as these countries consolidate their democratic systems the increase in political stability translates in less annual variation, and that transitions become smoother in time. This trend is clearer in the case of Brazil.

A second analytical dimension involves a slightly different conceptual angle, and measures the likelihood of variations in the organizational charts subject to turnovers in political principals. The next graph compares the countries in terms of the extent to which second and third level units change depending on turnovers (TORs) of the ministers in the parent unit during the previous year. If, for example two thirds of the lower level organizational units are changed from one year to the next, and of these, two thirds changed after a ministerial turnover, the bar in the graph would total 0.66, with the black portion (chart change with TOR) representing about 0.44 points and the grey one representing about 0.22. The measure gives an accurate picture of the extent to which incoming leaders 'appropriate' the bureaucratic structures in order to facilitate their mandates.

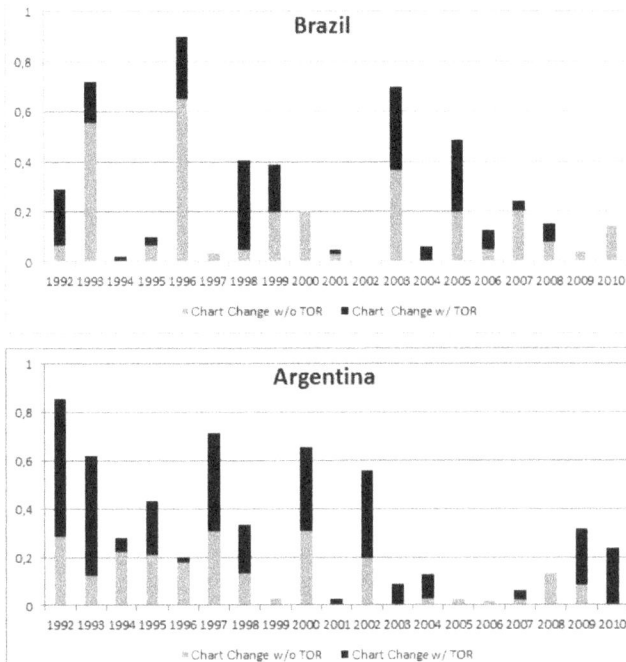

Figure 11.2 Organizational Chart Changes Subject to Political Turnover in Argentina and Brazil, 1990–2010

It can be observed that with few exceptions the proportion of organizational chart changes associated to turnovers is substantially higher in Argentina. To further test this statistically, I run a basic probabilistic analysis testing whether ministerial turnovers are significant in determining the probability of organizational chart change:

Table 11.1 Probability of Organizational Chart Change Subject to Political Turnover in Argentina and Brazil, 1991–2010

Year	Brazil	Argentina	Year	Brazil	Argentina
1992	0.656	0.421	2002	(omitted)	0.357
	(0.001)	(0.082)			0.009
1993	−0.718	0.778	2003	−0.065	(omitted)
	(0.000)	(0.000)		0.669	
1994	(omitted)	−0.682	2004	(omitted)	0.580
		(0.001)			0.067
1995	−0.296	0.045	2005	0.206	(omitted)
	(0.120)	(0.836)		0.163	

(Continued)

Table 11.1   (Continued)

Year	Brazil	Argentina	Year	Brazil	Argentina
1996	−0.572 (0.014)	−0.970 (0.001)	2006	0.202 0.340	(omitted)
1997	(omitted)	0.159 0.311	2007	−0.805 (0.000)	0.205 0.453
1998	1.049 (0.000)	0.225 (0.096)	2008	−0.042 (0.778)	(omitted)
1999	−0.041 (0.803)	(omitted)	2009	(omitted)	0.548 0.003
2000	(omitted)	0.072 0.775	2010	(omitted)	1.758 0.000
2001	−0.150 0.637	(omitted)			

Note: Probit estimations. Intercepts for each year are omitted.
Source: author's compilation.

These probit coefficients estimate increases or decreases in the probabilities that any subunit (secretaries and undersecretaries) is modified one year after a ministerial turnover occurs in the parent ministry. Data is therefore computed for the first time in 1992 based on turnovers between 1990 and 1991. Negative coefficients mean that increases in ministerial turnovers decrease the predicted probability of organizational chart change. Whenever all changes occur either with or without turnovers the estimations are naturally omitted. A positive and significant relationship can be observed seven times in Argentina, while only twice in Brazil throughout the period.

The overall picture suggests that although in both countries the centralized administration (cabinet offices) is largely adaptable, in Argentina this adaptability is substantially larger.

Predictability. Regarding bureaucratic predictability, I capture different patterns related to the behaviour of independent agencies in the two countries. Higher marks in these predictability patterns signal less tightly coupled political and administrative realms.

Discretionary political intervention in regulatory, administrative and coordination agencies is understood as a major obstacle for policy predictability. The agencies in the database are autonomous in legal terms, meaning that they were granted the right to self-govern, enjoy fixed mandates for its governors and, for the most part, define their own budgets. Although governors are formally appointed by the executive, their duration in office is meant to be independent of any political cycle.

The histograms next show the number of presidential appointments of independent agencies' governors in the days following the start of the respective presidential mandate, with fifty-day gaps:

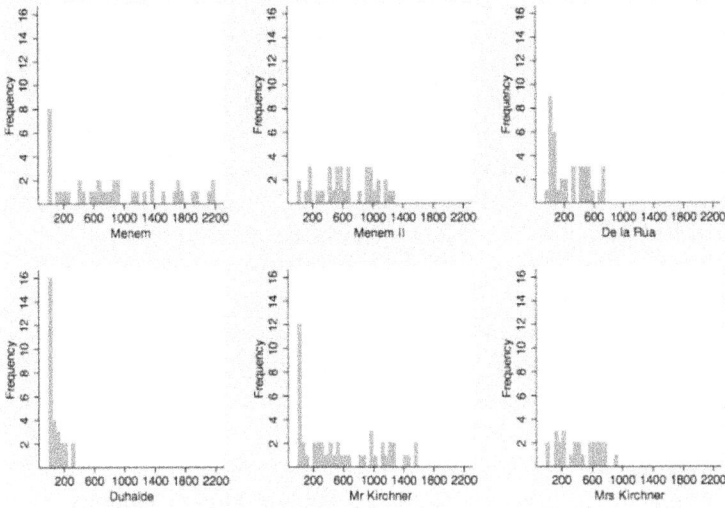

Figure 11.3   Argentina: Appointment of Agency Leaders after New Administration (days)

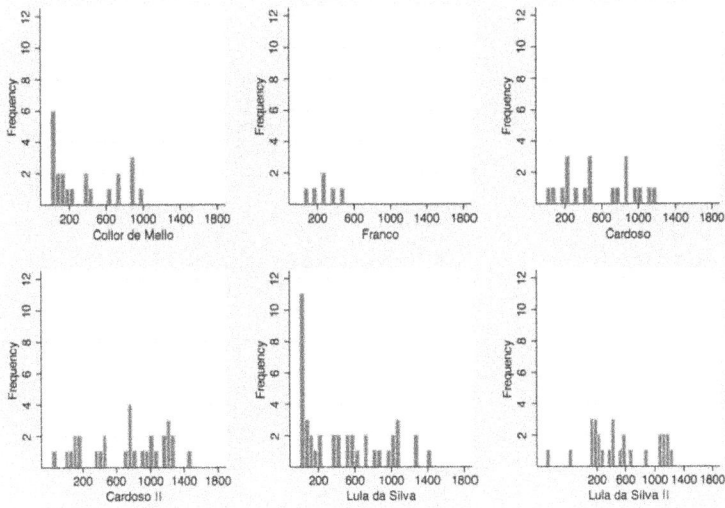

Figure 11.4   Brazil: Appointment of Agency Leaders after New Administration (days)

With the exception of the second Menem administration, and Mrs Kirchner's mandate (which could arguably be considered a continuation of Mr Kirchner's mandate), all new Argentine presidents have intervened agencies by appointing a large number of governors during their first 50 or 100 days in office. In Brazil the pattern differs more among presidencies. While Cardoso and Franco show a rather uniform distribution, signalling respect for independence, Lula da Silva and to a lesser extent Collor de Mello appointed a large number of governors at the start of their mandates compared to the following years.

Finally, some comparative patterns in the career paths of agency officials further illuminate the overall dynamics of the relationship between bureaucrats and politicians, and give hints about both predictability and adaptability trends.

The pie chart below shows some basic patterns of job mobility for those officials who were heads of independent agencies at some point during the twenty-year period. The first chart shows that while in Argentina 22 per cent of all officials also took positions in the central government (either as minister, secretary, or undersecretary of state), this percentage represents 13 per cent in Brazil. Also, while in Argentina most of these officials were political appointees in the cabinet prior to their agency appointments; only a minority followed this path in Brazil.

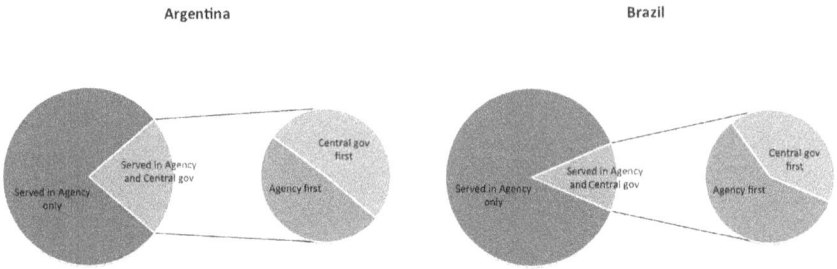

Figure 11.5   Career Paths of Agency Leaders I (1990–2010)

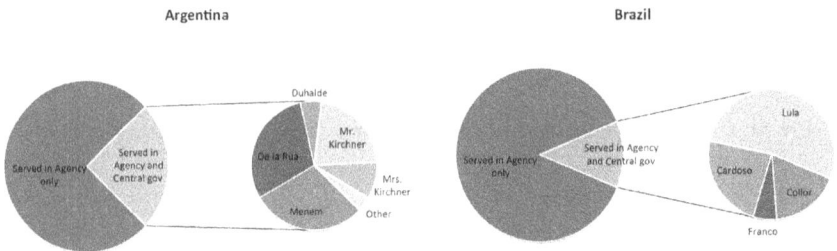

Figure 11.6   Career Paths of Agency Leaders II (1990–2010)

The second pie chart shows the presidencies under which these 'political' agency leaders served: while in Argentina no particular presidency stands out, in Brazil more than half of them served under Lula da Silva's administration.

The overall picture suggests that Brazil relies on bureaucratic structures that provide more stable regulation and predictability than Argentina, even though there is greater variance among presidencies. In the next section I delineate some of the political economy reasons behind this contrast, taking into account a corpus of literature on institutions in the region. These findings confirm our initial expectation that Brazil's political economy is conducive to less tightly coupled political and administrative realms than in the case of Argentina.

CONCLUSIONS

In this chapter I propose a comparative study of the bureaucratic features in Argentina and Brazil informative of the respective matrices of opportunities they offer for clientelistic and neopatrimonial practices. I developed an empirical model able to capture the dynamics of the interaction between the political and administrative realms in the two countries, and assessed how loosely or tightly coupled they have been over a twenty-year period. Through these dynamics I am able to evaluate the potential each country has to develop policy adaptability and predictability capacity. I argue that both are essential and yet dichotomous features of state capacity. The former is favoured by a stronger interdependency between the political and administrative realms, while the latter benefits from a more insulated public administration. I argue that while adaptability may be very beneficial in order to implement changing democratic preferences a potential downside may be a more generous matrix of opportunity for neopatrimonial practices, given that elected or politically appointed leaders have a deeper control over permanent bureaucratic structures. This, in turn, has the potential of distorting the design of policies in favour of those actors willing to engage in patronage.

All in all, I find that Brazil has a bureaucracy that has come a longer way in building its predictability capacity. In the Argentine case, there is an overall dominance of the political representatives over the permanent bureaucracy, favouring adaptability over predictability. It remains for future discussion, however, to which extent these adaptability technologies are at the same time potential sources of policy volatility, and to which extent too much predictability may result in policy-making rigidity or stalemate.

The reasons behind the resulting contrast between the countries are multiple and for the most part consistent with the institutional literature. Interestingly, and in line with traditional theories on veto players, a more fragmented decision-making arena has led to a more stable policy-making matrix in Brazil, while a majority-driven decision-making process has led to an intertemporally and intersectorally fragmented bureaucratic structure in Argentina. Several determinants have been portrayed: (a) the stronger congressional influence over the bureaucracy in Brazil; (b) its highly proportional electoral system and its subsequent encouragement of inter-party agreements; (c) the more important role played by the judiciary in enforcing administrative laws; and (d) the influence of an already existing professional bureaucracy when Brazil democratized in 1985. Also, state reforms of the 1990s were more comprehensive and strategically thought in the former country. Finally, Brazil's diversified economic structure is at the same time a cause and an outcome of a more independent bureaucracy that resisted political capture more successfully.

In sum, a diverse and plural political arena generated more incentives for a professional and stable public service in Brazil, while a more diversified economic structure has had a similar effect. I also observe that economic cycles affect the opportunities for administrative independence: while turmoil favours political reforms of the state apparatus, macro-economic stabilization tends to favour more initiatives towards independence.

Counter-intuitively, however, I also find that deeply rooted institutions do not completely explain the dynamics of state structures. Other factors such as the nature of leadership and political will seem to have played an important role in shaping reforms in both cases, most notably during the Cardoso administration in Brazil. There is plenty of evidence suggesting that Cardoso particularly pushed in the direction of civil service professionalization and higher predictability.

It is contended here that the quality of a country's public administration is the most important pillar of development, and that the distortion of policies hinders the legitimacy of the democratic system. Although the search for highly capable bureaucracies has been a long-standing quest, we still know very little about how these processes are shaped in time. This chapter moves one step closer to this goal.

Many challenges remain unaddressed. Comparative public administration studies are still in need for better and more precise empirical measures, so that they can illuminate more specific causal mechanisms. Also, the connections between development economics and in-depth studies of bureaucratic features and institutions in general need further complementarity, with quantitative and qualitative methods interacting virtuously. I believe a renewed interest in comparative bureaucracies promises an eventful agenda in the near future.

NOTES

1. Refers to Law 25411 of March 29, 2001.
2. Amendment 32, September 11, 2001.
3. Law 3337.
4. In the case of Brazil, however, data is missing for the cabinet office (Casa Civil).
5. Data on organizational charts was extracted from the searchable databases of legislation, in Argentina the site infoleg.gov and in Brazil legislacao.planalto.gov.br. Data on appointments was collected from the scanned and digital copies of both countries' daily official gazettes: the Boletin Oficial in Argentina and the Diario Oficial da Uniao in Brazil.

REFERENCES

Abranches, S. (1988). Presidencialismo de coalizao: O dilema institucional brasileiro. *Dados*, 31(1):5–38.

Brans, M. (2003). Comparative public administration: From general theory to general frameworks. *Handbook of Public Administration*. London: Sage, pages 424–439.

Cheibub Figueiredo, A. (2011). Government coalitions in Brazilian democracy. *Brazilian Political Science Review*, 1(2):182–216.

Cingolani, L. (2013). *The state of state capacity: A review of concepts, evidence and measures*. UNU-Merit Working Paper Series 2013–053.

Cingolani, L., Thomsson, K., and de Crombrugghe, D. (2015). Minding weber more than ever? The impacts of state capacity and bureaucratic autonomy on development goals. *World Development*, 72:191–207.

Dahlström, C., Lapuente, V., and Teorell, J. (2010). *Dimensions of bureaucracy: A cross-national dataset on the structure and behavior of public administration*, volume 13. QoG Working Paper Series.

Erdmann, G., and Engel, U. (2007). Neopatrimonialism reconsidered: Critical review and elaboration of an elusive concept. *Commonwealth & Comparative Politics*, 45(1):95–119.

Evans, P. B. (1989). Predatory, developmental, and other apparatuses: A comparative political economy perspective on the third world state. *Sociological Forum*, 4(4):561–587.

Fukuyama, F. (2012). The strange absence of the state in political science. *The American Interest*. Blog entry, February.

Gaetani, F., and Heredia, B. (2002). *La economia pol tica de la reforma del servicio civil en brasil: los años de cardoso*. Technical report, Inter-American Development Bank.

Geddes, B. J. (1986). *Economic development as a collective action problem: Individual interests and innovation in Brazil.* Berkeley: University of California Press.

Grindle, M. S. (2012). *Jobs for the boys: Patronage and the state in comparative perspective.* Cambridge, MA: Harvard University Press.

Hanson, J., and Sigman, R. (2011). *Measuring state capacity: Assessing and testing the options.* APSA annual meeting paper.

Hendrix, C. S. (2010). Measuring state capacity: Theoretical and empirical implications for the study of civil conflict. *Journal of Peace Research,* 47(3):273–285.

Lapuente, V. (2007). *A political economy approach to bureaucracies.* Doctoral dissertation, Oxford: Oxford University Press.

Longo, F. (2004). *Merito y exibilidad: la gestion de las personas en las organizaciones del sector publico,* volume 102. Editorial Paidos.

Longo, F. (2005). *Diagnostico institucional comparado de sistemas de servicio civil: Informe nal de s ntesis.* Technical report, Inter-American Development Bank.

Mattos, P. T. (2007). *The regulatory reform in Brazil: New regulatory decision-making and accountability mechanisms.* University of San Andres, New York University Law School, Buenos Aires.

Montero, A. P. (2001). After decentralization: Patterns of intergovernmental conflict in Argentina, Brazil, Spain, and Mexico. *Publius: The Journal of Federalism,* 31(4):43–64.

Oszlak, O. (1997). The argentine civil service: An unfinished search for identity. *Research in Public Administration,* 5:267–326.

Pacheco, R. S. (2000). Escolas de governo: tendencias e desafios. Enap-Brasil em perspectiva comparada. *Revista do Servico Publico,* 51(2).

Praca, S., Freitas, A., and Hoepers, B. (2011). Political appointments and coalition management in Brazil, 2007–2010. *Journal of Politics in Latin America,* 3(2).

Scherlis, G. (2013). Designaciones y organizacion partidaria: el partido de redes gubernamentales en el peronismo kirchnerista. *America Latina Hoy,* 62:47–77.

Sikkink, K. (1993). Las capacidades y la autonom a del estado en brasil y la argentina. un enfoque neoinstitucionalista. *Desarrollo Economico,* 543–574.

Villoria Mendieta, M. (2007). *El servicio civil de carrera en latinoamerica: diagnostico, causas y propuestas.* INAP, Madrid: INAP.

Von Soest, C. (2009). *Informal institutions compared-persistence and change of neopatrimonialism in various world regions.* In APSA 2009 Toronto Meeting Paper.

Wade, R. (2010). After the crisis: Industrial policy and the developmental state in low-income countries. *Global Policy,* 1(2):150–161.

Wilson, W. (1887). The study of administration. *Political Science Quarterly,* 2(2):197–222.

World Bank (2011a). *Argentina at a glance.* Technical report, Development Economics LDB database.

World Bank (2011b). *Brazil at a glance.* Technical report, Development Economics LDB database.

Zuvanic, L., and Iacoviello, M. (2005). *El rol de la burocracia en el PMP en america latina.* Inter-American Development Bank, Mimeographed, Washington, DC.

Zuvanic, L., Iacoviello, M., and Rodriguez Gustá, A. L. (2010). The weakest link: The bureaucracy and civil service systems in Latin America. C. Scartascini, *Ernesto Stein and Mariano Tommasi, How Democracy Works: Political Institutions, IADB Washington D.C.* Actors, and Arenas in Latin American Policymaking, pages 147–176.

Chapter Twelve

Conclusion

The Lessons Learned

Maria Spirova and Saskia Ruth-Lovell

This volume sets out to investigate the consequences of clientelism for the system of democratic representation. In this effort, it brought together research on clientelistic practices in second- and third-wave democracies (and one electoral autocracy) across three continents to look at how the input and output sides of the democratic process are influenced by this phenomenon. While we look at clientelism in a variety of contexts, we deploy a minimal definition focusing on those aspects that directly relate to the representative process. More specifically, we follow definitions that see it as an electoral mobilization strategy, and, hence, we focus on those types of practices where selective benefits (such as consumer goods, access to social security programs, or jobs) are exchanged for political support (e.g., Hicken 2011; Kitschelt and Wilkinson 2007; Stokes et al. 2013). Most importantly, we focus on the practices of vote-buying and political patronage. In this, we differ from other works on clientelism which conceive of clientelism in much broader light or limit it exclusively to either one or the other practice (e.g., Kopecký, Mair, and Spirova 2012; Piattoni 2001; Schaffer 2007).

The first chapter in this volume introduced our theoretical arguments and posited that we expect clientelism to have two distinctive implications for the process of democratic representation. We developed a vision of democratic representation with the processes of *accountability* and *responsiveness* at its core and presented it graphically in Figure 1.1. Within that framework, and building on previous research, we see clientelism as potentially distorting the representative link between parties and voters on the input side of the democratic process and challenging the traditional conceptions of accountability. In this regard, clientelism will impact the legitimacy of the representative link between parties and voters by distorting the potential of substantive representation. It does so by perverting the roles individual voters or social groups play and by altering the function of political parties and party systems in electoral politics (see, especially, Stokes 2005). Moving to the throughput and output side of the representative process, we set out an expectation that clientelism might lead to low (policy) responsiveness of the political elite to the interests of their clients. Instead of responding to their voters, clientelistic parties will be mostly interested in introducing new policies that expand their ability to provide clientelistic benefits of various kinds. As a result, clientelistic political actors will be more likely to engage in rent-seeking behaviour and in generating targetable private goods – able to finance clientelistic networks – instead of universalistic public policies (see Abente Brun and Diamond 2014; Weitz-Shapiro 2014).

The chapters in the book that followed addressed these two major themes in turn and pointed out important ways in which clientelism does, in fact, leave a variegated imprint on both the input and output side of the representative process. This conclusion will review the main findings of the contributions in this volume and point to the main insights into the relationship between clientelism and representative democracy as suggested by these findings in more general terms.

CLIENTELISM, VOTERS, AND PARTIES

The research presented in the volume suggests that clientelism concerns all actors involved in the process of democratic representation: how voters see themselves, how they relate to political parties and the political process, whether they vote or not and the way their preferences get translated into votes, and the overall systemic and social context within which elections take place. That clientelism impacts the link between voters and parties is not a new observation, but the evidence presented in the first part of the volume highlights the variegated ways in which this linkage type impedes the beneficial by-products of substantive representation (most importantly, responsiveness), an underexplored aspects of this phenomenon (e.g., Kitschelt and Wilkinson 2007; Powell 2004; Stokes et al. 2013).

Therefore, the first two chapters in this section set out to investigate how clientelistic practices distort substantive representation of most likely clients (e.g., poor and ethnic voters). To this end, Saskia P. Ruth-Lovell (chapter 2) looks at party-voter congruence – an often-used indicator of policy responsiveness – to assess to what extent clientelistic linkages impact the match between voters' policy preferences with their parties' policy pledges. Using a cross-sectional data set of eighty political parties covering eighty Latin American democracies, she concludes that 'clientelistic parties more likely misrepresent their supporters to the right (free market) end of the economic scale than to the left (state interventionist) end of the economic dimension' (Ruth-Lovell, 31), which is especially problematic having in mind that clientelistic parties' most likely targets are poor voters who should benefit most from leftist policies. Similar questions about the proper translation of voter preferences into representative institutions are raised by Petr Kopecký and Maria Spirova, in chapter 3. Exploring the links between ethnic parties and clientelism in Bulgaria and Romania, Kopecký and Spirova argue that ethnic parties, as such, are more likely to engage in vote-buying and extensive patronage practices, compared to their non-ethnic counterparts, thus putting into question the quality of the representation of the interests of minorities, which is already under pressure in many democracies. As a result clientelistic ethnic parties might also undermine any benefits descriptive representation might be bringing to the political system.

Further, Frank de Zwart examines the interplay of affirmative action, clientelistic practices and caste identity in India, in chapter 4, and observes how the persistence of clientelistic practices turns caste identity into an important commodity and leads to even further social, political, and administrative fragmentation (de Zwart, 76). In that way, it is not only the political process that is transformed by clientelism but also the very fabric of society into which it is embedded. Taking the democratic process one step further, Inga A.-L. Saikkonen, in chapter 5, examines clientelism in Russia by focusing on selective turnout buying, which links selective benefits to the likelihood of voters to participate in elections. In electoral autocracies such as Russia, where support for the ruling party is a given, voter turnout 'is a central part of the stabilization of electoral authoritarian regimes' (Saikkonen, 96). As such, clientelism helps to perpetuate non-competitive elections and impedes voters to hold their representatives accountable for their actions in office.

Finally, in chapter 6, Sergiu Gherghina and Clara Volintiru turn their attention to the party system level in Romania to discern the emergence of a new model of clientelism that factors in the interaction of parties, business elites and the state, extending the distorting consequences of clientelism for democratic representation even further. Analyses of Romanian parties between 2008 and 2012 illuminate the networks that have been built to link vote-buying practices by political parties to the financial resources provided by private firms in exchange for preferential access to public procurement.

Clientelism, these chapters showed, envelops all links of the input chain of representation and, if kept unchecked, can alter the very basis for the principles and workings of democratic representation. It systematically impedes the translation of voter preferences into political power for both poor and ethnic voter groups and may lead to the manipulation of the institutional and social context through affirmative action policies, turnout buying, or business influence to the benefit of those who run clientelistic networks.

CLIENTELISM, POLICIES, AND PUBLIC GOODS

Taking the discussion to the throughput and output side of the representative process, clientelism, we have argued, is likely to influence the way public goods are distributed. Only recently have researchers turned their attention towards disentangling the relationship between clientelism and distributive politics (see De La O 2015; Golden and Min 2013; Stokes et al. 2013). The second part of the book contributes to this ongoing research area by looking at how clientelism leaves an imprint on the patterns of public spending and social policy, in general, as well as specific sectoral expenditures, political reforms and the role of the bureaucracy. It thus delves into the intricacies of the mechanisms that mark the responsiveness of clientelistic political actors to their clients.

In chapter 7, Juha Ylisalo investigates an old question in a new light: the link between the size of governmental coalition and its likelihood to increase public spending. However, he qualifies the argument to assert that it is not the simple number of coalition partners but the extent of their clientelistic linkages that makes it more likely for a government to increase public spending. Using data from the EU, he support this with empirical evidence to conclude that taking into account clientelism linkages eliminates the link between fragmentation of the party system and public spending thus demonstrating clearly how clientelism distorts the patterns of public spending across democracies.

In chapter 8, Sarah A. Berens and Saskia P. Ruth-Lovell, explore the link between clientelism, social policy advocacy and social policy outcomes in the Latin American region. They show that clientelistic parties are less supportive of universal social policies while more clientelistic party systems are linked with lower social welfare, especially for the poor. Taken together, these conclusions point to 'a serious hurdle to political reforms toward more universal social welfare states in Latin America' (Berens and Ruth-Lovell, 168) and further illustrate how pernicious clientelistic practices might be for the legitimacy of democratic policy-making, and as such for the democratic political system overall.

Looking at a much more specific context, Francesco Stolfi, in chapter 9, investigates whether the degree of clientelism in Italian regions influences spending by regional governments for electoral reasons. Using quantitative analyses across the Italian regions, he shows that political budget cycles in health personnel spending are larger in more clientelistic regions. This calls into question fundamental assumptions in fiscal policy-making, as it demonstrates that how well rules work 'depends on relatively long-term features of national or even sub-national jurisdictions' (Stolfi, 188).

Chapter 10 moves into the study of the consequences of the New Public Governance reform of the health care sector in Croatia. Anka Kekez Kostro describes the benefits of this reform such as more interactive horizontal management and soft steering mechanisms, but also points out to the blind spots created by this reform that allow for patronage to be carried out by local elites. Detailed analysis of the developments in Croatian regions demonstrates that such reforms can 'enable politicians to create opportunities and resources for political patronage and to use these opportunities and resources for advancing political objectives' (Kekez, 217).

In the final substantive chapter of the book (chapter 11), Luciana Cingolani takes us further into the interplay of administrative reform and clientelism and back to Latin America. Exploring the development of administrative systems in Argentina and Brazil, she describes the dichotomy of their development in leading Brazil into a trajectory of policy predictability capacity and Argentina into a policy adaptability capacity. The latter, she argues, allows for opportunities for various neo-patrimonial practices because of high levels of control that politicians are given over administrative structures. This, in turn, leads to 'a potential of distorting the design of policies in favor of those actors willing to engage in patronage' (Cingolani, 240).

These chapters highlight that a diverse set of actors in clientelistic contexts face incentives to implement policies that undermine the interests of the groups that are particularly vulnerable in society and thus limit their policy responsiveness. Clientelism may, for example, induce national governments to engage in more public spending, irrespective of the size of governments, and hinder the expansion of social policies over time, due to the overrepresentation of regressive welfare state preferences. Moreover, the implementation of social policies as well as their reforms, even when they are designed by national politicians to improve the quality of services, may foster clientelism if policy-makers do not account for both the incentives of political actors on the local or regional level and the role and incentives of public service officials.

These diverse studies of the interplay of clientelism, public policy outcomes, party platforms and structures of the public sector demonstrate the variegated implications of the phenomenon of clientelism. It transforms the way parties relate to voters, and thereby the most important features of the democratic representative link: responsiveness and accountability. Thereby, it distorts both inputs into the representative process as well as the outputs that result from political representation. Thus, clientelism undermines all components of the process of democratic representation. Further research is to delve into the even more fundamental questions about the consequences of clientelism on the system of representation – its long-term effects. Many questions – such as what is the impact of clientelistic practices on the public support for democracy, how does clientelism transform the political elite and the system of representation itself, and ultimately, whether we can observe a long-term feedback impact on the preferences of voters – remain unanswered. Still, they become immediate because of the work presented in this volume.

REFERENCES

Abente Brun, D. and L. Diamond. 2014. *Clientelism, Social Policy, and the Quality of Democracy*. Baltimore: Johns Hopkins University Press.

De La O, A. 2015. *Crafting Policies to End Poverty in Latin America*. Cambridge: Cambridge University Press.

Golden, M. A., and B. Min. 2013. Distributive Politics Around the World. *Annual Review of Political Science* 16 (1): 73–99.

Hicken, A. 2011. Clientelism. *Annual Review of Political Science* 14 (1): 289–310.

Kitschelt, H. and S. I. Wilkinson, eds. 2007. *Patrons, Clients, and Policies: Patterns of Democratic Accountability and Political Competition*. Cambridge: Cambridge University Press.

Kopecký, P. P. Mair, and M. Spirova. 2012. *Party Patronage and Party Government in European Democracies*. Oxford: Oxford University Press.

Piattoni, S. 2001. Clientelism in Historical and Comparative Perspective. In *Clientelism, Interests, and Democratic Representation*, ed. Simona Piattoni. Cambridge: Cambridge University Press. 1–30.

Powell, G. B. 2004. Political Representation in Comparative Politics. *Annual Review of Political Science* 7 (1): 273–296.

Schaffer, F. C. ed. 2007. *Elections for Sale: The Causes and Consequences of Vote Buying*. Boulder, CO: Lynne Rienner.

Stokes, S. C. 2005. Perverse Accountability: A Formal Model of Machine Politics with Evidence from Argentina. *American Political Science Review* 99 (3): 315–325.

Stokes, S. C. Thad Dunning, Marcelo Nazareno, and Valeria Brusco, eds. 2013. *Brokers, Voters, and Clientelism: The Puzzle of Distributive Politics*. Cambridge: Cambridge University Press.

Weitz-Shapiro, R. 2014. *Curbing Clientelism in Argentina: Politics, Poverty, and Social Policy*. Cambridge: Cambridge University Press.

Index

accountability, 1, 3–4, 16, 22–23, 25, 96, 112, 133, 148, 153, 158–59, 216–17, 230, 245, 249

Argentina, 23, 32, 85, 221–29, 231–41, 249, 251; Banco Industrial (BI), 231–32; Institute for Public Administration (INAP), 228; Intransigent Radical Union Party (UCRI), 231; National System for the Administrative Profession (SINAPA), 228

authoritarian regimes, 83–86, 88, 96, 247

backward classes, 61–76, 77–79

bargaining, 108, 133–35, 139; inter party, 133, 135; process, 133–35

BJP. *See* India

BNDE. *See* Brazil

Brazil, 23, 32, 189n3, 221–40, 241n4, 241n5, 249; Brazilian School for Public Administration and Enterprise (EBAPE), 229; Department for Administrative Services (DASP), 228; Direcao e Assessoramento Superior (DAS), 230; Foundation for Administrative Development (FUNDAP), 229; Higher School of Financial Administration (ESAF), 229; National Economic Development Bank (BNDE), 228, 231; National

School of Public Administration (ENAP), 229–30; Partido de Reconstrucao Nacional (PRN), 227

Bulgaria, 8, 41–42, 45–56, 85, 137, 247; Democratic Alliance of Hungarians in Romania (UDMR), 47–50, 53, 115–16, 121, 126; Movement for Rights and Freedom (DPS), 46–53; Turkish Party, 48, 50, 53–54

bureaucracy, 70, 84–85, 198, 205, 221–25, 227–31, 233, 235, 237, 239–41, 248

cartelization, 8, 114–15, 124

cartels, 111, 115, 125

cash transfers: conditional (CCTs), 117, 151

caste(s), 61–78, 247, 251

civil service, 205, 221–22, 224–25, 227–28, 230, 240

clientelism, 1–3, 5–9, 15, 19, 21–22, 25, 29, 31, 34–35, 44–45, 52–54, 63, 70, 76, 83–85, 88, 90–91, 95–96, 105–10, 112–16, 124, 126, 132–36, 152–68, 175–82, 184–89, 222, 245–50; consequences of, 1, 245, 247; definition, 2; effects of, 1, 7, 29, 35, 153, 155, 163, 165, 167, 175; electoral, 83–85, 91; traditional, 2; vertical, 114–16, 124

About the Contributors

Sarah A. Berens is a postdoctoral research fellow at the Cologne Center for Comparative Politics at the University of Cologne. She completed her PhD in the International Max Planck Research School at the Max-Planck Institute for the Study of Societies and the University of Cologne. She has been a visiting researcher at Duke University and Columbia University. Her work explores the micro-foundation of welfare state politics and of labour market dualization in Latin America.

Luciana Cingolani is assistant professor for public administration at the Hertie School of Governance. She is associate researcher in the Horizon 2020 project on open data and digital transparency 'Digiwhist'. Her research interests include public management, administrative capacity building, transparency, digital technologies, and e-Government. Luciana holds a PhD in development studies and public policy from Maastricht University in the Netherlands and an MPhil in public policy from San Andrés University in Argentina.

Frank de Zwart holds a PhD in political anthropology from the University of Amsterdam. He was trained as a regional specialist in Indian studies. He works in the Department of Political Science at Leiden University and teaches on comparative politics, development, and institutionalist theory. His research focuses on the politics of patronage, and ethnic, caste, and racial diversity.

Sergiu Gherghina is lecturer in comparative politics at the Department of Politics, University of Glasgow. He holds a PhD in political science from Leiden University and has previously studied political science at Leiden

University and Central European University Budapest. His research interests lie in party politics in Central and Eastern Europe, legislative and voting behaviour, democratization, and the use of direct democracy.

Anka Kekez is a postdoctoral researcher and lecturer at the Faculty of Political Science at the University of Zagreb, Croatia. She holds a PhD in political science from the University of Zagreb. Her research focuses on policy implementation and service delivery, public management reforms, political meta-governance, and clientelism.

Petr Kopecký is professor of political science at Leiden University and co-editor of the journal *East European Politics*. His main research interests are political parties and party systems in contemporary democracies. His current research focuses on the relationship between political patronage and the processes of party building and party organizational transformation and on the politicization of recruitment of appointed elites. His other research interests include comparative (East) European politics, democratization, comparative political institutions, legislative behaviour, and civil society.

Saskia Ruth-Lovell is a research fellow at the German Institute of Global and Area Studies in Hamburg, Germany. Her research focuses on the consequences of populism and clientelism for the quality of democratic governance with a special focus on the Latin American region. She has published articles in *The Journal of Politics*, *Latin American Politics and Society*, *Political Studies*, as well as *Swiss Political Science Review*.

Inga A.-L. Saikkonen is an Academy of Finland Research Fellow at the Social Science Research Institute, Åbo Akademi University (Finland). She holds a DPhil in politics from the University of Oxford and has previously studied at the London School of Economics and the University of Oxford. Her work focuses on clientelism, electoral mobilization, electoral authoritarian regimes, and sub-national democratization.

Maria Spirova is senior lecturer of comparative politics and international relations. She holds a PhD in political science from the University of Wisconsin – Milwaukee and has previously studied political science at the Central European University and the American University in Bulgaria. She works in the area of comparative politics, and her research interests include political parties, party patronage and corruption, and the democratic representation of ethnic minorities.

Francesco Stolfi is lecturer in the Department of Modern History, Politics, and International Relations at Macquaire University. He holds a PhD in political science from the University of Pittsburgh. His current research is on the impact of austerity and European integration on Southern European public administrations and on the political economy of the liberalization of professions in Europe.

Clara Volintiru is lecturer at the Department of International Business and Economics, Bucharest University of Economic Studies. She holds a PhD in political economy and is currently a PhD candidate in political science at the London School of Economics and Political Science (LSE) where she also graduated an MRes in political science, and an MSc in comparative politics, in the Government Department. Her research is focused on institutionalism, institutional distortions, party politics, and clientelism.

Juha Ylisalo is a postdoctoral researcher in political science at the Department of Philosophy, Contemporary History, and Political Science, University of Turku. His research interests include political economy, electoral systems, and accountability relations in representative politics.

www.ingramcontent.com/pod-product-compliance
Lightning Source LLC
Chambersburg PA
CBHW022351280326
41935CB00007B/155